OUTSIDE LOBBYING

OUTSIDE LOBBYING

PUBLIC OPINION AND INTEREST GROUP STRATEGIES

Ken Kollman

PRINCETON UNIVERSITY PRESS   PRINCETON, NEW JERSEY

Library of Congress Cataloging-in-Publication Data

Kollman, Ken, 1966–
Outside lobbying : public opinion and interest group strategies / Ken Kollman.
p.   cm.
Includes bibliographical references and index.
ISBN 0-691-01740-9 (cloth : alk. paper) — ISBN 0-691-01741-7 (pbk. : alk. paper)
1. Lobbying—United States.   2. United States. Congress—
Constitutent communication.   3. Pressure groups—United States.   I. Title.
JK1118.K65   1998
324′.4′0973—dc21   97-39536   CIP

This book has been composed in Times Roman

http://pup.princeton.edu

Printed in the United States of America

10   9   8   7   6   5   4   3   2   1

10   9   8   7   6   5   4   3   2   1
(Pbk.)

To Colleen

Contents

Figures

Tables

Preface _____

OUTSIDE LOBBYING by interest groups is both the attempt to communicate public support to policymakers (what I call *signaling* in the book) and the attempt to increase that public support among constituents (what I call *conflict expansion*). It therefore has two purposes corresponding to the two audiences targeted, and these purposes often reinforce each other. Interest group leaders want to shore up their popular support, because the more support they can credibly demonstrate, the more influence the groups have among policymakers. Thus group leaders try to expand the conflict to improve the very thing that they are trying to signal to policymakers. The dual purposes make outside lobbying a powerful tool in the hands of interest group leaders.

Sometimes the purposes are at odds, however, and interest group leaders must undertake careful, targeted outside lobbying campaigns. Too much conflict expansion can provoke opposition groups or swing momentum to the other side if a group does not have the requisite underlying support among constituents. Or poorly timed outside lobbying can disrupt valuable coalition building around compromise legislation. Therefore, outside lobbying occurs selectively across issues, across time, and across interest groups.

In this book I explain under what circumstances interest group leaders want to use outside lobbying and how they go about it. The two purposes of outside lobbying—signaling and conflict expansion—are examined in detail. The unique data drawn from American politics are the first to connect information about interest group strategies and information on public opinion over a wide range of policy issues. I show that public opinion is a serious constraint on interest group strategies because it limits the claims of popular support that group leaders can make in representing constituents. Moreover, the book provides evidence from case studies and interviews with policymakers and lobbyists to bolster the theoretical claims.

I have many people to thank for help with this research. Benjamin Page in particular has been a reliable source of encouragement (and valuable criticism). Jane Mansbridge and Dennis Chong helped in the early stages of the project. Dani Reiter, Kathy Cramer, Doug Helmreich, Jessica Sysak, Ryan Garcia, and Robert Hamilton all provided able research assistance. John Huber, Nancy Burns, Ann Lin, Pradeep Chhibber, Doug Dion, Chris Achen, Arthur Lupia, Scott Ainsworth, Robert Axelrod, John Chamberlain, John Kingdon, Becky Morton, Roy Pierce, Richard Hall, Scott Page, Tim Feddersen, Cathie Jo Martin, David Meyer, David King, Alistair Smith, John Mark Hansen, and Burdett Loomis have commented on the research or on the manuscript. Frank Baumgartner and Laura Stoker provided special assistance later in the research process. Malcolm Litchfield has been a patient and supportive editor, and Ellen Broudy also helped pull it all together. Funding for gathering data and for research assistance, which I gratefully acknowledge, came from a Dissertation Year Grant at Northwestern University, the Horace H. Rackham School of Graduate Studies and the Office of Vice President for Research at the University of Michigan, and the College of Literature, Science, and Arts at the University of Michigan. The Center for Political Studies and the Department of Political Science at the University of Michigan also provided assistance and release time. Data from the American National Election Study were made available by the Inter-University Consortium for Political and Social Research at the University of Michigan, which bears no responsibility for analysis or interpretation presented here. Finally, this book is dedicated to Colleen, without whose support I surely would not have completed the project.

OUTSIDE LOBBYING

1

Introduction

THIS BOOK concerns the lobbying strategies of interest groups in the United States. In particular, the focus is on outside lobbying among Washington-based organizations. *Outside lobbying* is defined as attempts by interest group leaders to mobilize citizens outside the policymaking community to contact or pressure public officials inside the policymaking community.[1] It represents a viable and effective strategy for many interest groups trying to influence representative government between elections. What better way is there to win favorable legislation in Congress, for example, than to mobilize a significant number of constituents to contact key legislators? Old-fashioned inside lobbying, the personal access and contact with legislators so necessary for maintaining good relations with government, may have only limited effectiveness today. Just as elected officials in Washington feel the need to monitor and assuage public opinion through polls and public relations, modern lobbying increasingly requires sophisticated methods of public mobilization.[2] Lobbying in Washington is not just a game among well-paid lawyers, ideological activists, and legislators in the Capitol. The outside public is increasingly involved.

Mass expressions of public concern directed toward the federal government are rarely spontaneous. Behind most telephone calls, letters, faxes, and E-mails to members of Congress, behind marches down the Mall in Washington, D.C., and behind bus caravans to the Capitol, there are coordinating leaders, usually interest group leaders, mobilizing a select group of citizens to unite behind a common message. At the most basic level, an interest group leader seeks to persuade policymakers that what the members of the group want (as specified by the leader) is good public policy and/or good politics. And the leader uses outside lobbying to demonstrate first, that the

---

[1] There are other terms used colloquially that are similar to outside lobbying, such as "working the district," "coalition building," "using local organizations," "using the rank and file," and most commonly, "going grass roots." Outside lobbying subsumes many of these notions and includes appeals made to business elites, interest group members, potential campaign donors, news organizations, and of course, ordinary citizens not affiliated with the interest group. Also, throughout the book, I sometimes use the term *outside lobby* as a verb, where "to outside lobby" obviously means to engage in outside lobbying.

[2] Kernell (1986) claims that presidents over the course of the twentieth century have increasingly "gone public," or appealed to the general public over the heads of Congress and the Supreme Court.

members of the group are in fact united behind the leader, and second, that many other constituents agree with what the group leader wants. Faced with organized groups of constituents making noise about this or that policy issue, not many members of Congress could afford to ignore these efforts completely. Any leader who can organize thousands of citizens to write letters to their congressional representative, for example, can with some probability organize a good number of voters on election day to support or oppose the incumbent. For all the apparent benefits of outside lobbying to an interest group—sending a strong message to policymakers or reinforcing to voters that the group represents a credible source of political information—it is surprising nonetheless that outside lobbying is not undertaken more often by groups with an interest in controversial policy issues.

Outside lobbying, however, is in fact applied selectively, and lobbyists and interest group leaders spend precious hours and resources crafting careful public campaigns of persuasion. On some policy issues, groups on all sides use outside lobbying intensively. On other policy issues, only groups on one side of the issue use outside lobbying. There are many issues, even those considered extremely important to specific interest groups, where no groups use outside lobbying. And of course, groups try to time their public appeals for maximum effect. As every lobbyist (or salesperson, parent, or leader) knows, persuasion is a subtle business, and careless lobbying strategies can backfire. It is not always the case that outside lobbying, even when it generates a substantial public response, wins over the policymakers targeted.

The selective application and timing of outside lobbying strategies raises important questions. Obviously, outside lobbying is not always influential, even when interest group leaders on only one side of an issue use it. Who or what captures the attention of Washington policymakers? When are demonstrations of popular support effective in influencing policymakers? How do outside lobbying campaigns compare to financial donations or inside lobbying in influencing policymakers? V. O. Key raised similar questions nearly four decades ago, and he found answers difficult to come by. In the 1961 book *Public Opinion and American Democracy*, he expresses doubts about the influence of outside lobbying activities. "Their function in the political process," he writes in reference to "propagandizing campaigns" by interest groups, "is difficult to divine" (528). Outside lobbying activities are "rituals in obeisance to the doctrine that public opinion governs" and are "on the order of the dance of the rainmakers. . . . Sometimes these campaigns have their effects—just as rain sometimes follows the rainmakers' dance. Yet the data make it fairly clear that most of these campaigns do not affect the opinion of many people and even clearer that they have a small effect by way of punitive or approbative feedback in the vote" (528).

Why and when, Key is really asking, do policymakers pay attention to outside lobbying? Certainly many organizational leaders consider outside lobbying potentially influential; otherwise, they would not do it. The leaders of the major labor unions, peak business organizations, and civil rights and environmental groups use outside lobbying regularly enough to indicate that they believe outside lobbying is more than the dancing of rainmakers. Even corporate leaders use outside lobbying occasionally. And policymakers admit that organized groups of constituents influence their decisions. One congressional staff member justified his boss's vote to repeal catastrophic health insurance in 1990, little more than a year after voting for the insurance bill, by explaining, "It was a no-brainer. He got over five thousand letters for the repeal of the insurance, and literally eight letters in favor of the current insurance. He didn't have much choice really. He had to vote for repeal."[3]

But beyond the relatively uninteresting claims that interest group leaders consider outside lobbying effective and that policymakers sometimes consider it influential, the topic deserves more attention than it receives. If, as most observers claim, interest groups wield considerable power in Washington, and if interest groups spend resources using outside lobbying fairly regularly, then outside lobbying should be an important part of the process by which these groups wield their power. Precisely when, why, or how outside lobbying operates to enhance group influence, however, is not well understood.

Our evaluations of the normative effects of outside lobbying are similarly imprecise. We know very little about whether outside lobbying serves to improve the correspondence between what constituents want and what their representatives do or whether it merely confuses representatives with meaningless information or reinforces inequalities in access to representatives that accrue from campaign contributions and other less edifying activities of interest groups. Surprisingly, many depictions of outside lobbying in the national press are as unfavorable as those of lobbying in general. The image of fat-cat lobbyists shoving money in the pockets of legislators has been supplemented by negative images of farmers, teachers, truckers, or public employees demonstrating at the Capitol or flooding Congress with telephone calls for a bigger slice of the budgetary pie, or of business lobbyists spending money to generate so-called astroturf (in contrast to real grass-roots support) to save a valuable tax provision. The press depiction of interest group activities has had either a large influence on Americans or has tapped into deeply negative sentiments among the general population. Recent polls show that a vast majority of Americans are cynical about the power of special interests. In the 1992 American National Election Study (ANES), when asked whether "the government is pretty much run by a few big interests looking out for themselves or [if] it is run for the benefit of all the people,"

---

[3] This quote and all other unattributed quotes in the book are taken from personal interviews conducted by the author. Unless otherwise indicated, the persons quoted request anonymity.

78 percent of those offering a response answered, "a few big interests." Common wisdom, it appears, holds that some interest groups have their way in Washington, and that outside lobbying either reinforces existing inequalities in access or is irrelevant to the real game of special interest lobbying.

The cynicism of the press and the general public toward interest groups is not shared by many political scientists. Studies have tended to describe a more sanguine climate of bargaining and information gathering between interest groups and policymakers in Washington. Descriptions of interest group activities and influence from the last four decades range from the near impotence of business lobbyists during legislative conflicts over free trade (Bauer, Pool, and Dexter 1963) to subtle forms of persuasion and pressure that influence legislation marginally (Hansen 1991; Rothenberg 1992; Austen-Smith and Wright 1994). Many studies of policymaking or interest groups have concluded that other pressures on policymakers besides interest group lobbying—colleagues in the House or Senate, public opinion in the district, the White House, party leaders—were more important in determining policy (Kingdon 1989; Miller 1983; Browne 1988; Jacobs 1992; Dahl 1961; Ginsburg 1986; Heclo 1977). Even those who ascribe considerable power to special interests suggest that that power is wielded subtly or silently, without the intense lobbying activity so common in Washington (Gaventa 1980; M. Edelman 1964; Ferguson 1995).

One reason the press and the general public may tend to exaggerate the influence of interest groups is that the news overemphasizes dramatic instances of graft, exploited campaign finance loopholes, or extraordinary pressure exerted on members of Congress by organizations like the National Rifle Association. Successful outside lobbying campaigns and increasingly large campaign contributions due to the reporting of the Federal Election Commission attract attention and are visible manifestations of group power. Inside lobbying in the form of interpersonal contacts, while an everyday occurrence for nearly all interest groups, is harder for the mass media to observe on a regular basis and has more of the flavor of relationship building and coordination among lobbyists and legislators than of outright pressure. Thus, the media fail to report adequately on the effects of inside strategies, and if they were to do so, it would probably bring the popular evaluation of interest group power more into balance.

In contrast, some of the conclusions of political scientists about the muted influence of interest groups may have something to do with the lack of research on outside lobbying. Researchers have tended to focus on inside lobbying, campaign contributions, and especially organizational formation. For each of these subjects, conclusions of researchers have highlighted the limitations of organized interests. Inside lobbying rarely changes legislators' positions on policy issues (Bauer, Pool, and Dexter 1963; Kingdon 1989; Hall and Wayman 1990; Hansen 1991). Campaign contributions seem to correlate only weakly with legislative or electoral success (Hall and Wayman 1990; Morton and Cameron 1992). And groups are hard to form because of collective action problems (Olson 1965; Hardin 1982). Given all the obstacles interest groups presumably face, one wonders why there are more than seven thousand registered organizations in Washington, and why so many of them spend precious resources trying to influence policymakers. Interest groups work hard to influence legislation, and it is difficult to believe that their money and efforts go to waste.[4]

Part of the problem for political scientists may be that they fail to see the role that outside lobbying serves in enhancing the inside lobbying of interest groups. Interest groups choose lobbying strategies at the same time policymakers are trying to please constituents. Groups thus choose strategies intended to convince policymakers that group goals align with constituent goals (Hansen 1991). If successfully wielded, these strategies can enable interest group leaders to be quite influential in shaping public policies. While this seems apparent, outside lobbying does not get the attention it deserves in interest group research. Simply put, outside lobbying has rarely been studied systematically.[5] The kinds of interest group activities the mass media tend to highlight are precisely those that political scientists tend to understudy, and the differences in coverage among the two affect conclusions about interest group power. This book, in attempting to answer three questions—Why do groups use outside lobbying? When does outside lobbying work? Who benefits from outside lobbying?—is an effort to rectify the imbalance in interest group research.

Of course, interest group leaders are not the only ones who find it in their interests to mobilize citizens to pressure American policymakers. Political party leaders, politicians (especially the president), and even newspapers and mass media personalities actively encourage citizens to contact their elected representatives. The question of when it is advantageous in a democracy to mobilize citizens to pressure policymakers is considerably more general than the more specific question of when interest groups should do so. Many of the ideas in this book about outside lobbying by interest groups should certainly apply to other actors in the political system.

---

[4] Of course, it could be that interest groups are content to influence policy only some of the time. If lobbyists are influential only one time out of twenty, then that appears, by scientific standards, to be a null. In my own discussions in Washington, the most optimistic lobbyists tell me that many of their everyday efforts go for naught. While there may be little tangible evidence of systematic influence, an interest group may perceive itself to have enough of an effect to make its continued existence worthwhile. Regardless of whether the average interest group is influential on one piece of congressional legislation in five years, or on five blockbuster bills a year, precisely how, why, and when lobbying matters in policymaking is not well understood.

[5] There are many case studies of outside lobbying. See Petracca (1992b) and the latest edition of Cigler and Loomis (1991) for examples.

Overview

Outside lobbying is important because it is a common means (perhaps the most common means except for elections) for elite policymakers to experience pressure in the form of popular participation. Were it not for outside lobbying from interest groups, many policy decisions would take place solely among a relatively insulated group of Washington insiders. Instead, interest group leaders call upon people outside of Washington to remind policymakers that a sizable portion of their constituents is paying attention. At least potentially, outside lobbying can pressure policymakers to adopt more popularly supported policies than they would in the absence of outside lobbying.

Outside lobbying accomplishes two tasks simultaneously. First, at the elite level it communicates aspects of public opinion to policymakers. The many forms of outside lobbying—publicizing issue positions, mobilizing constituents to contact Congress, protesting or demonstrating—have the common purpose of trying to show policymakers that the people the group claims to represent really do care about some relevant policy issue. These tactics say, in effect, "See, we told you constituents were angry about policy X, and now you can hear it from them."

I refer to this role for outside lobbying as *signaling* because it has many characteristics of basic signaling models in game theory. An interest group (the sender) tries to signal its popular support (its type) to a policymaker (the receiver). To understand this role for outside lobbying, we shall want to answer similar questions addressed in game theory models that feature costly signaling. What are the conditions under which interest group leaders want to send signals? When do the signals sent by interest group leaders actually influence policymakers' behavior?

The noteworthy characteristic of outside lobbying, however, is that it is not just an elite-level phenomenon. It is intended to influence members of the mass public as well. The second role for outside lobbying is to influence public opinion by changing how selected constituents consider and respond to policy issues. I shall call this its *conflict expansion* role in reference to the theoretical legacy of Schattschneider, who wrote in 1960 that the "most important strategy of politics is concerned with the scope of the conflict. . . . Conflicts are frequently won or lost by the success that the contestants have in getting the audience involved in the fight or in excluding it, as the case may be" (3–4). As Schattschneider emphasized, political elites, when faced with intransigent opposition, can bring attention to their cause, invite constituents to participate in the policy process, and hope to swing momentum to their side.

For both of these roles, the salience of policy issues to constituents, an often-overlooked characteristic of public opinion, lies at the center of interest group politics. It is not the popularity of policies that is mostly communicated or altered through outside lobbying. For one, the popularity of policies tends to stay relatively fixed over long periods of time, even given the outside lobbying activities of interest groups (Page and Shapiro 1992). But even more important, policymakers tend to have good information on the popularity of policies, primarily through opinion polls, but also because such popularity stays relatively constant and they can learn about it over time. Salience, however, defined as the relative importance people attach to policy issues, is an aspect of public opinion that policymakers perpetually running for reelection want to know but cannot learn about from ordinary opinion polls and experience. Policymakers want to know what proportion of constituents, when voting in the next election, will weigh the actions of their elected representatives on a particular policy issue. More salient policy issues will weigh more heavily on voting decisions than will less salient policy issues, and policymakers rely to a considerable extent on interest groups for current information on which issues rank high on salience. Because they can mobilize constituents to speak for themselves and can occasionally increase the salience of issues to those constituents, interest group leaders have a comparative advantage in sending credible signals on this precious information.

In sum, interest group leaders can turn their informational and leadership advantages into policy influence. They can try through inside lobbying to convince policymakers that voters care about an issue and are on the side of their group on the issue. But outside lobbying goes a step further in making a costly, public demonstration that, one, the issue is in fact salient to voters and, two, the interest group can make the issue even more salient.

The distinction between the two roles can be quite fuzzy, especially in practice. Consider two analogous situations. An opposition leader in an authoritarian regime wants to hold a large rally in the capital. The rally, if it successfully gathers hundreds of thousands of people as planned, accomplishes the two tasks just specified. It both communicates to the current regime the swelling sentiment among the population that the current regime is offensive *and* coordinates or mobilizes the opposing citizens on a particular course of action: support the opposition leader and work to topple the current government. To the government the rally signals the status of the opposition, and to the citizens in the rally it reinforces the notion that the effort to topple the regime is important and worthy of risky collective action.

Outside lobbying is also similar to the marketing behavior of business entrepreneurs promoting new product ideas to consumers and investors at the same time. Entrepreneurs do their own brand of inside lobbying among investors, hawking their product ideas and wooing support among a small group of people. At the same time, they gauge consumer demand for their products, communicate that level of demand to potential investors, and even try to stimulate more demand among consumers. Success among one audience (consumers) will likely lead to success among the other audience (investors). Just as investors try to assess potential consumer response to the entrepreneur's marketing efforts because future investments will succeed or fail based on consumer behavior, elected officials look to constituents' responses to outside lobbying because reelection efforts may hinge on the interest group success in mobilizing constituents. For interest groups, as with entrepreneurs, there are two audiences in mass marketing, but the overall goals converge because one audience relies very much on the other audience. This analogy between business entrepreneurs and interest group leaders has been made previously in an innovative paper by Ainsworth and Sened (1993).

The duality of purpose makes outside lobbying a powerful tool in the hands of interest groups. It can simultaneously fan the flames of constituent anger and bring the heat of those flames to the attention of representatives far away, whose job it is to put out or contain the fire. However, while the two roles can get mixed together in practice, there are important conceptual distinctions between them. In the signaling role, the salience of a policy issue must be considered *exogenous* in that there is something fixed and unknown to policymakers about salience that the group claims to be able to demonstrate through outside lobbying. Perhaps it is the potential salience of an issue that interest groups want to communicate. In this case, the "fixed" element of public opinion being communicated is the latent salience of an issue. The group is confident it can expand the conflict to a certain point, and it wants to communicate that confidence through outside lobbying. In the conflict expansion role, the salience of a policy issue is *endogenous*, in that the strategy is intended to influence the very characteristic of public opinion that is being communicated in the signaling role.

The two roles can be represented briefly in a simple graphic. (It will be useful in later chapters to analyze the roles separately.) Figure 1.1 shows a picture of three possible trajectories for the salience of an issue. An interest group's leaders might know the current salience of an issue to their members is s, but they are very confident that through outside lobbying the group can raise the salience among constituents to s^{+++}. A policymaker, meanwhile, is uncertain about the values of s and the anticipated value of salience. In a slight abuse of microeconomics terminology, we might say that the policymaker is uncertain, and is especially concerned, about the elasticity of salience and the latent salience of the issue. The process of raising s to another level through outside lobbying is the role of conflict expansion, and the process of communicating the values of s, s^+, s^{++}, or s^{+++} to policymakers is role of signaling. A policymaker wants to know which three trajectories has occurred or will occur in response to outside lobbying by the group.

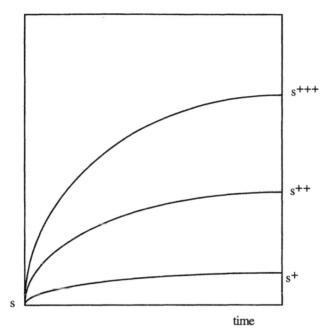

s^{+++}

s^{++}

s^{+}

s

time

Figure 1.1. Hypothetical Trajectories of Salience

Later chapters are devoted to explaining signaling and conflict expansion in more detail. I argue in chapter 3 that conceiving of outside lobbying as signaling is useful because it offers a language and systematic method to understand how communication costs, policy preferences, and reputations influence the communicative aspects of outside lobbying. Communication costs in particular are relevant to the study of outside lobbying because the costs of successful outside lobbying are related systematically to the existing state of public salience on an issue. Precisely because outside lobbying is costly, and the strategies of interest groups conditional on those costs offer clues to the underlying public salience groups are trying to communicate, outside lobbying can influence policymakers. Policymakers learn about salience by making inferences from the revealed efforts of interest groups.

When group leaders are confident they can expand the conflict—raise public awareness of an issue or frame issues in different ways to their advantage—additional considerations besides the advantages of signaling to policymakers become important. What information should a group present to constituents to convince them the issue is worth costly collective action? When in the course of legislation should conflict expansion happen for maximum impact? How should a group frame the advantages of one policy over another policy? In general, when there are opportunities to expand the conflict, decision making over strategies turns on how potential increases in salience (or sometimes popularity) will benefit interest group goals, rather than on how the current level of popular support will play with policymakers.

As a first cut at understanding conflict expansion, we might think it benefits groups that do not have ready access to policymakers. Much of our understanding of this comes from Schattschneider. Schattschneider believed not only that outsider groups would want to outside lobby, but also that such groups tend to have advantages in the realm of public opinion. According to Schattschneider, "It is the weak who want to socialize conflict, i.e., to involve more and more people in the conflict until the balance of forces is changed" (1960, 40), the assumption being that groups with concentrated wealth or power would eschew politics involving broad popular participation and do not stand to gain from increased salience.

Schattschneider's ideas, however, do not completely square with contemporary interest group politics. In an age when all kinds of organizations, including large corporations, wealthy trade associations, and professional groups outside lobby on policy issues of great concern to millions of Americans, clearly there are times when the strong and those groups with considerable inside access want to expand the scope of the conflict as well. In chapter 5 I supplement and expand on Schattshneider's basic ideas. I argue that groups deciding over conflict expansion, regardless of how powerful they are currently, have to consider important elements of public opinion and the policy context surrounding an issue.

Two aspects of the policy context that influence outside lobbying are discussed in detail in that chapter: the stage of legislation and the policy alternatives confronting policymakers. The stage of legislation—whether a policy problem is just being introduced to the government or whether well-defined alternatives are being considered by legislators—will have a large effect on both signaling and conflict expansion decisions (Kingdon 1984). In decisions over lobbying strategies or tactics, groups facing policies in earlier stages, when they merely try to raise consciousness on a new policy issue, will be less concerned about popular support for their policy positions than will groups facing policies in later stages, when they fight to swing a few key votes in a congressional committee. The stage of legislation shapes the way public opinion constrains interest group strategies mostly by varying the benefits groups attain in signaling the current salience of an issue versus in trying to increase the salience of that issue or the popularity of specific policies.

Policy alternatives, or more specifically the relative popularity of policy alternatives, matter a great deal because they also determine whether increasing salience is a good idea for a group. What may not be overwhelmingly popular—say, needle exchange programs—may be more popular than the most prominent policy alternative, increased spending on drug rehabilitation programs. Thus, as for influencing outside lobbying decisions, the popularity of policies must be regarded as relative, not absolute, a consideration that carries implications about whether a group benefits from conflict expansion.

This book provides considerable evidence from systematic data and from recent policy battles that outside lobbying occurs for these reasons. The data I collected and used for most of the analyses are the first available that combine public opinion information with lobbying strategies and tactics to provide a more complete picture of the environment shaping interest group decisions. Obviously, interest groups adapt their techniques to different situations, but data available prior to this point have been limited in that they have not allowed researchers to study how contexts that change across policy issues, especially public opinion, might affect group strategies. The unit of analysis for much of my data is a group-issue pairing, so there are multiple cases for each interest group studied. In short, with these data I can test for patterns of public salience, popularity, and lobbying strategies and tactics across policy issues that are consistent with my arguments.

These data, from lobbying decisions in the early 1990s by many interest groups across many policy issues, reveal that the salience of policy issues relates to lobbying decisions in ways consistent with the notions of signaling and conflict expansion. An interest group can be considered to have its own "good news" to signal about public opinion if constituents who agree with the group's goals care a great deal about the issue, enough to condition their vote in the next election on how policymakers behave on the issue. I find that the better the news interest groups have to signal about salience, the more they use outside lobbying. Moreover, the stages of legislation and the role of policy alternatives matter in lobbying decisions as well, especially as strategies relate to the popularity of policies. Groups deciding over signaling or conflict expansion pay more attention to the popularity of their issue positions in certain stages of legislation than in others. And finally, groups appear to behave differently depending on the popularity of the status quo relative to their preferred alternatives.

Most us would presumably like to see outside lobbying coming from groups supporting popular policies on salient issues. Instead, the empirical conclusions of this study are mixed. I find that outside lobbying, contrary to the view that most of it produces phony grass-roots support, is far from artificial. It is actually a good way for policymakers to learn what their constituents care about. My data show that outside lobbying on average works as a policymaker might hope: it communicates fairly accurately the salience of policy issues to large numbers of constituents, and it often influences the salience of policy issues to benefit the more popular side of an issue. At the same time, however, and more often than we would like, outside lobbying springs forth from intense groups pursuing relatively unpopular policies (especially early in the legislative process), and in this regard, it falls somewhat short in reinforcing the majority's preferences. Outside lobbying, in sum, does not distort the policymaking process nearly as much as many people like to claim, but it does a better job in communicating salience information than in bolstering popular pressure for majoritarian policies.

↳ so not as bad as originally thought?

The Players

There are three main kinds of players involved in outside lobbying: interest groups, policymakers, and constituents. Interest groups—or, more precisely, their leaders—make decisions over lobbying strategies, and because they are the main players throughout the book, data from interviews of group leaders about their group strategies form the basis of the empirical part of this study.[6] Policymakers, as the ones who make the policy decisions interest groups care about, provide the reasons for lobbying at all. We can assume that the primary goal of lobbying is to influence policy decisions, and interest group leaders who carry out lobbying strategies without close attention to the constraints facing policymakers will undoubtedly fail much of the time. And constituents, the most immediate targets of outside lobbying campaigns, constrain the actions of politicians and interest groups by controlling through their collective action whether the politicians get reelected, the interest groups get funded, and the outside lobbying campaigns result in any real public pressure.

Interest Groups

Interest groups are both numerous and enormously diverse in the United States. I use the term *interest group* to include any nonparty organization that regularly tries to influence government policy. This definition subsumes organizations as different as Waste Management, one of the world's largest corporations, and the Gay and Lesbian Task Force Policy Institute, a public interest group promoting civil rights for gays and lesbians. In the mid-1980s, Schlozman and Tierney (1986) estimated that seven thousand interest groups operated in Washington, D.C. A vast majority of interest groups, they found, are business trade associations, professional associations, or corporations,

---

[6] Note that I restrict attention to interest groups rather than to the lobbying specialists they hire. (See Heinz et al. 1993 for a comprehensive study of hired lobbyists.) Most of the time interest group leaders make final decisions on lobbying strategies, especially at the level of generalization used throughout this study.

but there are also sizable proportions of public interest groups and labor unions. A public interest group, part of a broad category, is defined as an organization that "seeks a collective good, the achievement of which will not selectively and materially benefit the membership or activists of the organization" (Berry 1977, 7). Within each of these categories, and of course across categories, there exist vast differences in group resources, organizational structures, and propensities for certain lobbying strategies and tactics. In the public interest group category, for example, groups range from the National Committee to Preserve Social Security and Medicare, with an annual budget of $33 million, to the tiny Consumers for World Trade, with an annual budget of $100,000 and three part-time staff persons. And major corporations like Allied-Signal are in most respects an entirely different species than more familiar interest groups like the U.S. Chamber of Commerce, the Teamsters, or Common Cause.

Surprisingly, there is enough similarity in the behavior of such diverse organizations as Waste Management and the Gay and Lesbian Task Force to warrant comparisons of strategies across all the different kinds of groups. While organizational characteristics matter a great deal in determining which strategies are more common for a particular group, to a large extent the toolbox available to all groups is fairly uniform. Corporations and trade associations, for example, increasingly resort to mobilizing employees to call members of Congress, a tactic that was for a long time the strategic province of labor unions and public interest groups. And labor unions now hold educational seminars in exotic places to expose members of Congress to the value of certain pro-union policies. It used to be that only business groups offered these boondoggles. With the exception of a few tactics, such as protesting (corporations never protest), all kinds of interest groups use outside lobbying strategies and tactics to some degree.

The data in this study come from a great variety of interest groups. The two major sources of data were extensive interviews conducted with participants in the battles over the North American Free Trade Agreement (NAFTA) in 1993 and health care in 1993 and 1994, and systematic, structured interviews with more than sixty-two interest groups active on numerous policy issues in 1992. Here I shall summarize the relevant characteristics of the 1992 data, the basis for much of the empirical analysis in the book. A listing of the groups and persons interviewed, and various other pieces of information on the data collection, are given in appendixes A, B, and C.

The systematic data collected from interviews with group leaders are organized in two distinct ways. In the first data set, the unit of analysis is a group. This construction allows for comparing behavior across groups, and most other interest group data are organized in this fashion. Data collected and analyzed in three prominent studies by Jack Walker (1991), by John

Heinz and others (1993), and by Kay Lehman Schlozman and John Tierney (1986) are organized by group.

The units of analysis for the second data set are group issues. In contrast to every other set of systematic data on American interest groups I am aware of, this data set allows for the comparison of lobbying strategies across issues for the same interest group. Most interest groups lobby on more than one issue, and many potentially relevant factors that influence lobbying strategies or tactics may vary across issues. For example, the National Restaurant Association expressed strong concern over business regulation, national health care policy, trade policy, and employment issues, so there are ten cases for the group in the group-issue data set (on various specific policy issues related to the four general issues), plus for each case there are data on the policy issue itself, such as public opinion information, the positions of the group on that issue, and the group's perceptions of the political environment surrounding that issue. Another trade association, the Bankers Association for Foreign Trade, expressed interest in only one issue, foreign trade policy, so only two cases, each having to do with foreign trade policy, are included in the group-issue data set for the group. Some of the most important interest groups, like large unions, peak business associations, or major public interest groups, expressed interest in up to fifteen different issues. Using this construction I have deliberately weighted the data toward the most important, broadly focused interest groups.

The data in both of my sets incorporate information on the organizations and the political environment facing the organizations, including public opinion information for specific issues. I organized a large amount of public opinion data into the group-issue data set. Among other things, I compare public opinion on an issue to the official position of the group on an issue. Thus with the use of public opinion marginals (percentage of the sampled public giving each possible answer to a polling question) and salience information (percentage of the sampled public giving this issue as an important problem facing the country), I can construct measures of public opinion on the given issue as it relates to group goals and behavior.

I restrict the study to groups active on issues for which public opinion data were available. Thus, to sample interest groups, I started with a collection of public opinion questions and public responses available in spring 1992. Questions were chosen that dealt with controversial policy issues in 1991 and 1992 asked of national samples fewer than eleven months before the research began. All in all, there were seventy-seven public opinion questions of high quality concerning anywhere from ten to twenty topics of national policy (depending on how the questions are classified) from the Roper Public Opinion Archives at the University of North Carolina.

I compiled a large list of 328 interest groups that fit the following criteria: (1) they were registered as lobbying groups in Congress in 1990, with several exceptions;[7] (2) their headquarters were in Washington, D.C., *or* they had a significant office in Washington, D.C.; (3) and their lobbying concerns overlapped with issues in the seventy-seven public opinion questions, as categorized in the *Washington Information Directory*.[8]

To include corporations, I chose the twenty top PAC (political action committee)-giving corporations for the 1990 campaign cycle, plus the five top PAC-giving corporations in eight industrial sectors strongly affected by the policy concerns in the seventy-seven public opinion questions. These twenty corporations were not chosen randomly from all possible corporations to be included in the large list of 328 because it was important to survey corporations with strong interests in government policy. The PAC data served as a proxy for the determination of "strong interests." While their inclusion on the large list was not randomly determined, whether or not these corporations were chosen to be interviewed out of the 328 *was* randomly determined. Since even with corporations having strong interests in politics we see limited variation in strategies across these groups, choosing other corporations less interested in politics would only limit what we learn about corporate political action. Had I sampled from all corporations active in politics—a very difficult (if not impossible) task, to be sure—the overall results of the study would likely have not changed.

From this list of 328 groups, I randomly sampled 70 groups and interviewed 50.[9] Group leaders could request any level of anonymity for the data and the interviews, but only four of those interviewed asked for some level of anonymity. The frequency of the classes of groups interviewed is comparable to that of other surveys. Table 1.1 lists the frequencies of classes of groups as they compare to the data used in the well-known study by Schlozman and Tierney (1986).

I interviewed an available person within each group who had a "broad understanding of the group's political activities." This person was usually the president or the legislative director. At the beginning of each interview, I asked whether certain policy areas were "of major importance," "somewhat important," or "not important" to the group. I asked the representative of the group the exact public opinion questions on those areas of policy coded

---

[7] A few groups were included that failed to register in 1990 because they were of national prominence and had registered in the past.

[8] The following sources were used to compile the large list of interest groups:

Washington Information Directory. 1991. Congressional Quarterly Press.
American Lobbyists Directory. 1990. Gale Research.
Public Interest Profiles. 1992–93. Foundation for Public Affairs and Congressional Quarterly Press.

[9] There were 12 additional groups interviewed that were not randomly chosen and therefore do not appear in any quantitative analysis in the book. They were interviewed because of special outside lobbying campaigns.

TABLE 1.1
Percentage of Cases in Interest Group Classes

	Public Interest Groups	Labor Unions	Trade Associations	Corporations	Professional Associations	N
Group data	28	14	34	16	8	50
Group-issue data	32	23	28	14	3	323
Scholzman-Tierney data	25	11	26	30	7	175

"major" or "somewhat" to get a measure of the popularity of the group's issue positions.[10] I then asked the representatives about the lobbying tactics used on the specific issues, plus assorted other questions shown in the questionnaire in appendix B. The entire set of public opinion questions asked of interest group leaders (after they had expressed the requisite interest on the topic) numbered 323, the number of cases in the group-issue data set.

To illustrate the advantages of these data, let us compare two tables. Table 1.2 presents a standard summary from the group data set, and table 1.3 summarizes a simple result from the group-issue data set. Table 1.2 is very similar in format and results to a prominent table in Schlozman and Tierney

TABLE 1.2
Percentage of Groups Using a Particular Tactic

	Public Interest Groups	Labor Unions	Trade Associations	Corporations	Professional Associations
Talking with the press	100	100	100	88	100
Organizing letter-writing campaigns	93	100	91	75	100
Mobilizing group members	93	100	94	87	100
Advertising policy positions	79	71	35	25	50
Protesting	64	100	0	0	0

[10] It is important to note that I requested the official positions of the organizations, not the representatives' personal opinions.

(1986, 173). Both table 1.2 and the Schlozman and Tierney table report the frequency of outside lobbying activities by the common group classification of corporations, unions, trade associations, professional associations, and public interest groups. Table 1.2 shows that nearly all groups talk with the press and organize letter-writing campaigns. As tactics like advertising and protests become more expensive or controversial, the frequency of use declines, especially for business and professional organizations.

The group-issue data can answer further questions about factors that change across issues. For example, how might perceptions of popular support by group leaders influence lobbying techniques? Table 1.3 reveals the confidence that groups have in their public support and the possible influence of that confidence on outside lobbying activities. Each cell gives the percentage of group-issue cases for a class of groups where the group leaders using the tactic believed "a majority of the public agrees with" the group's position on the issue. For example, in the first column and first row, of the cases where public interest groups held press conferences or hired public relations firms, in 71 percent of these cases the leaders of those groups involved felt they had majority public support for their position. Union leaders felt, surprisingly, that the majority of the public supported them 100 percent of the time they held press conferences or protested. Unions and public interest groups in general appear to tailor their strategies or tactics to their perceptions of public opinion, but corporations and trade associations do not seem to follow suit. It is also the case that unions tend to be remarkably confident that they are on the popular side of major public issues, as indicated by the bottom row. For 92 percent of group issue cases facing unions, including even those for which they did not use outside lobbying, the union leaders felt they had majority support among the public. This contrasts with the benchmark of 65 percent of all group-issues cases where the group leaders believed they had majority support (data not shown).

The results in table 1.3 should be interpreted with caution, however. Not only are there few cases in each cell, but there are many other influences on lobbying techniques left out of this simple analysis. And I do not examine here a comparison of perceptions of public opinion between the group-issue cases involving outside lobbying and those group-issue cases not involving outside lobbying. A multivariate analysis of lobbying decisions, as in chapter 4, is more appropriate to control for other influences and to compare across many cases. In chapter 4 I broaden this result to show that real public opinion data (mostly about the salience of issues), and not just data on perceptions of public opinion, correspond to outside lobbying decisions.

It is also interesting to note that these same data reveal a general hubris among group leaders, at least as they communicate their confidence to the public and to academic interviewers. Fewer than one-third (30 percent) of all group-issue cases involved a group leader admitting that a majority of the

TABLE 1.3
Percentage of Group-Issue Cases Where Group Leaders Believed They Had
Majority Support of Public

Ci+izen group / Public Interest Groups	Labor Unions	Trade Associations	Corporations	Professional Associations
Holding press conferences	71	100	14	NA	50
Mobilizing group members	73	92	21	50	100
Advertising on policy positions	90	64	33	20	0
Protesting	53	100	NA	NA	NA
All group-issue cases	64	92	48	57	44

Note: These are conditional percentages. For example, for all group-issue cases involving public interest groups using press conferences, 71 percent gives the proportion of these cases in which the group leaders felt they had majority support. The bottom row, however, is conditioned only on whether the case involves the particular class of group, not on whether the group used outside lobbying.

public disagreed with the group's position on an issue. In contrast, as mentioned, for 65 percent of group-issue cases, group leaders believed they had majority support. There is a slight tendency for group leaders to get it right, especially if they acknowledge they are on the unpopular side of an issue. Let us set an objective standard for public support as a simple dichotomy: whether or not the group position on a public opinion question is the same as that given by a plurality of the public.[11] Among the cases where the group leaders believed a majority of the public agrees with their groups, 58 percent of these cases involve group policy positions with plurality support. Yet among the cases where the group leaders believed a majority of the public disagrees with their groups, 67 percent of these cases involve group policy positions without plurality support. In short, group leaders on the whole definitely exaggerate popular support for their groups' issue positions (no surprise), but those who admit to pursuing unpopular policies are more reliable for a given issue than are those who brag about pursuing popular policies.

[11] I do not use the standard of majority support for the actual public opinion data because there is an incomparability across questions that provide two, three, or more possible answers to the question.

These data, having been collected for the purpose of examining how strategies and tactics change across issues, allow for many of the internal characteristics of groups to be held constant. Previous research on lobbying strategies has often tended to emphasize factors that stay constant across issues, even though strategies change across issues for the same groups. Walker (1991), for example, considers funding sources as critical to the tendency of groups to use specific strategies. Berry (1977), in explaining grass-roots strategies among public interest groups, focuses on a number of factors that do not change across issues, such as whether a group has a history of mass mobilization. And Hill and Rothschild (1992) explain grass-roots strategies as following from organizational culture. Undoubtedly, internal characteristics, such as the ones these authors highlight, are relevant in explaining outside lobbying. The national labor unions tend to use outside lobbying often, especially mail campaigns directed at particular members of Congress and personal visits to legislators in home districts. They have large, paid memberships, federated structures, and histories of activism that make them ideally suited for certain kinds of outside lobbying tactics. These are important resources readily available to lower the costs of outside lobbying for unions. But these resources stay relatively constant for groups. Data that can connect lobbying techniques to the resources or opportunities that change across issues, like the policy context or the public support for a policy or public salience of an issue, will help to explain the variation in techniques across issues.

In the remainder of the book I continue to devote attention to the external environment interest groups face and how that environment shapes the choices of group leaders. Mostly left out of this study are two important interest group activities that other researchers focus on, the maintenance of the organizations themselves and the internal decision making processes. Both how group leaders organize and maintain members and how group leaders solve internal conflicts have been the subjects of many studies, and deservedly so. But once collective action problems have been solved, and once internal dissension has been stifled, organizations invariably make decisions for which they or their leaders are held accountable. Therefore, interest groups in this book are assumed to be unitary actors led by appointed leaders, and the group leaders are assumed to make decisions over strategies and tactics to maximize the chances of their favored policies becoming enacted. While this sweeps many elements of interest group politics under the rug, I seek to isolate the influence of specific external factors on group strategies.

Policymakers

The preferences of and options available to policymakers are crucial to the story of outside lobbying. For this study, policymakers are assumed to seek information regarding their constituents for the purpose of making decisions consistent with the goal of reelection. Whether an interest group tries to convince policymakers to change policy or to avoid changing policy, outside lobbying is intended to demonstrate to policymakers that their interests coincide with the interests of the group and the constituents the group represents. Since policymakers want to win reelection, the possible situations can be simplified to two: (1) if an interest group wants a policymaker to do something that hurts his or her chances of reelection, then the interests of the group and the interests of the policymaker do not coincide, and (2) if an interest group wants a policymaker to do something that helps his or her chances of reelection, then the interests of the group and the interests of the policymaker do coincide. The critical information for policymakers is which situation actually exists. Naturally, interest groups want the policymaker to think that the second situation exists.

Policymakers, of course, try to learn their constituents' preferences and issue salience in many ways, such as through polls, the press, visits to the home district, and, yes, through interest groups. The depiction of interest groups as providers of information is nothing new, although there has been considerable disagreement about whether the relationships between policymakers and interest groups are primarily adversarial or primarily cooperative. The nature of these relationships is crucial to the nature of the communication that can occur between the two kinds of players. Bauer, Pool, and Dexter (1963), for example, comment that "the lobbyist becomes in effect a service bureau for those congressmen already agreeing with him, rather than an agent of direct persuasion" (353). These conclusions have been challenged by a number of researchers (Wilson 1981; Austen-Smith and Wright 1992, 1994). And recent theories by Hansen (1991), Ainsworth (1993), and Austen-Smith (1993) boil down to the proposition that interest groups try to inform policymakers about the consequences of policies; whether the relationships are adversarial or cooperative depends on the particular policy and the degree of convergence in preferences over policy outcomes among the various players involved.

From my own interviews with policymakers and their staff, I believe that most policymakers do not view their relationships with interest groups as adversarial, at least not most of the time. Many lobbyists have a great deal of expertise and provide useful information (Browne 1988). They often help policymakers craft legislation and decide on difficult issues. Simultaneously, however, interest group leaders, when talking about outside lobbying, tend to use a language indicating that their goals are to make life uncomfortable for policymakers. They brag about "holding their feet to the fire" and "reminding congressmen who elected them so they vote right," to use actual quotes from my interviews with an environmental lobbyist and a labor lobbyist, respectively. These are hardly the statements of lobbyists as pseudo–staff members at the beck and call of policymakers. These group leaders repeatedly invoke their responsibility to change policymakers' minds when the situation calls for it.

To a large extent this seeming contradiction between how policymakers refer to interest groups and how interest groups refer to policymakers reflects one of the important differences between inside and outside lobbying. For inside lobbying, the more common strategy by far, the preponderance of time spent in conversations between lobbyists and policymakers involves fairly placid negotiation, coordination, and information exchange. Inside lobbying, part of the everyday activity of interest group leaders and hired lobbyists, rarely includes overt conflict or even impolite attempts at persuasion. It very often involves explicit collusion between lobbyists and policymakers who tend to agree with each other about some policy matter. This is what policymakers refer to as helpful in describing interest groups, and this is the subject of the famous study by Bauer, Poole, and Dexter (1963) on business lobbyists. Outside lobbying, in contrast, is a clear step above in intensity, and usually follows the determination by the group leaders that unless they resort to it, policymakers will act against the policies their group advocates. Outside lobbying is often targeted at undecided policymakers. The very nature of outside lobbying more often than not means that policymakers feel that groups put them in an adversarial position. And interest group leaders prefer to talk about their triumphant lobbying strategies, which usually include outside lobbying and convincing undecided or (ex ante) opposing policymakers to decide on a course of action favorable to the groups.

Thus adversarial relationships between policymakers and interest groups are perhaps the exception rather than the rule, much as outside lobbying campaigns, in contrast to everyday inside lobbying, are the exceptions rather than the rule. But the exceptions are not all that rare and can be extremely significant in deciding the fate of legislation. Following the general adage that friends and enemies are only temporary in Washington, D.C., a given interest group and a given policymaker can cooperate and be friendly on most issues, but find themselves adversaries on other issues. In fact, many interest groups resort to outside lobbying when a policymaker the group leaders expected to support the group's goals turns out to waver on the policy or even oppose the group. Moreover, policymakers grow quite bitter when they think interest groups contribute to constituents' anger. The more outside lobbying results in significant increases in issue salience (conflict expansion), the more apt policymakers are to feel that their problems with angry constituents are caused by interest groups rather than merely communicated by interest groups. This bitterness multiplies, of course, when policymakers feel interest group leaders deliberately mislead constituents about policies and turn them against those the policymakers think are good for them. An

example of these kinds of accusations occurred during the battle over catastrophic health insurance in 1989, the subject of a story in chapter 2.

Constituents

Understanding outside lobbying requires consideration of the people at
whom the appeals are most directly targeted. The average congressional constituency is quite diverse; people have a multitude of opinions, fears, desires,
group affiliations, and degrees of knowledge about politics. Many of them
communicate regularly with elected officials, whether they intend to or not.
Every act of voting, answering opinion polls, writing letters to editors, sign-
ing petitions, contributing to causes, and even subscribing to certain magazines communicates something valuable about constituents to policymakers.
Sometimes the entire nation reacts with near unity on public issues, such as
condemnation of domestic terrorist activity. More often, constituents are divided and send conflicting messages to their representatives. In a hypothetical congressional district with cities, farms, and ports, some people want
price supports for farmers above all, others want lower food costs without
consideration for farmers' incomes, and still others want to import foreign
food at lower costs because their jobs at the docks depend on it. Public
opinion in a constituency, however manifest, reflects many interests that
overlap and conflict.

   Although the public is quite diverse, what elected officials often want to
know about their constituents is simpler. The vital information can be boiled
down to two elements about public opinion: what proportion of constituents
supports a given policy (popularity) and how important is a given policy
issue to constituents (salience). The distinction between popularity and salience is important for many points made in this book. Let us examine two
differences here.

   First, whereas public preferences are relatively easy to discover, issue salience is not. There are hundreds of poll results published every year on
public policy preferences, including those conducted by candidates within
electoral districts. Preferences can be communicated credibly and quickly.
Even on obscure issues that affect few constituents, policymakers can usually tap the preferences of these constituents over these issues. However, the
salience policymakers are concerned about—whether a given issue will figure into constituents' voting or contributing decisions—is notoriously difficult to discern. This is partially because the salience of issues is not the
subject of many opinion polls. Policymakers look to interest groups, among
others, for this information on particular issues, assuming that interest
groups specialize in particular issue areas and can substitute for good polling
data. Certainly interest groups in a particular issue area are likely to have

more information about the public salience of the issue than are policy-makers.

Second, aggregate public preferences change infrequently on major policy questions, but the salience of issues to voters changes fairly rapidly and frequently over time (Page and Shapiro 1992; Tom Smith 1985). Salience rises and falls with news coverage, presidential speeches, world events, and most relevant for our purposes, the activities of interest groups. To take one example, the percentage of national samples answering that they favor "national health insurance, which would be financed by tax money, paying for most forms of health care," barely fluctuated, from 64 percent in October 1990, to 60 percent in June 1991, to 65 percent in January 1992, to 66 percent in July 1992, and finally to 63 percent in January, 1993.[12] Meanwhile, pollsters using a common measure of salience—the percentage of respondents in national polls volunteering health care as the most important problem facing the country—found that the salience of health care went from 6 percent in December 1991, to 12 percent in April 1992, to 18 percent in January 1993, and then to 28 percent in September 1993. That is an increase of 466 percent of Americans mentioning health care as important. The causes of such an increase in salience during this short period certainly include the many Americans losing health insurance coverage during the early 1990s recession, the presidential election campaign, introduction of and debate over Bill Clinton's health care plan (which eventually failed), and incessant television commercials by various interest groups. The uncertainty of elected officials about the salience of issues stems partially from such volatility. Interest groups not only, through signaling, try to communicate public salience on an issue at a given moment and the future salient issues in the next election; they also, through conflict expansion, try to influence the salience of issues.

While salience of an issue may be more malleable than aggregate policy preferences, it is not completely pliant. Information in this book implies that public opinion in various forms plays a central role in inhibiting the influence and constraining the activities of Washington-based interest groups. It is less likely for interest groups to use outside lobbying if they do not have the requisite popular support (both popularity and salience) than if they do. Together policy preferences and issue salience among ordinary people comprise public opinion, and a useful image is to think of public opinion as the landscape upon which interest groups and elected officials operate. The landscape is not fixed (groups, and others, can alter the landscape), but it is sturdy, and it does present considerable constraints on behavior by limiting the claims interest groups can make about public support. For example, the

---

[12] These are measured by CBS/New York Times polls, as reported in *Public Opinion Quarterly* in various issues from 1993.

public as a whole consistently cares more about the economy, for example, than about policies toward AIDS research. No matter how much presidents, party leaders, or interest groups try to influence the public, the American economy will not, in the near future, become less salient to the average American than, say, AIDS or the fate of the war refugees in parts of Africa. The final word on salience among constituents rests with, well, constituents.

Thus public opinion sets limits on the success of lobbying in general. Key recognized this when he wrote, "The world of pressure politics becomes more a politics among the activists than a politics that involved many people. Yet politics among activists occurs in a context of concern about public opinion, a concern that colors the mode of action if not invariably its substance" (1961, 526).

One more thing must be said about constituents. An important aspect of constituency behavior and opinion is left out of this study for practical reasons. Constituents, as distinct from interest group leaders and elected officials, are not assumed to act strategically. For example, the mass public in the signaling model in chapter 3 is modeled as "reduced form," or, that is to say, the public behaves somewhat mechanically. It is assumed that interest group leaders, with enough resources, can get group members or sympathetic citizens to behave in favorable ways outside of the voting booth.[13] This is a deliberate, if unfortunate, analytical choice. I am concerned mostly with the decisions of elites, and to understand these decisions I assume that elites consider constituents as a largely fixed but slightly movable constraint or force to be reckoned with. Also, there are many interesting theories incorporating strategic voters or citizens (Olson 1965; Lohmann 1993; Ainsworth and Sened 1993). In chapter 5 I discuss these theories briefly. It might be straightforward to append these other published theories onto the ideas proposed here, but that is beyond the task set out for this book.

Synopsis of the Book

The remaining chapters provide a detailed account of outside lobbying and lay out the implications of signaling and conflict expansion by interest groups. Chapter 2 contains an empirical summary of outside lobbying in the United States and demonstrates the differences between inside and outside lobbying. The data indicate that outside lobbying occurs selectively but in relative abundance, and that a great variety of groups use various forms of the strategy. The use of outside lobbying, however, appears in patterns, and those patterns can help to explain the role of outside lobbying in interest group politics. In chapter 3, I summarize and justify a signaling model of

---

[13] Interest groups have a more difficult time influencing behavior inside the voting booth. This topic will be discussed in later chapters.

outside lobbying. The model offers a consistent argument about the communicative role that interest groups play in transmitting salience information to policymakers. In chapter 4, I show that data on outside lobbying are consistent with a particular equilibrium in the signaling model. The prevalence of this equilibrium behavior means that the cynicism surrounding outside lobbying is only partially warranted. Salience information and outside lobbying are systematically related, and so there is nothing artificial about outside lobbying. Few groups use outside lobbying when they represent constituents with low salience on an issue. But popularity and outside lobbying are only mildly related, and so many groups supporting unpopular policies use outside lobbying too.

Two elements of the policy context that influence outside lobbying decisions, the stage of legislation and the policy alternatives, are examined in chapter 5. These are especially relevant when group leaders try to expand the conflict. I show that interest groups benefit differently from conflict expansion depending on the stage of legislation. Also, the policy status quo has a large effect on groups' propensities to expand the conflict.

Chapter 6 presents a case study of outside lobbying over trade issues. Decision making by interest groups and by legislators over NAFTA conforms well to the signaling and conflict expansion models presented in chapters 3 and 5. One additional feature is discussed as well. The biggest outside lobbyist in the case of NAFTA in 1993 was President Clinton. His involvement adds a new wrinkle to the outside lobbying story, as his strategies influenced what interest groups did and how other policymakers responded to interest groups. Chapter 7 concludes with a brief discussion of real grass roots versus astroturf, First Amendment rights, and the potential dangers of policymakers granting access to the well organized.

what about a counterfactual??

2

Tactics and Strategies

The Story of the Hat Trick

One beautiful August morning in 1989, Leona Kozien took the bus from near her home in Chicago to the Copernicus Center for senior citizens on the city's northwest side. Kozien, who was sixty-nine years old, had no idea at the time that she was going to become a brief media star and a figure of political lore. All she knew was that she was angry with the politicians in Washington. In particular, she felt betrayed by her congressman, Dan Rostenkowski, chairman of the Ways and Means Committee of the House of Representatives. Kozien was upset by a new policy from Washington that caused her husband to pay a surtax for catastrophic health care insurance. In her mind, it was an unfair attempt by the federal government to make senior citizens pay unreasonably for health care.

Rostenkowski knew many seniors were angry, but he did not know the extent of the anger. Since the unveiling of the policy a year earlier, a policy that he and the largest seniors lobby, the American Association of Retired Persons (AARP), had sponsored and supported all through the legislative process, he had been reluctant to meet with smaller senior citizens' groups, even those from his own district. National groups separate from the AARP, especially the National Committee to Preserve Social Security and Medicare, run by James Roosevelt, son of President Franklin D. Roosevelt, had been mobilizing grass-roots opposition to the policy for more than a year. The AARP then decided to oppose the new policy. Partly as a concession and partly as a compromise, Rostenkowski had agreed to meet with a few of the leaders of local senior citizens groups. The meeting was held at the Copernicus Center, right in the heart of Rostenkowski's district.

After prodding by her husband (who could not attend), Kozien joined approximately one hundred seniors who waited in the main hall of the center for Rostenkowski to emerge from the meeting with the group leaders. She and other seniors had been given signs to wave at Rostenkowski. The signs indicated displeasure with the current policy: Congressman Rostenkowski, Don't Tax the Seniors and Read My Lips: Catastrophic Act Is a Seniors Tax.

While Rostenkowski met with group leaders, Kozien and her own group were holding a meeting of their own in the main hall. Participants were taking turns telling the rest of the group why the catastrophic health policy was bad for seniors. The group waiting for Rostenkowski agreed that the catastrophic "tax" had to go, but they also agreed on something else. They wanted Rostenkowski to speak to them in person.

"A lot of people felt they were owed something," one local interest group leader recalls. "They just wanted to see him. He was right there, and they felt this was their opportunity [to tell him what they thought of the policy]."

Rostenkowski emerged from his meeting and headed for the exit. The group waiting for him booed and hissed. Before the congressman could get to the door, a television crew stopped him to ask questions about events in Poland, a topic of keen interest to many of his constituents. This pause gave a small group of seniors enough time to run out of the building and surround Rostenkowski's car. Kozien led the charge.

Kozien shouted, "Where's his car parked? I'm going to make him talk to us!"

A small mob followed Kozien outside, and pretty soon there were fifteen to twenty seniors surrounding the congressman's car, while television crews stood nearby. Rostenkowski, meanwhile, fought through the crowd and got in the car.

"Coward!" "Shame!" "Impeach Rottenkowski!" The seniors stood in front of the car and waved placards. The congressman's driver honked the horn and moved the car a few inches. The front bumper brushed against Kozien's thigh, and she staggered a bit. Some man shouted, "You knocked her down! You hurt her!" This same man then turned to Kozien and said quietly, "Lay down under the car."

"Are you crazy? No way, he'd run me over!" retorted Kozien, who was barely over five feet tall. The car moved again, and this time Kozien fell on the hood of the car. Her face was inches from Rostenkowski's, with glass separating them. She was still carrying her placard, and from inside the car, Rostenkowski saw her placard, her face, and her body sprawled across the windshield.

"Killer! Killer!" the crowd shouted.

Rostenkowski then got out of the car and ran through a parking lot while angry seniors chased after him. The driver maneuvered through the crowd, drove around the block, and caught up with Rostenkowski down the street from the center. Rostenkowski jumped in, and the car sped off.

"It was a funny picture," recalled one local politician present, "because it was a true chase. The seniors would move faster, and Rosty would move faster. He gets in the car, and they stand in front of the car."

The scene made for dramatic television. The Chicago film crews, delighted with the footage, distributed it immediately to the national networks. All three major television news shows carried the story prominently that evening, earning the interest group leaders what they call "a hat trick," in reference to a hockey player scoring three goals in one game.

Kozien, meanwhile, the activist and agitator for that day, was an unlikely hero. She had never before been active in politics. She knew little about the seniors groups at the Copernicus Center. Her relatives called that evening, expressing amazement at their "crazy Aunt Leona." Over the next several years politicians, prior to speaking at senior citizen events, would ask her to accompany them onstage. She always refused.

She likewise downplayed her heroism. "We just wanted answers. Had he answered our questions, there would have been no incident." Yet the incident was a bonanza for the leaders of the interest groups. The image of Kozien on the hood of Rostenkowski's car was used for years afterward on network news to symbolize the potency of the senior citizen lobby.

The catastrophic insurance program, which had passed the House in June 1988 by a vote of 328 to 72, was soon after repealed. The vote was not even close. The House voted 360 to 66 in favor of repeal in October 1989. Incidentally, Rostenkowski stood firm, voting to oppose repeal.

Many members of Congress had heard from people like Kozien, though presumably not from atop the hoods of their cars. Two Florida legislators reported getting more than seventy-five thousand pieces of mail, each opposing the policy. One staffer reported to me that his boss received more than two thousand mail pieces in favor of repeal, and eight mail pieces against repeal. The turn of events on catastrophic health insurance had people shaking their heads.

To some, the outside lobbying gave a large voice to a small number of people. "It was a case of the House of Representatives being stampeded by a small, vocal group of seniors," said Pete Stark, a Democratic congressman from California. "Ambushed is how a lot of people here feel now," Tim Penny, a Democrat from Minnesota, said at the time. "Every member of Congress was getting accosted at town meetings," said Senator John McCain, Republican from Arizona.

Others were more positive about the outcome, preferring to think that the outside lobbying tapped into a widespread sentiment. "We made a mistake last year [in 1988]," said Brian Donnelly, a Democratic congressman from Massachusetts. "This time, we listened to the voters."

Significance of the Story

The story of the Rostenkowski incident in north Chicago, while hardly typical of stories of outside lobbying, is useful for several reasons. For one, it shows in dramatic fashion how interest groups can instigate or facilitate collective action through outside lobbying. Contrary to what interest group leaders were claiming afterward, the mobbing of Rostenkowski was not all that spontaneous. The meeting between Rostenkowski and the interest group leaders was set up by the interest group leaders, and seniors from around the neighborhood were encouraged to attend by the interest group leaders. The interest groups leaders, not Rostenkowski's staff, had invited the networks to the meetings at the Copernicus Center. Rostenkowski's staff wanted to avoid media attention. And the interest group leaders made the placards and distributed them to Kozien and other seniors.

Interest group leaders also knew that the seniors attending were unusually angry about the new policy, and the leaders wanted to communicate that anger forcefully and make it seem less than fully staged. The seniors at the Copernicus Center were to represent the tip of the iceberg of constituent opinion. As for the seniors, their reactions could not have been better for the group leaders. The leaders provided a small, low-cost spark and let it turn into a conflagration. The behavior of Kozien and others was spontaneous and chaotic enough to indicate that the seniors were just plain mad. After all the preparations, events got out of control at the right time and at the right level. "Just barely out of control" might be the optimum level of behavioral response interest group leaders want from constituents in an outside lobbying campaign.

Therefore, what was communicated loudly and clearly to policymakers was the ease with which interest group leaders mobilized Kozien and her fellow seniors. The low costs involved for the interest groups to get hundreds of seniors to stampede the car of a powerful committee chairman counted for much more than the stampede itself. In trying to signal the "true" level of public salience over an issue, an interest group that succeeds with little effort can gain credibility. I shall discuss this important point in more detail in the next chapter.

Most of the conflict expansion on the issue had occurred well before that fateful day. National seniors organizations like the Gray Panthers and the National Committee to Preserve Social Security and Medicare had been running advertisements for months, and they had successfully framed the issue as one of unfair taxation for all seniors as opposed to one of health care benefits for a vast majority of seniors. By one reasonable interpretation, through the summer of 1989 interest groups had increased the level of salience among seniors on the issue. Then, as the salience of the issue peaked in late summer, interest group leaders had only to signal to policymakers the salience of the issue among those seniors who opposed the new policy. The Rostenkowski incident was timed perfectly. The conflict had been expanded, and the time had come to let policymakers know about it.

The story also neatly illustrates the roles assumed by the main players described in the previous chapter. Interest group leaders, the ones who had invited people like Kozien in the first place, set the stage for the famous confrontation (though they got lucky when it succeeded beyond their expectations). A policymaker, in this case a powerful House committee chairman,

TABLE 2.1

Reconsidering Catastrophic Health Insurance: Number of Members of the House of Representatives Voting For or Against Original Bill and Repeal

	Original Bill	
Repeal	Yea	Nay
Yea	240	64
Nay	60	1

Note: This takes into account turnover from the 100th to 101st Congress, in that only members who voted on both bills are included. One member, Larry Hopkins, a Republican from Kentucky, voted against the original proposal and against repeal. The original bill was HR 2470, Catastrophic Health Insurance/Rule. The repeal was HR 3299, Amendment to Budget Reconciliation, Repealing Catastrophic Health Insurance Surtax.

found himself the target of outside lobbying efforts by interest group leaders and constituents. And the ordinary constituents like Kozien, who behaved in both an organized and disorganized manner, made the lives of policymakers more difficult through simple expressions of anger.

The story is useful as well for highlighting the potential influence of outside lobbying. The renegade senior citizens groups, those distinguishing themselves early on from the AARP on the catastrophic health care policy, appear to have had an effect on Rostenkowski's colleagues in the House. As table 2.1 indicates, 240 members of the House switched their votes from supporting catastrophic coverage in June 1988 to supporting repeal of catastrophic coverage sixteen months later. This is a remarkable instance of collective reconsideration. Only 124 members, or approximately half of the number that switched votes, voted the "same" way for both bills—that is, 124 either voted against the original bill and for repeal, or they voted for the original bill and against repeal. The latter vote, on the amendment to repeal the Catastrophic Coverage Act, was the first time Congress had ever voted to repeal a major social benefit it had created.

"An event of about 150 elderly people changed the tide of the thing," recalled Jan Schakowsky, at the time a leader of the Illinois State Council of Senior Citizens, one of the groups that mobilized seniors on that day. "It was a pivotal event." It was pivotal not because it changed Rostenkowski's mind (which it did not), but because it had such an influence on his colleagues. As the story and its aftermath remind us, a well-publicized event among a small number of people can send very strong signals about, and enhance the reputation of, a group numbering many thousands or even millions of people. More than five years later, members of Congress referred to the Rostenkowski incident as cementing the reputation of the senior citizens lobby. This, according to people in Washington who are inclined to slight hyperbole, is one group in the population they do not want to cross.

Another revealing aspect of the story is that the Rostenkowski event happened because of a grave miscalculation on the part of the chairman and his colleagues. They enacted the original policy because they were led to believe that seniors were behind it, but they gambled and lost when interest groups tapped into a undiscovered level of antipathy among certain groups of seniors.[1] In general, legislators try to estimate the policy preferences and issue salience among their constituents, yet these estimates are shots in the dark on many controversial issues. They never know how some groups will respond, or which issues their next electoral opponent will use against them. They need to do the near impossible: anticipate how latent constituent opinion will manifest itself in the coming years.[2] Rostenkowski was probably warned when he led his committee to recommend the original policy. Like anyone facing a difficult decision, however, he listened to the people who had previously established a credible reputation for electoral power, the AARP. Yet until Kozien and her fellow seniors let him know loudly and clearly their preferences, he could not have been certain about the consequences of his previous actions. The response among seniors led Rostenkowski and other policymakers to move toward repeal.

The Rostenkowski story is unusual, of course. Rarely are outside lobbying efforts as successful. Famous examples, such as this one, become lore around the Capitol. Another example from the early 1980s still generates discussion around Washington. During the successful outside lobbying efforts in 1982 by the American Bankers Association to repeal tax withholding from interest-bearing accounts, 22 million postcards from depositors flooded into Congress within days of the passage of the tax bill containing the provision. Every congressional district responded, according to the staff of Robert Dole, the chair of the Senate Finance Committee at the time. The marvel is that bankers, of all people, were able to make an issue more salient through conflict expansion, and at the same time were able to signal that salience to policymakers with a successful outside lobbying campaign. They did all of this without hiding their identities as bankers, indicating that latent salience among constituents is a great resource for all groups, not just for those with popular images or credibility as electoral powerhouses.

---

[1] In truth, even the AARP was caught off guard. Dissident elderly groups, those opposed to the policy all along, begun stirring opposition until the AARP changed its policy on the issue. Then, once the AARP was opposed to the policy, it galvanized further action by the dissident elderly groups.

[2] Arnold, in his study of Congress (1990), found that much contemporary legislative behavior can be explained by legislators' anticipation of the campaign issues opponents may use against them in future campaigns. These anticipated campaign issues reflect, in turn, what issues legislators think constituents will consider important at election time, or what issues will be salient. There are strong parallels between Arnold's argument and the arguments about signaling in this book.

Interest Group Strategies and Tactics

The tactics used at the Copernicus Center were not typical of outside lobbying strategies either. Constituents waving placards, shouting, and surrounding cars have the advantage of capturing attention, especially if news cam-
eras are rolling nearby. But the strategy of outside lobbying, while intended
in the end to accomplish what the hat trick accomplished—namely, to influence policymakers' perceptions of the salience of policy issues to subsets of
constituents—encompasses a variety tactics, most of which are more common and less dramatic than noisy demonstrations. How common are various
outside lobbying tactics? For that matter, how common are outside lobbying
strategies in general?

Answers to these question will depend on the way data on lobbying techniques are organized and represented. Previous research has drawn conclusions on lobbying tactics at the group level, and while this approach has a
number of disadvantages, which I discussed in chapter 1 and will discuss
again shortly, the approach is helpful in discovering the tendencies of classes
of groups to undertake certain lobbying strategies or tactics.

Measuring Outside Lobbying Frequency by Group

Interest groups essentially have a common toolbox; each tool fits a different
situation and carries with it different risks and costs. Understanding how
group strategies and tactics change across issues, which is the purpose of
much of the empirical analysis in this study, requires that data be organized
by group issue rather than by group. But there are clear tendencies among
groups. Groups undoubtedly rely on tools they are familiar with and that fit
their organizational structure and culture. And not only are some tactics unlikely to be used by specific groups, there are tactics that are never used by
whole classes of interest groups. For instance, corporations never protest
with placards or marches. Other classes of groups, in contrast, use as many
tools as the law allows. Labor unions, especially the large national organizations like the Teamsters and the United Auto Workers, use a great variety of
tactics on many issues. Finally, tactics such as personal contact with members of Congress or their staff are used by virtually every interest group in
Washington. Data organized by group can provide a picture of the range of
tactics used by any one group in a given period.

Studies by Schlozman and Tierney (1986) and Walker (1991) are based on
group differences, and they reveal several interesting patterns among interest
groups, which are largely replicated in my own study. The information in
table 2.2, for example, leads to conclusions similar to those from another

TABLE 2.2
Percentage of Interest Groups Engaging in Particular Activities

	Regularly	Occasionally	Never	N
Inside Lobbying				
Contacting Congress personally	96	4	0	50
Testifying in Congress	70	30	0	50
Presenting research to government	68	32	0	50
Contacting agency personnel	67	33	0	49
Contributing to campaigns	54	10	36	50
Testifying at agency hearings	39	49	12	49
Serving on public advisory boards	27	52	21	48
Participating in litigation over policy	22	51	27	49
Outside Lobbying				
Talking with the press	76	22	2	50
Mobilizing group members	56	38	6	50
Organizing letter-writing campaigns	54	36	10	50
Presenting research to the press	49	49	2	49
Holding press conferences	29	50	21	48
Publicizing voting records of candidates	24	4	72	50
Endorsing candidates	22	2	76	50
Protesting	10	22	68	50
Polling the public on policy issues	8	28	64	50
Advertising policy positions	6	46	48	50
Hiring public relations firms	4	32	62	50
Contributing personnel to campaigns	4	4	92	49
Organizational Maintenance				
Entering coalitions with other groups	80	18	2	50
Sending letters to group members	72	4	24	50
Polling group members on policy issues	40	24	36	. 43
Fund-raising with direct mail	24	8	68	49
Advertising to attract new members	6	26	68	50

prominent table in Schlozman and Tierney (150). Table 2.2 summarizes the percentage of groups in my study that undertake interest group tactics "regularly," "occasionally," or "never." The information in table 2.2 goes beyond that contained in the Schlozman and Tierney table in that it categorizes the tactics into three sets, as part of inside lobbying strategies, part of outside lobbying strategies, or part of organizational formation or maintenance. Recall that inside lobbying is defined as communication or interaction directed at policymakers or their staffs, and outside lobbying is defined as an appeal toward persons outside the policymaking community. Organizational formation involves those tactics intended to help the group, or a coalition of groups, solve collective action problems, that is, communicate with members, raise money, provide selective benefits, and coordinate behavior with other groups in some way.

Most, though not all, of the categorizations of these tactics are straightforward. The first four tactics listed in table 2.2 are clearly inside lobbying. Note how every interest group interviewed uses the four tactics at least occasionally. These data, and the data from the Schlozman and Tierney study, highlight an important fact: interest groups do not choose either inside lobbying or outside lobbying, as though the strategic choices were mutually exclusive. Rather, all groups inside lobby to some extent all the time, and especially, as the group-issue data show later, on issues their leaders or members care about. Choices are then over which tactics to use above and beyond the basic inside lobbying tactics, personal contacts and testimony at hearings. Additional tactics include other inside lobbying techniques, like filing suit or giving campaign contributions, and outside lobbying techniques, like organizing letter-writing campaigns, holding press conferences, and running advertisements.[3] Groups can also forge coalitions and improve membership communication or enrollments, though these are indirect tactics that may bolster group resources. I consider these part of organizational maintenance. Several techniques are difficult to categorize, such as urging influential members of the organization to lobby, contributing personnel to campaigns, and direct mail advertising. I shall consider all but the last of these outside lobbying, though this coding makes little difference for any conclusions drawn throughout the study.

While inside lobbying is prevalent in some form among all interest groups, outside lobbying occurs less often, and only among a subset of groups. This too is similar to the findings of Schlozman and Tierney. The most common forms of outside lobbying are low-cost activities like talking with the press and urging group members to write letters to lawmakers. In contrast, tactics that force groups to choose sides in electoral competition— like publicizing a candidate's voting record, making endorsements, and contributing personnel to campaigns—are undertaken sparingly and by few groups. This is partially because groups need to maintain tax status as a nonpolitical organization. A bit surprising is that 36 percent of groups in my data participate in polling the general public about policy issues, a finding that gives an idea of how important public opinion polls have become in policymaking, especially given their expense. And 52 percent of groups fund or help fund advertisements on policy issues. It appears, from the frequency of these last two tactics, that interest groups acknowledge the importance of public opinion in the success of lobbying efforts, and that, sometimes at

[3] Filing suit or giving campaign contributions can be interpreted as outside lobbying, but given my definition of outside lobbying as appealing to persons beyond the policymaking community, lawsuits and campaign contributions can reasonably be placed in the inside lobbying category.

TABLE 2.3
Percentage of Interest Groups Engaging in Outside Lobbying
Strategies for Specific Issues Raised in Interviews

Mobilizing group members	70
Advertising policy positions	52
Holding press conferences	26
Protesting	20
Hiring public relations firms	16
N	50

great expense, they actively try to engage constituents in lobbying or try to gauge potential public reaction to outside lobbying.

Unlike in surveys from previous studies, I asked groups not only about their general lobbying practices, but also about their lobbying techniques on specific issues. The data summarized in tables 2.3 and 2.4, while still referring to group-level tendencies, are somewhat different from the data summarized in table 2.2. Tables 2.3 and 2.4 refer to responses about specific issues discussed in depth during interviews. For example, only if a group advertised on any of the issues mentioned in the interview would its answer be given as affirmative for advertisements in tables 2.3 and 2.4. There were, however, many issues discussed in the interviews, so these tables provide a good depiction of the extent of outside lobbying. The first row in table 2.3 shows that 70 percent of groups urged members to lobby policymakers on at least one issue discussed in the interviews.

This low-cost tactic, urging members to contact policymakers, is certainly the most common form of outside lobbying, a finding comparable to that of Schlozman and Tierney. They found that 84 percent of groups inspired letter-writing or telegram campaigns, and 80 percent of groups mounted grass-roots lobbying efforts. Unless an interest group has thousands of members in each congressional district, a luxury enjoyed by only a handful of groups, this tactic hardly ranks as a major instrument of national conflict expansion. For most interest groups, since they either tend to be concentrated in a small number of districts or states or tend to have a small number of members in each district or state, urging members to contact policymakers essentially involves convincing a few hundred constituents of specific legislators to call, fax, E-mail, or write their opinions on selected issues.

More than half of the groups advertised in some form on at least one of the issues discussed, and one-fourth held press conferences. Other forms of outside lobbying are also relatively common. Table 2.4 takes a closer look at advertising. Usually, advertising is highly targeted, though with one notable exception. Elite national newspapers, like the *New York Times, Washington Post,* or *Wall Street Journal,* are common platforms for interest groups. On

TABLE 2.4

Percentage of Interest Groups Engaging in Advertising Strategies for Specific Issues
Raised in Interviews

	Among All Groups	Among Groups That Advertised
Newspapers—elite, national	26	54
Newspapers—local, targeted	26	54
Magazines—targeted at policymakers	16	33
Magazines—local, targeted at citizens	14	29
Television—targeted (cable, other)	8	17
Radio—targeted (religious, age group, race)	4	8
Magazines—elite, national	4	8
Radio—general audience	4	8
Television—general audience	2	4
N	50	17

the selected issues in the interviews, approximately one out of four groups
advertised or participated in (contributed to) advertising in these newspapers
within the year previous to my interviews. Note that this understates the
extent of interest group advertising in the elite papers because other issues
not discussed in my interviews are not included in table 2.4.

As for the tendency of a certain class of groups like labor unions to adopt
a standard set of tactics and return to them time and again, the data reveal
that this undoubtedly occurs. For example, an analysis of the group data
reveals that when corporations and trade associations use outside lobbying,
they tend to hire public relations firms, sponsor issue advertising, or encourage business executives (and occasionally a wider group of employees) to
contact members of Congress. Labor unions rarely hire public relations
firms, but they do run advertisements and frequently try to mobilize their
members to contact Congress. Professional associations rely almost exclusively on membership mobilizations, although these mobilizations are almost
never on broad policy themes like social welfare or employment issues.
They focus instead on narrow, technical issues on which their members can
claim expertise.

Behavioral patterns also emerge for specific groups. One insurance corporation surveyed found it useful to advertise on television their position on
health care reform. Another professional association, the American College
of Surgeons, advertised its position on AIDS research funding repeatedly
in national magazines. And a particularly ambitious public interest group,
the Liberty Lobby, published its own newspaper, held its own radio talk
show, publicized voting records of lawmakers, and held small protests. This

TABLE 2.5
Factor Scores for Group Data Set

	Maximum Likelihood Estimates (Lambda)		Factor Scores	
Lobbying Behavior	Inside Factor	Outside Factor	Inside Factor	Outside Factor
Testifying at agency hearings	1		0.044	
Testifying in Congress	1.265***		0.286	
Contacting Congress personally	0.194*		0.086	
Contacting agency personnel	0.991**		0.116	
Participating in litigation	1.763***		0.127	
Presenting research to government	0.456**		0.035	
Serving on public advisory boards	0.784**		0.029	
Advertising policy positions		1		0.050
Talking with the press		0.622***		0.043
Polling the public on policy		0.264		0.009
Presenting research to the press		0.593*		0.031
Holding press conferences		0.970**		0.032
Organizing letter-writing campaigns		1.358*		0.067
Fund-raising with direct mail		1.686***		0.049
Mobilizing group members		1.113***		0.061
Protesting		1.53***		0.09
Endorsing candidates		2.044***		0.094
Publicizing voting records of candidates		1.955***		0.072
Correlation among Factors			0.379	
Chi-square (df = 34)			247.75	
Goodness of fit index			0.654	
Adjusted goodness of fit index			0.559	
Root mean square residual			0.055	

Note: Numbers listed are MLE coefficients and standard errors (in parentheses) for the first two columns, and factor scores for the latter two columns.

$*p < .1$, $**p < .05$, $***p < .01$

group's leaders, surprisingly and virtually alone among public interest group leaders, never tried in 1992 to mobilize letter-writing or telephone call campaigns among its members targeted at Congress.

As will now be shown, the tactics recorded in my data tend to cluster into inside and outside strategies, thus revealing group-level patterns of strategies consistent with past research. Gais and Walker, for example, used exploratory factor analysis on Walker's group-level data to indicate inside and outside tendencies among membership organizations (1991, 110). They found two variance patterns that correspond to inside and outside strategies. Table 2.5

summarizes results of a confirmatory factor analysis on my group data. Confirmatory factor analysis differs from exploratory factor analysis in that with the former the researcher specifies a model in advance and sets the number of latent variables. In the latter, neither the model nor the number of latent variables are specified in advance, and the latent variables emerge from the variance patterns discovered (through a variety of possible methods) in the observed variables.

For this confirmatory analysis, two latent variables representing inside and outside strategies are posited and then the procedure tests whether the observed tactics summarized in table 1.2 have common variances among one another and with the latent variables. The model is a basic maximum likelihood confirmatory factor model estimated using LISREL.[4] One observed variable for each factor is held constant at one, and the model is identified. To help with interpretation of the coefficients and factor scores, note that each observed variable ranges from zero to two, corresponding respectively to the "never," "occasionally," and "regularly" from table 2.1. Note also that left out of the analysis are observed variables with little common variance with either factor.[5]

The maximum likelihood estimates in table 2.5 are similar to regression coefficients in that they are unstandardized measures of how much each observed variable explains the latent variable, if the other observed variables are held constant. The factor scores, meanwhile, help to form an index of inside or outside tendencies for a particular group. The two indices can be formed by multiplying (weighting) an observed variable by its corresponding factor score, and summing across all the tactics under a particular strategy. So, for one public interest group, the Americans for Democratic Action, its inside index was calculated as follows:

$$.004*(0) + .286*(2) + .086*(2) + .116*(1) + .127*(1) + .035*(2) + .029*(0)$$

The numbers in the parentheses correspond to the three possible responses, "never" (0), "occasionally" (1), and "regularly" (2), and the multipliers are the factor scores for the various tactics shown in table 2.5.

The coefficient estimates (which are highly significant statistically) and the factor scores confirm the presence of the two hypothesized strategies. This is fully consistent with the Gais and Walker findings. Furthermore, the two indices offer measures of group tendencies to adopt the two strategies.

[4] The standard confirmatory factor model in LISREL has symmetric covariance matrices, uncorrelated errors, and no endogenous factors.

[5] Direct mail fund-raising was included in the outside lobbying index because it was strongly correlated to the outside factor and because it was used by many of the groups as a method of mobilization. Strictly speaking, direct mail fund-raising is organizational maintenance, but it is included here as part of outside lobbying as a nod to letting the data, and the group leaders I interviewed who use direct mail fund-raising, speak for themselves.

Groups do tend to use one or the other strategy more, as indicated by the correlation coefficient between the factors, though an important caveat for the inside index must kept in mind. For a few of the inside lobbying tactics—the first four listed in table 2.2—there is little variation across groups. All groups use the tactics, so all groups use some form of inside lobbying on issues they care about. The inside index is still useful, however, because the remainder of the inside lobbying tactics, especially testifying in agency hearings and serving on governmental boards, tend to reflect a group's insider status as indicated by government invitations to participate in decisions. Some groups receive government overtures to participate in hearings and provide expertise to policymakers, and these invitations suggest a legitimacy bestowed on selected groups. The inside index therefore is not a straightforward measure of group's tendency to decide to use inside lobbying. Rather it is a measure of a combination of interest group leaders' decisions and the insider status accorded to a group by policymakers in the government.

Differences across five group classes can be measured using the two indices. Figures 2.1 and 2.2 show the distributions of the two indices for all the groups, and then for the five classes of interest groups. Both indices were rescaled to range from zero to one. Figure 2.1 indicates that, other than a set of groups bunched down at very low ranges, the inside index has a left skew. Many groups inside lobby extensively and receive government invitations to consult with policymakers. The pattern does not change very much across classes of groups. Yet figure 2.2 on the outside lobbying index is a telling contrast. Among all groups, the outside lobbying index has a right skew, indicating that most groups bunch at the bottom of the scale. Of the five classes of groups, public interest groups and labor unions comprise the bulk of the organizations using outside lobbying tactics, while professional and trade associations and corporations comprise the bulk of the organizations at the lower end of the scale.

My group data therefore reveal three patterns worth summarizing, all of which are consistent with previous research. First, inside lobbying is ubiquitous among groups, and outside lobbying is less common but still fairly prevalent among most groups. Second, tactics tend to cluster slightly into inside and outside strategies at the group level. And third, certain classes of groups, especially labor unions and public interest groups, use a wider variety of outside lobbying tactics more consistently than do their business and professional counterparts.

Measuring Outside Lobbying Frequency by Group Issue

If we want to know the frequency of outside lobbying strategies, group level data has distinct limitations. Interest group leaders can say that their organizations use a tactic "regularly," but this response has no referent to the num-

All Groups

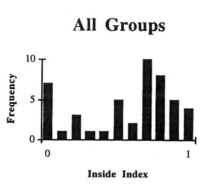

Professional Associations

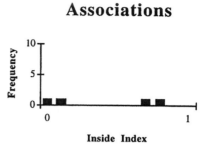

Public Interest Groups

Corporations

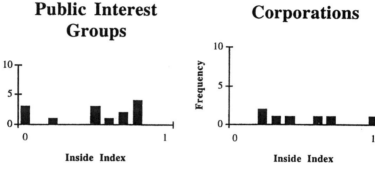

Trade Associations

Labor Unions

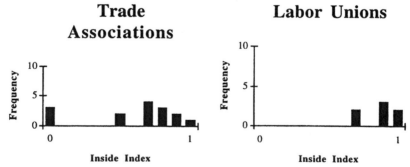

Figure 2.1. Distribution of Inside Index (Group Data)

ber of issues a group takes on or the scale of the use of the tactic in any particular set of circumstances. Moreover, many interesting questions concerning the relationship between group strategies and the political environment facing groups cannot be addressed with group data. How do interest groups respond to hostile public opinion? Do group resources override pub-

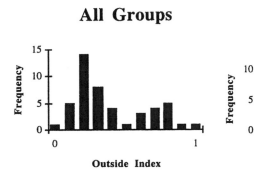

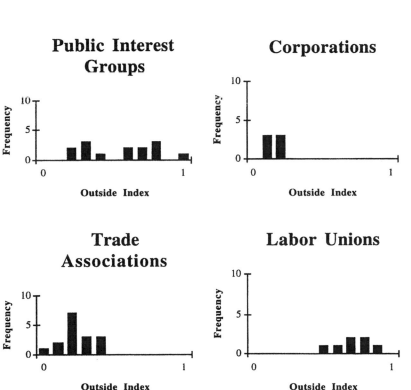

Figure 2.2. Distribution of Outside Index (Group Data)

lic support in determining outside lobbying strategies? How do outside lobbying strategies change over the course of legislation? Because factors that change across issues may influence strategic decisions over lobbying strategies, group level data are inadequate.

Group-issue data, such as I have collected, can provide a more complete

TABLE 2.6
Percentage of Group-Issue Cases Involving Outside Lobbying

Mobilizing group members	57
Holding press conferences	25
Advertising policy positions	16
Protesting	13
Hiring public relations firms	7
N	323

picture of the extent of outside lobbying. The data, by construction, are weighted toward those groups with interests over more issues. Thus, table 2.6 presents data on the frequency of outside lobbying tactics among the group-issue cases, and these measures can be interpreted as giving the proportion of decisions facing interest groups when their leaders chose to use outside lobbying. Or, to put it another way, these measures offer the proportion of *potential* outside lobbying strategies that actually end up as outside lobbying.[6] The tactics in table 2.6, among all the ones considered part of outside lobbying strategies in table 2.2, are those that vary across issues.

Once again, according to table 2.6, urging group members to lobby is very common, used on over half of the cases. Press conferences are used in one-quarter of the cases. More expensive or controversial tactics, however, drop dramatically in frequency from the group data. We know from table 2.3 earlier in this chapter that more than one-half of groups advertised on policy issues, but table 2.6 shows that these advertisements are bought very selectively, at a rate of about one in six group-issue cases. Protesting and hiring public relations firms are even more rare in the group-issue data. The dropoff in percentages for particular tactics from table 2.3 to table 2.6 is revealing; the less frequent tactics are used selectively, perhaps because they are expensive, risky, or effective only in specialized circumstances. So, for example, many groups use advertising, but not many group-issue cases involve advertising.

Simply counting tactics used on a given issue does not reflect the full range of choices available to interest groups deciding over strategies. As important as the particular tactic used is the scale of outside lobbying. How many citizens is the group trying to reach? How targeted are the outside

---

[6] The one caveat is that the decisions being considered by interest groups in these data follow the initial decisions to show interest in a policy issue at all. Recall that at the beginning of my interviews with interest group leaders, I asked them which issues they considered to be important. There are prior decisions for groups, like whether or not to pay attention to the policy issue (which may or may not relate to the various concepts studied here), that are unfortunately unexamined.

lobbying strategies? Consider that advertising in elite, national newspapers is outside lobbying on a large scale. In some cases, interest groups hope to reach every citizen in the country with television advertising. The famous Harry and Louise television commercials, sponsored by the Health Insurance Association of America to fight President Clinton's health care proposal in 1994, were promulgated to reach the largest possible audience. The ads ran during popular sports programs, sitcoms, and news broadcasts. Anti-NAFTA advertisements by the AFL-CIO in 1993 were on a huge scale as well.

More often, outside lobbying occurs on a smaller scale. A notch below the mammoth television campaigns are advertising and letter-writing campaigns targeted at readers of specific periodicals or viewers of specific television programs. The American Association of Railroads (AAR) in 1991 ran what they consider a highly successful series of advertisements in the *Washington Post* and the *New Republic* to oppose deregulation proposed by the trucking industry. The American Trucking Association (ATA) at the time was trying to convince Congress to allow trucks in all states to pull up to three trailers behind their rigs. More trailers on trucks means more efficient trucking, and more efficient trucking is bad for the railroad business. The AAR, clearly out for its members' own economic interests, emphasized in the ads the danger long trucks pose to automobile passengers. "Some Trucking Companies Want Them," say the ads, referring to a picture of double and triple trailer trucks, "Do You?" Cutouts and postcards were sometimes attached to the advertisements for people to send the Congress, and the AAR distributed film footage to national TV networks of trucks swerving on rain-drenched highways so the networks could work the film spots into news broadcasts. The campaign appeared to serve its purpose, and the proposed deregulation was left out of the year's highway bill.

The ATA, on a side note, knows the value of outside lobbying on that scale. The ATA in 1993 generated tens of thousands of telephone calls to Congress protesting President Clinton's fuel tax increases. As there are approximately 2.7 million professional truck drivers in the United States, a large number from every congressional district, any attempt to mobilize the entire trucking profession would count as relatively large scale outside lobbying.

By far most instances of outside lobbying involve a few thousand citizens or less. In a typical outside lobbying campaign, an interest group targets several legislators on a key committee, contacts their group members in the districts of those legislators, and urges them to write letters, send faxes or E-mails, or make telephone calls to either the legislators' Washington offices or district offices. Many groups, especially labor unions and public interest groups, undertake these tactics themselves, using regular staff and local representatives in their organizations. Other kinds of groups hire specialized public relations firms to mobilize a small number of citizens.

Quite a few consulting firms in Washington, D.C., specialize exclusively in mobilizing very targeted grass-roots pressure on Congress. Most of their clients are businesses. Bonner and Associates in Washington, D.C., was the most famous of these firms in the early 1990s. A list of their clients includes the Pharmaceutical Manufacturers Association, American Bankers Association, Nonprescription Drug Manufacturers Association, United States Tobacco Company, Nationwide Insurance Companies, and the LTV Corporation. Jack Bonner's strategy is to find influential people to contact Congress who have no explicit connection with the business organizations doing the lobbying. So when the largest American automobile manufacturers hired Bonner in 1990 to fight proposed extensions of the Clean Air Act, Bonner contacted representatives of the elderly and handicapped, and urged them to write Congress about the benefits of big cars. A few hundred calls or letters from the right people can mean a lot, and several controversial measures, including tailpipe standards, were defeated. The Northrop Corporation hired Bonner to generate pressure in support of the B-2 bomber in 1991 and 1992, and Bonner followed through by convincing several hundred leaders from religious, elderly, and veteran groups to write or call Congress that the bomber saved lives in the 1991 Gulf War.

The nature of the group membership will matter a great deal in determining the number of citizens the interest group leaders feel they can or must mobilize. A labor union or an environmental group will contact thousands of their members in a single district. This kind of outside lobbying, according to activists in these groups, is "small" scale because it is so targeted in one or two districts, and it is small relative to other outside lobbying campaigns these groups undertake. In contrast, a favorite small-scale tactic for trade associations is to fly a handful of chief executive officers to Washington for consultation with the home member of Congress. "There isn't anyone as effective as the CEO," says one lobbyist (Birnbaum 1992, 198). In a few cases, interest groups will bring in a celebrity or someone with a gripping story to testify at congressional hearings. Hollywood stars are an increasingly common phenomenon on the Hill, testifying, for example, for environmental regulation or against gun control. And on crime bills, sorrowful stories told by crime victims can be heard in testimony around the Capitol. These victims are usually invited by a law enforcement group or a pro–gun control group.

The group-issue data allow for the scale of outside lobbying to be incorporated into the analysis of group decision making. Not only can we expect that tactics change across issues, but even more likely the scale of those tactics changes, especially in relation to the amount of public support that group leaders feel they can generate. I therefore coded three of the outside lobbying variables using ordinal scales to correspond to the number of citizens the interest groups were trying to mobilize. The scales were created from the range of outside lobbying campaigns I found in the data and are intended to cut the data into equal percentiles (for those cases for which the groups used outside lobbying; the number of cases using none of particular tactic will always be larger than the other categories). The scales reflect the number of citizens targeted and the degree of discrimination—how much the tactics were targeted at specific groups of constituents—in the outside lobbying campaign. The codings for the group-issue data are given below. Numbers in parentheses are the codes given to each level.

Protesting
No protests (0)
Small, local protests (1)
Moderate, regional protests (2)
Large, national protests, or on the Mall (3)

does this mean small protests on the mall?

Advertising
No advertising (0)
Advertising targeted at fewer than 1,000 persons (e.g. policymakers) (1)
Advertising targeted at fewer than 1 million persons (2)
Advertising targeted at more than 1 million persons (3)

Membership Mobilizations
No membership mobilizations (0)
Mobilizations targeted at fewer than 100 persons (1)
Mobilizations targeted at fewer than 500 persons (2)
Mobilizations targeted at fewer than 200,000 persons (3)
Mobilizations targeted at fewer than 1 million persons (4)
Mobilizations targeted at more than 1 million persons (5)

why these 5

The three variables coded for the scale of outside lobbying, plus a fourth dichotomous variable indicating whether the interest group held a press conference on the issue, were included in a confirmatory factor analysis summarized in table 2.7.[7] This analysis is very similar to the one summarized in table 2.6, though the group-issue data were used (in contrast to the group data) and only one factor, outside lobbying, was specified in advance. Since inside lobbying does not vary much across issues, an inside lobbying index was not created.

Once again, the maximum likelihood estimates in table 2.7 give an unstandardized measure of the effects of the observable variables on the latent factor. These estimates should be read with the audience codings in mind because the codings provide the numerical scaling of the observed variables. And the factor scores provide the means to create an outside lobbying index

[7] Hiring public relations firms did not correlate with the latent variable outside lobbying and was dropped from the analysis.

TABLE 2.7
Factor Scores for Group-Issue Data Set

	Maximum Likelihood Estimates (Lambda)	Factor Scores
Lobbying Behavior	*Outside Factor*	*Outside Factor*
Mobilizing group members	1	0.540
Advertising audience index	0.184***	0.166
Protesting audience index	0.215***	0.337
Holding press conference	0.12***	0.461
Chi-square (*df* = 2)		7.45
Goodness of fit index		0.988
Adjusted goodness of fit index		0.942
Root mean square residual		0.018

Note: Numbers listed are MLE coefficients and standard errors (in parentheses) for the first column, and factor scores for the second column.
$*p < .1, **p < .05, ***p < .01$

to use for the group-issue data. To create the index, the observed variables are multiplied (weighted) by the factor scores and the weighted variables are summed, as in the previous indices for the group data. The resulting index (rescaled to be between 0 and 1), which measures the common factor among the observed outside lobbying tactics, can be interpreted as the scale of outside lobbying used on the issue by the group. The index includes a variety of tactics—advertising, press conferences, membership mobilizations, broad letter-writing or telephone campaigns, and protesting—because these tactics are part of the same basic process, expanding the number of constituents informed and mobilized in a given policy conflict. This variable, which I call OUTSIDE, is the major dependent variable used in the remainder of the book.

Figure 2.3 displays the frequency of various levels of outside lobbying across the group-issue cases. The OUTSIDE index is highly skewed to the right over all the cases, as the figure shows. On more than one-third of the cases (37 percent) , interest groups did not use any outside lobbying. This is not at all surprising, as there are many reasons for a group to avoid outside lobbying on an issue. Further, the patterns for the classes of groups only strengthen the conclusion from the group data that public interest groups and labor unions comprise the bulk of cases where outside lobbying is used. (Note that, unlike for figures 2.1 and 2.2, the vertical scales change across histograms in 2.3.) Among the business and professional groups, a small number of cases involving trade associations resulted in extensive outside lobbying, but otherwise, professional groups and corporations showed limited outside lobbying action on the specific issues collected for the group-issue data.

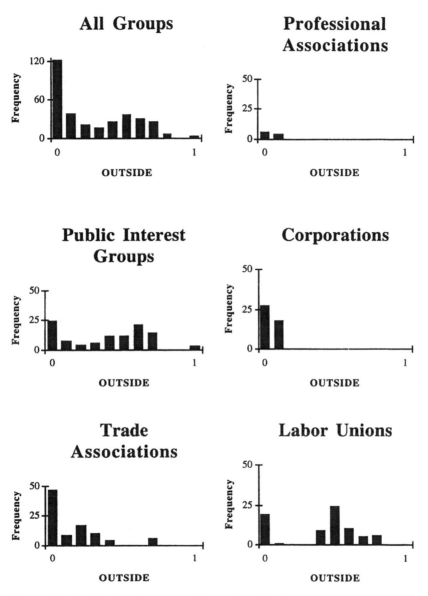

Figure 2.3. Distribution of OUTSIDE (Group-Issue Data)

More on Group Differences

Dividing interest groups into the five recognized classes, as in figures 2.1, 2.2, and 2.3, is more than merely following the labels the group leaders ascribe to their organizations. There are obviously real organizational differences between, say, a corporation and a public interest group that relate to the kinds of tactics the two groups will use to influence policymakers. The purposes of the organizations, the membership qualifications of the organizations, and the kinds of resources available to group leaders are all important to lobbying decisions and overlap somewhat with the group classifications.

Olson (1965), for one, argues that groups which form and exist for reasons other than politics—such as corporations, professional associations, most trade associations, and even labor unions—would have advantages over purely voluntary political organizations, such as most public interest groups. The groups that can lobby the government as a *by-product* of their other organizational activities will not have to solve difficult collective action problems every time they face a political threat. Their resources, especially staff, communication networks, field offices, and expertise, are already in place. For instance, Olson writes, "the impressive political power of the American Medical Association and the local groups that compose it is a by-product of the nonpolitical activities of organized medicine" (140).

This could cut both ways, however. Olson may be right when he says groups that can lobby as a by-product have many of the tools in place to begin with. There is no need to solve difficult collective action problems in forming the organization. At the same time, we ought to expect that when it comes to outside lobbying, groups that maintain constant contact with their members, often for reasons having to do with organizational maintenance, may be advantaged. From figures 2.2 and 2.3, public interest groups appear to be *more* likely to use outside lobbying than are other classes of groups that would fall under Olson's description of lobbying as a by-product. Their members are used to being called on to contribute to the efforts of the group, whether it be giving money, contacting Congress, or showing up at meetings. If, as it seems reasonable, interest groups continually facing the challenge to mobilize members just to maintain the organization can wage outside lobbying campaigns more successfully than groups not facing this challenge, then this turns Olson's idea on its head. A habit of solving collective action problems can be beneficial when the time comes to mobilize members in an outside lobbying campaign.

A more politically charged distinction among groups is whether an organization represents a "special" interest or whether an organization represents "public" interests. The self-described public interest group movement in the 1970s chose the label knowing the contempt many Americans feel toward interest groups representing specific economic interests. Public interest groups do not have the monopoly on representing "public" interests, but they do stand apart from the other classes of groups in at least claiming to represent interests that are not linked specifically to members of the groups. And as we have just seen, public interest groups often feel confident in demonstrating the public nature of their support.

There are other ways to distinguish groups by the degree of specialization. For example, many Americans would consider representative groups from particular industries to epitomize the term "special interest." Thus industry groups and labor unions are derided accordingly. These groups are generally less popular and have less sympathy among the broad public than, say, environmental or child welfare organizations.[8] Accordingly, if public sentiment influences lobbying decisions at all—for example, by limiting how receptive policymakers are toward unpopular groups—then groups that are part of particular industries may lobby differently from the way other kinds of groups do. They may feel the need to control the content of their messages because of hostile reporters or because the public may automatically discount their messages (Schlozman and Tierney 1986, 171).

My data indicate that in fact there is little difference in overall levels of inside and outside lobbying between groups that are part of particular industries and groups that are not part of particular industries. Even over the various tactics, differences are, for the most part, negligible. Several exceptions should be noted. Groups that are not part of particular industries tend to use direct mail and protests more frequently than do their counterparts. And groups that are part of industries tend to be invited to be on governmental boards and testify at agency hearings more often than do their counterparts.

As for memberships, different group classes have distinctive membership qualifications that lead to some tactics being used regularly by one class of groups and avoided completely by another class of groups. Corporations do not have members in the same way that labor unions do, and certainly not the kind of members that are willing to protest with placards and slogans. Corporations do, however, urge their employees, especially their executives and managers, to write to Congress on occasion, and they do occasionally advertise on public policies and announce at press conferences their positions on issues. Trade association and professional association memberships range from the very specialized (e.g., the Gas Appliance Manufacturer's Association) to the very broad (U.S. Chamber of Commerce), and this has implications for outside lobbying that one might not expect. It is certainly the case that the larger, broader trade and professional associations outside

---

[8] For example, data from the American National Election Surveys show overwhelmingly that thermometer scores (ratings of positive or negative feelings toward something) reflect negative views of corporations and unions relative to environmental and women's groups.

lobby more often and on a larger scale than more specialized associations do. However, the broad cross-industry trade associations, for example, have a difficult time finding common ground among members and therefore choose fairly innocuous pro-business positions on public policies. In relation to the size of their memberships, their outside lobbying is not on that large of a scale. In contrast, although the specialized trade associations rarely tackle big public issues, when their industries are threatened they can put together impressive outside lobbying campaigns, albeit highly targeted at their business executives or other employees. Specialized professional groups, like those representing oral surgeons or group practice physicians, can also wage intense, targeted outside lobbying campaigns among their members.

Labor unions and public interest groups are the most ideally suited for regularized outside lobbying because they have large membership lists of individuals who are in the habit of joining collective action to try to influence policymakers. Public interest groups in particular attract people who are inclined to join collective efforts for a cause; thus, the groups can often overcome the individual incentives to free ride off the efforts of others.

That individuals form the membership bases of many groups and organizations form the membership bases of other groups is not a trivial difference. For some reason, perhaps having to do with the direct contact between Washington organizations and individual members, individual memberships matter in outside lobbying decisions. Table 2.8 compares outside lobbying among group-issue cases between those interest groups with organizations only as members and those interest groups with individuals as members. The difference in average OUTSIDE index between the two sets of groups is large and highly significant statistically by standard tests.

Table 2.8 contains other notable contrasts among groups. The mean values of OUTSIDE for the five group classes are provided, reinforcing the information presented in figure 2.3. Public interest groups and labor unions outside lobby heavily compared to other classes of groups. And the presence of local chapters leads to more outside lobbying (especially, in data not shown, with urging group members to lobby Congress), suggesting that organizational structure plays a role in decisions over lobbying strategies. The difference in means between groups with local chapters versus those without local chapters is highly significant statistically by standard tests.

The final difference between groups that I consider here—resources—may be seen at first glance as the most important. Simply put, some interest groups are wealthier than others, and outside lobbying takes resources. Resources, in many guises, should naturally play a large role in decisions over how to lobby. Groups like the U.S. Chamber of Commerce, if their members are united, wield enormous clout around the Capitol. The Chamber can command a huge array of resources, if necessary, to carry out effective lobbying. These resources include cash to hire consulting firms, staff to help with

TABLE 2.8
Mean Values of OUTSIDE by Various Categories

		N
Members		
Organizations only	0.17	91
	(0.22)	
Individuals	0.42	181
	(0.30)	
Interest group class		
Professional associations	0.05	10
	(0.06)	
Public interest groups	0.42	103
	(0.30)	
Corporations	0.06	45
	(0.06)	
Trade associations	0.17	91
	(0.22)	
Labor unions	0.44	74
	(0.29)	
Structure		
Local chapters	0.37	202
	(0.30)	
No chapters	0.16	121
	(0.20)	

Note: Standard deviations are in parentheses.

special projects, and members willing to work on local grass-roots efforts. All else being equal, the Chamber should have an easier time outside lobbying than less wealthy organizations, like the Society of Independent Gasoline Marketers of America.

Yet establishing which resources play a role in lobbying is not straightforward. What does it mean for one interest group to have more resources than another interest group? It depends on what the interest group wants to do, of course. Certainly money matters a great deal, and so General Motors or Exxon would seem to have a lot of resources. Interest group leaders always want there to be more money available to accomplish more goals. But General Motors and Exxon, it is reasonable to speculate, may envy the AFL-CIO or the AARP for their abilities to mobilize thousands of citizens for political action. A large membership base, or even a talented and charismatic leader, can be an invaluable resource in interest group politics. Assuming, for the moment, that money is always useful to all groups, it can be tricky to measure the monetary resources of interest groups, especially those of corporations. The assets of the corporations? That may be misleading in terms of their resources for political action. The budgets of their Washington offices? Such a measure may underestimate their political activities because corporations tend to use their public relations departments, their CEOs, and many paid lobbyists for their political work.

Several measures are available in my data, but most of them lead to comparisons that make little sense. The number of members, for example, is misleading because, to take an example, one trade association, the American Petroleum Institute, had 250 business firms as members and one public interest group, Common Cause, had 250,000 individuals as members. Clearly Common Cause is not more resource-rich than the oil companies' trade association, even though it has one thousand times the "members" of the trade association. And I do not have data on the number of employees in each business firm represented by the trade associations, but even if I did, it is not the case that for employment issues and other economic issues employees see themselves as represented by their company's trade associations. In short, who counts as a member is ambiguous enough to make membership comparisons difficult.

One measure, though not ideal, accounts best for problematic cases because it comes the closest to a common standard across groups. When corporations are excluded from the analysis, the correlation between groups' budgets and the number of full time staff for their Washington offices is $r = 0.82$ for the group-issue data set and $r = 0.80$ for the group data set. The size of staff offers a good approximation of the group's resources for political activities, and for corporations the number of people on staff in Washington is a good measure of the corporation's commitment to the public policy process. Corporations may have many more resources to use if necessary, of course, but the same can be said for trade associations and professional associations. I use the natural log of staff in order to reflect the common assumption that resources in organizations have decreasing returns to scale.

The log of number of staff is correlated with both the inside lobbying index ($r = 0.37$, $p < 0.01$) and the outside lobbying index ($r = 0.35$, $p < 0.01$) for the group data. Results for the OUTSIDE index for the group-issue data are more complicated. Taking all cases together, the correlation is indistinguishable from zero. However, if the group-issue cases where the group used no outside lobbying are dropped from the analysis, the correlation between the log of staff size and OUTSIDE is significant and similar to the results from the group data ($r = 0.31$, $p < 0.01$). Once groups decide to use outside lobbying, the scale of that outside lobbying correlates with the number of full-time staff. These relationships are not as tight as one might guess, but they are in the expected directions. The data indicate, quite reasonably, that groups with more resources lobby more actively, both inside and outside, than groups with less resources. As in just about anything in politics, resources matter in lobbying.

Moreover, a considerable portion of representatives in interviews complained about the lack of resources to use certain tactics. The data confirm that resources constrain some tactics more than others. The size of the full-time staff is positively correlated with two tactics: the scale of advertising used and the scale of membership mobilizations used. In contrast, interest groups also hold more press conferences and hire more public relations firms the smaller their full time staffs are. So it appears groups want to use outside lobbying in certain situations and they either rely on their staffs or members if they have them or they rely on the media or hired guns if they do not.

The relationship between resources, as measured by the number of staff, and one particular tactic, the scale of membership mobilizations, is misleading and must be interpreted with caution. The scale for membership mobilization was coded by considering the number of people targeted by the group to contact Congress. This coding was accomplished partially using information on the size of the memberships for the organizations; since the size of the memberships correlates with the number of full-time staff, the relationship between the scale of membership mobilization and the group resources comes very close to being expressed by the statement that membership mobilizations increase in scale when group memberships increase in size. The logic is nearly tautological, though not quite so empirically. A few groups with small memberships undertook massive letter-writing campaigns targeted at employees and other "members" by association, thus attaining high scores on the variable for scale of membership mobilizations. One example is the National Coalition for the Homeless, which counts only seventy thousand paid members but developed an extensive letter-writing campaign aimed at hundreds of thousands of citizens.

This caveat about membership mobilizations nevertheless brings us back to the ambiguity in assigning any single measure status as an indication of resources. Large memberships are valuable resources for any group. So are large staffs, large cash reserves, and at some level, reputations for integrity. By using the number of full-time staff, I have chosen a measure that correlates with many of these other possible measures, though imperfectly, but is comparable across groups.

To summarize the differences in lobbying strategies across different kinds of interest groups, there are four patterns identified. First, labor unions and public interest groups use outside lobbying more than their business and professional counterparts do. Second, groups with individuals as members use outside lobbying more than groups with organizations as members do. Third, groups with local chapters use outside lobbying more than groups without some version of a federal structure do. And fourth, groups with more resources tend to use outside lobbying more than less well endowed groups do, though the relationship is uneven across outside lobbying tactics.

These are group-level tendencies that show up even in the group-issue data and therefore transcend issue-specific differences in strategies. To a large extent, therefore, these findings are not at odds with previous research that has found differences in strategies at the group level. But moving beyond group-level differences is an important next step in understanding decisions over lobbying strategies.

Conclusion

This chapter began with a story of a famous incident that showcased many extremes of outside lobbying. The behavior of the players in the story, especially that of the senior citizens stampeding Rostenkowski and that of the many policymakers who changed their minds in the months following, was hardly typical. But the story demonstrates clearly the dynamics of successful outside lobbying, albeit in exaggerated form. Interest group leaders mobilize people outside the policy making community to show policymakers the salience of policy issues among their constituents, who will decide their fate in the next election. The policymakers are surprised by the response from constituents to the interest groups' entreaties, and having observed the response, many policymakers change their behavior.

The data on lobbying summarized in this chapter depict a more recognizable set of interest group strategies and tactics than those used to persuade Rostenkowski's colleagues. Across policy issues, group leaders often find it worthwhile to start letter-writing campaigns to Congress, advertise policy positions on issues, present to the media research information and policy positions, and even protest. The complete picture of outside lobbying, while not always as dramatic as the hat trick story, is still vigorous and impressive. Outside lobbying is remarkably common, and even groups considered among the wealthiest and most powerful bring the public into their lobbying efforts. The image of a mysterious community of insider lobbyists and policymakers does not capture accurately how interest groups operate.

One crucial piece of information from these data is that interest groups use outside lobbying selectively across policy issues. Previous research on interest groups has failed to acknowledge this point or to investigate its significance. Gais and Walker (1991), relying on information from Walker's group data, write,

> The assertion that interest groups adopt a dominant operating style early in their histories cannot be given a definitive empirical test with data from our cross-sectional survey, but we do not wish to create the impression that interest groups constantly shift their tactics as circumstances change. Established groups do some-

times alter their dominant strategies, but only after much discussion, and usually after their standard approach has proved unsuccessful time and time again. Most groups adopt a preferred style of political action early in their histories, and, when these early choices are being made, group leaders naturally emulate the tactics being employed at that time by the most successful groups. Once an inside or outside strategy becomes the association's dominant approach, it is very difficult to move in a new direction. (119–20)

At one level, Gais and Walker are correct. Groups adopt a "preferred style" of lobbying and stick with it, according to results from my data. Yet at another level, the exceptions to these preferred styles are immensely revealing. The times when interest groups behave at odds with their preferred styles can provide clues about the weight of various causes of outside lobbying. As an analogous research problem, consider that members of Congress vote with a majority of their party most of the time, but the exceptions when they break from their party are worth examining because these instances perhaps correlate with factors besides party affiliation that may be hypothesized to influence congressional voting decisions. To understand behavior at the margins in many different political or economic contexts, look at departures from the usual patterns.

Thus the group-issue data set will continue to be useful to examine outside lobbying decisions because other factors that vary across issues can be included in the analysis of the ordinary and the exceptional cases. So far we know from these data that group class, group resources, organizational structure, and the nature of memberships correlate with the use of outside lobbying both across groups and across issues. Next I examine the role that public opinion, something that definitely changes across issues, plays in lobbying decisions.

This chapter has focused on one side of the outside lobbying story: the behavior of interest groups. To continue with the story we must link the behavior of interest groups to the interests and preferences of policymakers and constituents. In the next two chapters I lay out a theory of outside lobbying as signaling and show that information from the group-issue data set are consistent with the theory.

3

Outside Lobbying as Costly Signaling

ACCORDING TO DATA summarized in the previous chapter, all interest groups in Washington use inside lobbying, and nine out of ten interest groups engage in some kind or level of outside lobbying at least occasionally. Not only do my own data record high percentages for outside lobbying, but data collected by Schlozman and Tierney (1986) and Walker (1991) record similar patterns. Moreover, among the group-issue cases collected, 63 percent of the cases involved outside lobbying by the group. Evidently, while some tactics are more common than others, and while specific groups and some classes of groups are inclined to use outside lobbying tactics frequently while other groups or classes of groups are inclined to stay away from certain tactics, outside lobbying as a general strategy is common. It is not reserved for groups with activist organizational cultures or histories of grassroots mobilization. Even corporations and professional associations get into the act at times, choosing to enlist their members or employees, and indeed, other constituents, to help make their case before policymakers.

What do interest groups gain by using outside lobbying? I have proposed that outside lobbying simultaneously communicates (signals) to policymakers the salience of policy issues among constituents and increases the salience of issues among constituents (expands the conflict). In this chapter I focus on the signaling aspect of outside lobbying, leaving conflict expansion for a later chapter.

The canonical signaling model in game theory has two players, a sender and a receiver. The sender signals a message to the receiver, and then the receiver takes an action that influences the utility of one or both players. In the model discussed in this chapter, an interest group (the sender) has an opportunity to use costly outside strategies to mobilize constituents for nonelectoral participation in order to demonstrate to a policymaker (the receiver) that the group has (or can generate increasing) popular support. The policymaker, using information from the outside lobbying, then decides whether or not to act on behalf of the interest group.

The purpose of this chapter, of course, is not to push the frontiers of signaling models, nor is it to describe in great technical detail a signaling model of outside lobbying. (I present a mathematical model in appendix D.) There are many published signaling models. Rather, the purpose is to summarize an applied model and make the case that this is a useful way to think about outside lobbying. The model demonstrates that under certain conditions that I claim are often present in interest group politics, accurate information about public opinion *can* be communicated through outside lobbying. Even when interest groups have incentives to be deceitful and policymakers have incentives to be skeptical of interest group claims of popular support, and even when the salience of issues to constituents changes across situations, there are reasons to be hopeful that outside lobbying can actually make policymakers better informed about the intensity of constituents' concerns.

Why the Concept of Signaling?

Conceiving of outside lobbying as signaling is useful for several reasons. First, signaling focuses attention on the informational aspects of lobbying, rather than on the simple power or wealth asymmetries between groups. This focus on information is consistent with the recent literature on lobbying. In particular, by assumption a signaling framework implies that advantages accrue to some interest groups because the groups' leaders know facts that policymakers do not know and can demonstrate that those facts are true. (I focus on facts about the salience of policy issues among constituents.) Why else would interest group leaders spend precious resources trying to convince policymakers that some policies have popular support? It must be the case that they are confident they can convince policymakers to change their minds about something.

Second, and more generally, a formal theoretical model can provide a language and logical structure to analyze the essence of a situation, often in ways that people from various research traditions can find interpretable. Granted, signaling models in game theory are highly abstract and extremely stylized. When applied to lobbying situations, they admittedly sweep many elements of communication and influence under the rug. For instance, no one has been able to incorporate competing interest groups, the different incentives of group leaders and group members, and various congressional institutions into a single analytical model of lobbying. All of these things are undoubtedly very important to interest group politics. Instead, formal theorists can analyze pieces of the puzzle in attempts to isolate relevant features of lobbying. Here I isolate the interaction between one interest group and one policymaker where the policymaker is skeptical of the group's claims of popular support. In my view, that is the essence of outside lobbying.

Third, signaling as an abstract concept can subsume many of the ideas about grass-roots mobilizing contained in other prominent theoretical traditions, but it does so in a way that highlights the strategic incentives of the players. In fact, one advantage of the model in this chapter is that it can be interpreted in a number of ways, depending on one's research tradition. Of course, I provide my own interpretation, which I think is consistent with my data.

As an example (there are more later in the chapter), resource mobilization theories emphasize the ability of interest group leaders to rely on existing organizations, social networks, and other resources in their target groups to lay the basis for wider social action (McCarthy and Zald 1977; Morris 1981; McAdam 1982). Left unexplored in this theoretical tradition are the strategic incentives for leaders to mobilize or not mobilize their groups in particular situations. In specifying a resource mobilization model, the resources that are the focus of attention can either be known to all players, in which case interest group leaders would have no need to signal them to policymakers (because they are known), or unknown to policymakers but known to interest group leaders, in which case the leaders can usefully signal about them.

And as another example, ideas in persuasion research can likewise be incorporated into a signaling framework. The focus of that research, in contrast to the signaling literature on lobbying, is on persuasion of the mass public instead of persuasion of policymakers. The studies do not explore the possible configurations of incentives among interest groups and policymakers under which persuasion of the mass public would be beneficial to the interest group leaders. Nevertheless, we can easily recognize that elites consider carefully their incentives to try to persuade the mass public over a variety of issues. They undoubtedly try to signal to other elites their capacities for persuading members of the mass public. Indeed, the empirical results of the most recent studies are consistent with the notion that elites have important facts—their capacity to exploit latent public opinion—to signal to other elites (Mutz, Sniderman, and Brody 1996). These studies have generally found that media and elite effects on mass attitudes are noticeable and politically relevant.

Signaling models have already been used to examine aspects of lobbying. For example, lobbyists are observed to devote considerable inside lobbying attention to their legislative friends. Austen-Smith and Wright (1992, 1994) propose a signaling model demonstrating the value to lobbyists of "counteractive lobbying," or lobbying legislative friends only after the friends have been lobbied by opposing groups. Potters and Van Winden (1992) demonstrate in a model with costly lobbying the preference conditions under which lobbyists can communicate anything credible to policymakers, and these conditions turn out to be relatively restrictive. Banks and Weingast (1992) model the interaction between interest groups and policymakers as a signaling game where the groups try to communicate bureaucratic performance to the policymakers, who then adapt bureaucratic institutions to account for the new information. And Ainsworth (1993), in a model very similar to the one described here, proposes a model where lobbyists spend resources to convince policymakers that they represent the people whom the lobbyist claims to represent.

The model discussed here is related to this previous research, particularly the Ainsworth model. In the Ainsworth model, costs of sending signals (lobbying) are constant, whereas in this model, the costs of signaling are systematically related to the information being sought by the receiver. This turns out to have important effects on the possibilities for communication. In the Ainsworth model something external to the model (such as a monitoring third player, or side payments) must be present in many instances for the receiver to learn anything from the signal, while in this model the correlation between costs and the information means that receivers have more opportunities to learn something from signals sent.

Let us first consider the model and its results, and then afterward address the critical questions of interpretation.

A Model of Outside Lobbying

By assumption, the sender in a signaling model has facts the receiver would like to know. The private information is referred to as the sender's *type,* which is unknown to the receiver. The sender's type can refer to something about the sender, like personal preferences or propensity for vengeful behavior, or it can refer to something that the sender knows about other people or circumstances in the world. In this case, the interest group leader knows something about the policymaker's constituents that the policymaker would like to know. The group leader's knowledge of the policymaker's constituents, therefore, is the group leader's type. There are multiple possible types (the group leader can have a range of facts about constituents), and the policymaker is uncertain about the group leader's true type but has well-defined (logically consistent) probabilities over all types.

For simplicity we can assume that an interest group can be a high type or a low type, where a high type means the group represents constituents who care enough about the issue to make the policymaker disagreeing with them uncomfortable in the next election, and a low type means the group does not represent constituents who care enough to make an offending policymaker uncomfortable in the next election. The policymaker, prior to any outside lobbying decision by the group's leaders, places some probability p on the possibility that the group is a low type and a probability $1 - p$ on the possibility that the group is a high type. The parameter p is known to both players.

There are three things to note about this setup. First, the limitation to two possible types for the interest group does not alter the conclusions of the model in any relevant way. Signaling models with continuous types are more complicated and for some purposes yield richer conclusions than models with dichotomous types, but we shall not be concerned with these purposes here. Second, as I will discuss later, other attributes of an interest group that might be useful in making a policymaker uncomfortable in the next election, such as a group's wealth, leadership characteristics, or its reputation for strong grass-roots support, are apt to be known by policymakers. The salience of the *particular* policy issue to constituents is reasonably assumed to be unknown to policymakers. That is why groups use outside lobbying. Thus, since we want to focus on information policymakers do not know for a given issue, and since by definition types in signaling models refer to fixed, private information, we can restrict the notion of different interest group types to different levels of salience on the issue among a group's members or other constituents the group claims to represent. And third, the idea that an interest group's leaders know its type with certainty, is restrictive, though for our purposes, as long as the group's leaders know more than the policymaker about the salience of a given policy issue, little is lost with this assumption. Similar results hold if both players are uncertain but the sender is slightly less uncertain. It is standard practice in these models to assume that the sender knows its type with certainty and the receiver is uncertain about the sender's type.

Following the conventional signaling literature begun by Spence (1973) and described in Banks (1991), the model has this sequence of events.

1. The policymaker is initially inclined to avoid helping the interest group on a policy matter. (This makes the situation interesting to study.)

2. The interest group's type on the issue, high or low, is determined by nature (some random, exogenous process), where the random process is known to both players but the actual type remains unknown to the policymaker; that is, the probability of the group being a high or low type is common knowledge.

3. The interest group's leaders can choose to use outside lobbying at some level, and this outside lobbying acts as a costly signal to the policymaker about the interest group's type, where the outside lobbying may or may not be accurate. In other words, the outside lobbying may or may not be consistent with the interest group's true type. The interest group's leaders can spend enough resources to make the group look like a high type regardless of its true type, but the resources necessary may be prohibitive (especially for low type groups).

4. The policymaker, upon observing the level of outside lobbying by the interest group (which could be zero), decides either to help the group or not to help the group on the policy matter.

There are further assumptions in the model. The policymaker prefers to help the interest group if the interest group is a high type, and prefers to avoid helping the interest group if the interest group is a low type. This means that the interest group's leaders and the policymaker have common interests when the interest group happens to be a high type. They have common interests in the policymaker supporting the group and pursuing the more popular policy among the group's members. When the interest group is a low type, however, the interest group's leaders prefer that the policymaker support the group, but the policymaker would rather not support the group. Their interests diverge in this situation.

The policymaker's action, to support or not support the group, is conditional on her beliefs (or knowledge) about the interest group's type, and these beliefs are represented as the probability that the group is a high (or low) type. The group's leaders, in contrast, prefer that the policymaker help the group regardless of the group's type. However, because outside lobbying is costly, the interest group's leaders prefer, all else being equal, to use no outside lobbying at all. Indeed, if the policymaker were going to support the group prior to any possible outside lobbying, the group's leaders would have no need to use outside lobbying.[1] The interest group's leaders are willing to use outside lobbying if the group's payoff from doing so exceeds remaining silent, which may occur of course if the outside lobbying potentially influences the policymaker's behavior.

The next two assumptions are critical to the results and require some justification. First, the higher the interest group's type, the lower the costs are to make the group appear to have a given level of popular support. And second, the interest group's level of true popular support is independent of the popular support demonstrated through its outside lobbying efforts.

To see that these assumption are reasonable, consider that ultimately what policymakers care about is how constituents will vote on Election Day, and they look to clues from outside lobbying for indications of this behavior. Therefore, there are two kinds of constituency behavior, what constituents do between elections and what they do on Election Day. Part of the notion of distinctive interest group types is that for low types, the link between these two modes of participation by constituents, nonelectoral participation and voting, is tenuous and cannot be assumed, and for high types, the link is likely to be very reliable. In other words, low types may have to "purchase" grass-roots support that will eventually wither away before Election Day. High types do not have this problem because through outside lobbying they are representing some true level of salience on the issue.

Furthermore, I simply note that it is no secret in Washington today that grass-roots support during the time between elections can, in most cases, be

---

[1] Costly signaling is not always necessary for communication to occur in signaling models. So-called cheap-talk models consider situations where signals are sent with zero costs (Farrell 1987; Matthews 1989). In cheap-talk models, players use signals to coordinate actions, though the possibilities for credible communication are more restrictive than in models with costly communication.

bought. Consulting firms and lobbying specialists can frame an issue in such a way and communicate the issue's urgency to constituents so as to generate any plausible number of telephone calls or letters to members of Congress. For enough money, someone will be willing to exert the effort to round up a sizable number of constituents for nonelectoral participation. However, the ease of rounding up constituents will vary depending on the true nature of public concern about the issue, and it is the low type group that will have to pay significant costs for outside lobbying. It is certainly not the case that a group spending a lot of money to mobilize citizens for nonelectoral participation can always do the same for electoral participation, especially for low type groups. There are too many alternative sources of information around Election Day (especially from the candidates themselves) for it to be assumed that interest groups carry as much weight among voters in elections as they do in the time between elections.

One way to think about the costs of outside lobbying is to compare how much it takes to mobilize one citizen for nonelectoral participation. How many citizens must the group contact in order to find one citizen willing to write a letter or make a telephone call? That number will depend crucially on the existent or latent level of salience of the issue. In general, a high type group will have to spend less of a scarce resource mobilizing one citizen than will a low type group. For very low type groups, the costs may be prohibitive to mobilize even a few citizens, though it may be possible in theory to spend the resources to find them. As Dan Weiss, the head lobbyist for the Sierra Club, boasted, contrasting the process of mobilizing his members with the actions of many of his adversaries, "If you spend enough money, you can generate results. But our people are willing to do these things for free. Remember Machiavelli: Don't hire mercenaries."

So in the model, the policymaker knows that the interest group's leaders may be making the group appear to be a more popularly supported than it is in fact. And the policymaker knows how much it would cost for each type to generate different levels of outside lobbying. Upon observing a certain level of outside lobbying, the policymaker applies standard Bayesian decision rules to update information and make a decision about whether to act on the group's behalf or not. (A tricky issue arises when we consider the endogeneity of salience. I will have more to say about this later.)

As in most signaling models, there are multiple equilibriums to this game. Under any equilibrium, neither player wants to change its behavior unilaterally, regardless of its type (though remember that only the interest group's type can vary in the model). Three kinds of equilibriums emerge. The most desirable kind of equilibrium from the policymaker's point of view is called *separating*, because the types undertake separate behaviors (send distinct signals). The policymaker can tell perfectly from outside lobbying the interest group's type. The policymaker then supports the group when the level of outside lobbying is above some threshold and does not support the group when the level of outside lobbying is below some threshold. This is also desirable from the point of view of the leaders of high type interest groups. They can successfully distinguish their groups from low type groups. Separation can occur when low type groups are not willing to pay the costs of outside lobbying to appear like high type groups, and high type groups get enough benefit from the policymaker's support to justify their relatively low costs for outside lobbying.

A second kind of equilibrium is called *pooling*, because all types of interest groups "pool" into a common strategy. That is, all types choose the same level of outside lobbying, and the policymaker cannot infer anything from the signal. When high type group leaders believe they cannot distinguish their group from low types, they might as well let policymakers guess and save the cost of outside lobbying. The policymaker must rely on information prior to outside lobbying (*p*) to decide whether to support the group or not. The outside lobbying is pure noise in this outcome; it does not communicate anything. Consequently, this is not desirable for either player, though it does not necessarily make either player worse off.

The most desirable kind of equilibrium from the point of view of the leaders of low type interest groups is the ability of low types to act occasionally like high types and convince the policymaker to occasionally (and mistakenly) support the interest group. In game theory terminology, the players play mixed strategies. Each player is not certain about the behavior of the other player, so the optimal response is to make sure the other player is not certain about one's own behavior. More specifically, low type groups should occasionally act like high type groups (use extensive outside lobbying) for the same reason poker players should bluff every now and then: it keeps the other players honest. These equilibriums are called *semi-pooling* because sometimes the different types pool and sometimes they separate.

The fact that there are multiple equilibriums leading to qualitatively different empirical hypotheses means that this model is not really predictive. It does not restrict our expectations about data in any way. Later, when we attach empirical measures of issue salience to interest groups and relate these measures to levels of outside lobbying, any particular empirical outcomes can be consistent with an equilibrium in the model. Both high and low types use outside lobbying under some equilibriums, and both types avoid using outside lobbying under other equilibriums.

What the model does indicate, however, is that under plausible equilibriums, outside lobbying *can* actually communicate accurate information about public opinion. And data can in turn indicate that behavior is consistent with particular kinds of equilibriums. So in the separating equilibrium, and occasionally in the semipooling equilibriums, groups divide into t. camps, and this division causes a correlation of types and behavior: gro representing constituents who are largely indifferent about a policy do not use outside lobbying on the issue (even though the group leaders would like policymakers to believe their constituents care), and groups representing constituents who really do care about a policy use outside lobbying on the issue. The model provides an explanation for why there might be a correlation between salience and outside lobbying. This separation of types, I contend, is not only possible and reasonable to expect, but to the extent that it occurs, it is important. Given that pooling equilibriums are not beneficial to either player on average, we might expect that either separating or semipooling will be the outcomes.

Depicting outside lobbying this way is normatively important because it leads to the conclusion that outside lobbying can improve communication between constituents and policymakers. Policymakers can learn more about the salience of policies to constituents through outside lobbying. And positively, this portrayal is important because it provides insight into some curious patterns of outside lobbying. More specifically on this last point, it paves the way for multivariate data analysis in the next chapter and anticipates our results.

The separating and semipooling equilibriums lead to several conclusions that we can examine empirically in the next several chapters. It is reasonable to expect there to be a positive correlation between interest group type and the levels and frequency of outside lobbying, where type is defined as the salience of the issue to the constituents the group claims to represent. Furthermore, the levels of outside lobbying observed on a given issue should decrease for higher type groups as the lower type groups on the same issues represent constituents with very low salience. This is because high type groups on those issues do not have to use much outside lobbying to distinguish themselves from lower type groups. Finally, and not surprisingly, outside lobbying on an issue should increase in intensity as interest group leaders value their favored policies more.

Interpreting the Model

We now turn to interpreting the model and its components. One of the more ~~ized~~ aspects of this model is that it depicts an interaction between an ~~group and a policymaker as a one-shot~~ game. Of course, this is not ~terest groups and policymakers develop relationships that allow ~ of honesty to develop. A repeated-game setting would be ~ accurate and would certainly make credible communica-~ard. Group leaders in a repeated model could develop ~and policymakers could learn through reputations ~ a group's claims to represent a large number of

constituents who care about an issue. Indeed, my choice of a one-shot signaling game sets up a distinct prejudice against credible communication.
Certain conditions must be present in one-shot signaling games for communication to occur, and so part of the task of interpreting this model is to
determine if these conditions enabling communication are present in interest
group–policymaker interactions.

For various reasons I consider the one-shot game more useful as a model
for outside lobbying. For one thing, by definition issue salience changes
across policy issues, and policymakers want to know, for a given issue, how
credible is an interest group's claim that this particular issue is highly salient
to large numbers of constituents. The central parameter of concern changes
across issues and across situations confronting the two players. While it is
certainly the case that a large part of the influence of an interest group is its
reputation for being a credible representative of constituents, there is always
some uncertainty on the part of policymakers whether in this particular instance the interest group is misrepresenting its mandate. Each new interaction between an interest group and a policymaker has a vitally important
"new" component, the true salience of the issue. In theory, the policymaker
faces a slightly different "player" each time she considers the action of an
interest group, even though the group leaders may be the same. The information the group leaders want to convey or conceal is different. Especially
when the interest group weighs the present very heavily relative to the future, one-shot games capture the situation nicely.

Moreover, reputations are not absent in one-shot games. The model here
includes p, the policymaker's prior expectation (prior to any evidence from
outside lobbying) on the possibility that the group's leaders are not telling
the truth and lack the claimed popular support. This prior expectation partially encapsulates a group's reputation. In effect, a repeated game is a series
of one-shot games, and if a group leader's information on issue salience
varies in each game, then it is the same conceptually as examining the single-shot game and adjusting the prior beliefs of the policymaker. Perhaps the
only important element lost in the one-shot game is the discounted future
benefits in deciding over lobbying strategies in the present, an omission I
maintain does not detract from my main argument.

Finally, if we can derive credible communication through outside lobbing
in a one-shot model, then we can certainly do so in a repeated-game model
as well. We do not need the repeated setting to derive communication if
certain conditions are met in the one-shot game. Similar results follow from
a repeated game as from this single-shot game, and one shot games are
easier to describe and analyze.

The remainder of the discussion of interpreting the model is centered
around two questions. What information is being signaled? How do polic
makers respond to the information being signaled? Answers to these qu

tions, especially the first, are critical in making a convincing case that data on outside lobbying can be better understood using a signaling framework.

What Is Being Signaled?

Signal theory of outside lobbying w/out side lobbying

I assert in the description of the model above that the information being signaled through outside lobbying is the salience of the policy issue to the constituents the group claims to represent. There is, of course, room for alternative interpretations.

Two modes of thought have dominated the study of American interest groups in twentieth century political science, and differences between the two are relevant to the question of what is being signaled. One is consistent with my interpretation, and the other challenges my interpretation.

The first, following on the classical pluralist writings of Bentley (1908) and Truman (1951) and based on ideas borrowed from sociology and social psychology, assumes a fundamental relationship between the organizational basis of a group in society and the amount of grievance felt by the members of that group. People have a natural tendency to band together with like-minded persons, especially when faced with a common threat. For Bentley and Truman, groups, defined as sets of citizens with shared attitudes and values, are the basis of all of politics. Political conflict can be understood as essentially conflict among groups in society. Organized interest groups are those among all groups that have been able to mobilize citizens with intense enough attitudes to warrant the costly behavior membership in a political organization implies: paying dues, traveling to Washington for marches, going to meetings, or writing letters to Congress. Until the late 1960s, the study of interest groups, following on Truman's ideas, operated on the premise that the existence of a well-organized, mobilized group of citizens petitioning the government indicates that there also exists enough people who care about a policy to contribute to the collective effort and make that effort noticeable in Washington.

The second mode of thought comes from economics and the study of public goods. Research on interest groups, and on many other fields in the social sciences, underwent profound changes soon after the publication of Olson's *Logic of Collective Action* in 1965. According to Olson, who feel very intensely about a public good may very well not influence the production of that public good, preferring in off the efforts of others. Among interest group scholars, how groups shape all of politics and how the pluralist many and varied grievances felt by citizens to- toward other groups, to how organizations form, how people resolve collective action problems, and how organizational leaders attract and maintain members.

To those in the Truman tradition, it seems perfectly apparent that intensity of preference over some policy issue corresponds to the willingness to pay costs to influence the policy outcomes. If policymakers want to assess how much an *individual* cares about a policy, they infer a good deal of information from the costs, in money, time, or effort, that the individual expends to influence the policy. The same goes for a group of citizens. If a group of citizens expends great effort to demonstrate their unhappiness with current policy, it is not unreasonable for policymakers to infer that those citizens feel intensely about the issue. The salience of the issue to the group as a whole and the costs expended on lobbying, one might say, are assumed to be positively correlated.

In contrast, Olson's book casts doubt on the pluralist notion that a successful voluntary organization signals the existence of a group of citizens with intense preferences over specific policies. Intensity of preference, Olson's theory implies, does not translate into political participation. There may be many citizens with very intense preferences over policies who have difficulty organizing themselves into an effective lobbying group. Instead of signaling the salience of an issue, a successful outside lobbying campaign, or even the existence of an organization, may signal merely that the interest group's leaders are good at solving collective action problems.

On the one hand, in the abstract it does not matter much for our signaling story which mode of thought one finds more appealing or useful. In fact, if all we are concerned to show is that outside lobbying is signaling, any kind of information will work, as long as the group's leaders knows more than the policymaker. There may be other pieces of information besides issue salience among constituents or organizational skill that are communicated through outside lobbying. An interest group's leadership, for example, would want a particular policymaker to know how much money the group has to influence voters or other politicians, or how much bravado the group has in publicizing controversial issues positions (e.g., animal rights activists). Regardless of whether policymakers want to know from interest groups the salience of issues to the members of an interest group or the ability of interest group leaders to solve collective action problems (or some other information), outside lobbying can still be thought of as signaling between group leaders and policymakers. In the former case, policymakers learn useful information directly about rank and file group members or ordinary constituents and can infer from this information something about potential electoral behavior in the next election. In the latter case, policymakers learn useful information directly about the organizational skills of interest groups leaders, and only indirectly about potential electoral behavior in the next election because this behavior may be dependent on the organizational skills of interest group leaders. Either way, outside lobbying signals something useful to policymakers facing reelection.

On the other hand, differences between the two interpretations have normative implications. I want to suggest that outside lobbying is a particular kind of signaling. The Truman interpretation, if true, and the subsequent interpretation of outside lobbying as signaling the intensity of preferences among constituents, if true, together offer a relatively favorable view of outside lobbying because interest groups transmit public opinion information fairly accurately. The organization of groups in society and the degree of mobilization of those groups at various points in time reflect to a large degree the underlying salience of the issue to significant groups of constituents. A policymaker can learn about the intensity of preferences by paying attention to whom he or she hears from. The Olsonian interpretation is not so sanguine. Policymakers will tend to hear from those groups wealthy (or lucky) enough to hire a skillful organizing leader or wealthy (or lucky) enough to offer a wider group of people selective incentives to join their organization. The link between public opinion and organized behavior does not logically follow in Olson's theory.

Which information is being signaled is largely an empirical question, and I shall discuss empirical evidence shortly, and then again in the next chapter. However, we can gain some ground on the problem by thinking through the logic of signaling. Consider the possible bits of information besides issue salience that can be signaled, such as money, activist bravado, and organizational skills. For signaling to be the proper theoretical model for a class of situations, we must be trying to explain the transmission of information that one player or set of players knows and the other player or set of players does not know. Policymakers, we can assume, tend to have a good deal of information on a group's resources like money, staff, and expertise, on a group's bravado, and perhaps even on a group leader's ability to solve collective action problems. These are organizational characteristics that do not change much in the short or medium term and can be learned by a policymaker after one experience with outside lobbying by the group, through a long-term relationship with the group leaders based on inside lobbying, or with public records. The salience of policy issues among many constituents, however, is something policymakers do not tend to know about precisely, and most importantly, *something about which they look to interest groups to inform them issue by issue*. Policymakers search for cues from outside lobbying campaigns to warn them of problems among a broad set of constituents.

Another way to say this is to use the language of statistics. We ought to focus on variables that change across issues and across time, as opposed to variables that stay (relatively) constant across issues and time. Outside lobbying, the variable we are trying to explain, varies across issues, so variables that might covary with outside lobbying cannot be those that stay constant across issues. Both in principle and, as we have seen and will see, empirically, group strategies and issue salience vary across issues and thus these two variables can at least potentially covary across issues. (According to data in the next chapter, they do in fact covary.) The same cannot be said for other relevant variables.

So issue salience makes a good deal of sense as the piece of information communicated through outside lobbying. But it is not enough to say that issue salience across issues is being communicated. Issue salience can change over time, and this may be a problem theoretically because interest groups themselves can affect issue salience. How do they communicate a piece of information that is endogenous to their own actions? Cannot they just push salience higher to get whatever they want?

Neither the variability nor the endogeneity of salience is incompatible with the notion of signaling. First, according to my interviews, interest group leaders in most situations think of public opinion as largely immovable in the period of time available before critical government action, and therefore the interpretation of what is being signaled (salience as a "fixed" piece of information) is fairly straightforward. Second, even if interest groups are expanding the conflict and influencing the salience of issues to constituents, signaling can still be a useful concept. The piece of information being signaled may be changing over time, but if the group is signaling the *movement* of that piece of information over time, then we are on firm conceptual ground. As long as the group and policymakers are confident that the group has information that the policymakers lack, such as the group's capacity to influence public opinion, the latent salience among the constituents, or the group's ability to mobilize voters in a later election, then the signaling framework can be of use. And of course, interest groups can increase issue salience only to a certain point, so it may be the maximum point of salience that a policymaker wants to know from the interest group (see fig. 1.1).

One more matter must be addressed. The information the group wants to convey through outside lobbying can be interpreted as the *net* effect of popular mobilization on a policymaker's reelection prospects. The information can encapsulate, in an indirect way, the ability of a group to mobilize its own sympathizers without provoking the opposition. Left out of the model, unfortunately, are the games opposing groups play with each other. Certainly groups do not want their own outside lobbying to strengthen the opposition's case. It is possible that a group can mobilize many constituents, but that mobilizing is essentially nullified by the reaction of groups on other sides of the issue. David Harris of the American Jewish Committee made this point clear in reference to his group's advertisements in the *New York Times*. They advertised, he said, to show that the ideas did not provoke a big backlash. "[We do this to show] a willingness to put this issue before the American people. And a kind of confidence, if you will, that many within American society will passively accept the message and therefore will provide a [supportive] backdrop against which decision makers can make decisions."

How Is a Policymaker Influenced?

Most of our attention to this point has been on interest groups, the senders of signals through outside lobbying. Conceiving of outside lobbying as signaling begs the question of what policymakers, the receivers of the signals, are doing as well. After all, they determine whether outside lobbying is influential or not.

By influential I mean that the signaling behavior of the interest groups changes policymakers' decisions. In its most blatant and noticeable form, interest group influence leads a member of Congress to switch from supporting a bill to opposing a bill, or vice versa. This is relatively rare. Most of the time, according to research, influence is more subtle or incremental, changing a policymaker from a mild supporter (or opponent) to an intense or vocal supporter (or opponent) (Hall and Wayman 1990). Either way, whether the influence is dramatic or subtle, the notion that signals can lead to changes in behavior still applies. Without the signaling action of the interest group, the policymaker would behave differently. The description of the model above uses the extreme case of changing the policymaker's behavior from opposing to supporting the group, but this can be made more general to include changes from uncertain support for the group to certain support, or certain opposition to uncertain opposition.

We know from casual observation that outside lobbying *can* be influential. In fact, members of Congress freely admit that outside lobbying affects their decisions at times. When a Democratic controlled Congress in 1994 passed its Family Leave Bill, it had cut the leaves to half the length originally proposed. Lawmakers from both major parties pointed to a vigorous outside lobbying campaign by the National Federation of Independent Business (NFIB), the largest organization of small businesses, as a major cause of the change. Furthermore, systematic interviews with members of Congress (as we shall see shortly) indicate that it is virtually a consensus in Congress and among interest groups that constituent appeals are the most effective way to lobby a wavering Congress (see also Kingdon 1989).

As a dramatic example, consider the case of Jim Slattery. During the 1994 health care debate, Slattery, a Kansas Democrat and a key member of the House Energy and Commerce Committee who happened to be running for governor of Kansas, changed his mind on policy directly following a vigorous outside lobbying campaign by the National Association of Life Underwriters (NALU), an association of small and medium size insurance companies. Prior to the outside lobbying, Slattery was publicly supportive of

Clinton's health care plan. On March 11, 1994, he admitted, regretfully, to members of another interest group (incidentally, the NFIB) that he supported employer mandates. Employer mandates meant that employers would be required to provide health insurance coverage for their employees. The NALU, learning of Slattery's revelation, mobilized on a large scale in Slattery's district. They organized meetings with constituents in many small towns, and convinced hundreds of Slattery's supporters to write him letters urging him to oppose employer mandates. Slattery later told a reporter that the NALU connected with those people in small towns who "sit on school boards, work for civic groups, head up charity drives, run for public office, and bankroll politicians. When you go to the town hall meeting or the Rotary Club, they're the ones who understand health care. When [insurance] agents tell people what the [Clinton] proposal will do, they listen." The agents were telling people that the Clinton plan would devastate small business and make people negotiate insurance with government bureaucrats. On April 22, little more than a month after Slattery's public announcement of support for the Clinton plan, he announced publicly that he could not support employer mandates and therefore could not support the Clinton plan.[2]

It is difficult to determine with confidence how often policymakers change their behavior in response to outside lobbying pressure. A different, and perhaps more manageable, question is, which activities do policymakers say influence them? Two confidential polls of members of Congress and congressional staff in 1992 asked this very question.[3] The responses are revealing. The findings of these polls, and my own research as well, clearly indicate that members of Congress put considerable weight on the willingness of ordinary citizens to participate in outside lobbying campaigns. To relate this to the earlier question of what is being signaled through outside lobbying, it appears that members of Congress do not profess much belief in the logic of collective action. They may experience it in their own chamber or in their own parties and campaign organizations, and they may simply be living in denial about it, but for all that social scientists know about free riding and selective incentives, the ideas behind Olson's theory do not appear to have permeated the Capitol. By their lights, if thousands of union members donate hard earned money and spend precious time contacting members of Congress, all to influence legislation on health care, it is a good sign of the high salience of health care to the union members. When a constituent posts a lengthy, handwritten letter that obviously took a good deal of time to com-

[2] The story on Jim Slattery is summarized in Johnson and Broder 1996, 337–42.

[3] The polls by Gallup and by Hart and Associates were commissioned by Bonner and Associates and by Burston-Marsteller, respectively. Not surprisingly, the polls resulted in findings favorable to the "grass roots" industry. It must be said, however, that my own interviews with congressional staff members and former members of Congress revealed similar information, as does the research of Kingdon (1989).

pose, that sends a strong message. Morris Udall, former congressman from Arizona, once said, "On several occasions I can testify that a single thoughtful, factually persuasive letter did change my mind or cause me to initiate a review of a previous judgment" (Frantzich 1986, 65).

As more systematic evidence, the polls lead to rankings of actions that affect a member's voting decisions. For both surveys of members of Congress, personal letters from constituents or leaders of local district groups were rated the highest. More than 70 percent of the members of Congress surveyed by Gallup rated nonform, personal letters from constituents as having a "great deal of influence." At the bottom of the list were computer-generated postcards, issue papers, editorials, and advertisements. Fewer than 25 percent of congressional members surveyed rated these as having a great deal of influence.

In my own interviews as well, I have found that interest groups and congressional offices engaged in an escalating game of attempted deceit and discovery over constituent mail from the early 1980s to the early 1990s. First, in the early 1980s, there was the flood of mail pouring into Congress after the widespread availability of computerized databases and mass mailing technology. Data on mail into Congress show a spike upward in the early 1980s, when more than 92 million pieces of mail flooded House and Senate offices (Frantzich 1986, 11). Once groups started sending mass mailings, according to interviews with veteran congressional staff, the marginal effectiveness of mass mailings declined.

Then there was the emphasis on handwritten letters. Jack Bonner told me, "You want letters that show that people understand both sides of the issue. If you're writing from the farm bureau, you want to communicate how farmers in Nebraska will be impacted. What makes it is the quality of the letter from a person or group. What's the content of the letter? Is it Xeroxed?"

Supposedly, for a time in the late 1980s handwritten letters "counted" more in Congressional offices than did stacks of mass-produced postcards. Legislators, nevertheless, eventually learn the tricks of the trade, and when mass-produced letters, appearing handwritten and on company stationary, were flooding Congress during the late 1980s, many on the Hill resented the attempted deceit on the part of lobbying consulting houses in Washington. By 1993, the state of the art consisted of coaching handwritten letters out of constituents over the phone. A caller from a phone bank would call a constituent, ask him or her to write a letter, send him or her information, and even dictate a suggested letter over the phone. This was a costly but effective way to produce quality mail to Congress.

The interest groups are never completely absent in nearly every case. A "quality" piece of constituent mail can mean a letter brimming with facts and well-reasoned argument, something interest groups can supply to constituents. And interest group leaders using a new technology count on time lags between the emergence of the technology that allows one to use the tactic, the tactic's widespread usage by many other groups, and its being discounted by congressional offices. Once congressional offices become widely aware of the new way consulting houses produce mail in bulk, the effectiveness of the tactic has already diminished. The technology spreads to other groups and consulting houses in Washington, producing a crowding effect in the industry. It pays to be one of the first organizations to exploit the new technology.

The key insight from the surveys and from the changes in congressional mail over the past decade or so is that constituent communications that seem to lack orchestration by a central organization, especially when they arrive in noticeable numbers, are more influential than obviously highly orchestrated ones. Taking this one step further, we might say that the less orchestrated the constituent communications are (because nearly all outside lobbying efforts are orchestrated to a certain extent) the more policymakers pay attention to them. Here, then, is evidence for one of the crucial assumptions in the model. What moves members of Congress, by their own admittance, is when constituents are willing to undertake costly collective action on behalf of some policy issue, without intense prodding by interest group leaders. A strong signal by interest group leaders occurs when these leaders expend *little* effort and produce big grass-roots results. Interest group leaders have incentives to push off the costs of outside lobbying onto constituents, not only to avoid paying costs but because doing so sends a strong signal.

For outside lobbying as signaling, therefore, it is implicit that the costs to an interest group of generating a particular level of outside lobbying on an issue are inversely related to the salience of the issue to constituents, and that these costs are common knowledge. This inverse relationship, in fact, is a crucial assumption in our model and drives much of the result that credible communication is possible.

Ironically, there is one aspect of the Olsonian tradition that has penetrated the Capitol. A crucial legacy of Olson's book, in the research of Salisbury (1969) and Moe (1980), was to disconnect conceptually the study of group leaders from the study of group members. The Truman tradition largely papered over differences between group leaders and the rank and file. For those in the Olsonian tradition, interest groups are not the single-minded vectors that exert pressure on policymakers. Instead, they are made up of different layers of activists with individual interests and incentives to free ride and/or act selfishly to attain prestige, power, or material goods within the organization. Policymakers see the distinction and are influenced by interest group leaders that can rely on high levels of activity among rank and file members.

Conclusion

Why do interest groups need outside lobbying to communicate to policy-makers the salience of policy issues to constituents? This appears to be a simple question: because, one might say, there are many group leaders claiming to deserve the attention of policymakers, and outside lobbying can place constituents' concerns directly in a policymaker's face. Outside lobby-ing forces policymakers to pay attention. But this answer is still filled with ambiguities. When should groups attempt outside lobbying? (Surely not al-ways.) Under what conditions are policymakers influenced? What outcomes are possible?

A signaling model, as I have described, provides a precise and logical accounting of how influential outside lobbying might work and when groups might use outside lobbying. The guts of the model, the assumptions made about interest group types and policymakers' beliefs and both players' possi-ble actions, are critical to the story and lead to results where influential outside lobbying (credible communication) can occur in a one-shot setting. The conditions that allow for outside lobbying as signaling to influence poli-cymakers include the following. First, the inverse relationship between the costs of generating a certain level of grass-roots support and an interest group's true type (salience of an issue to constituents the group represents) is known to both players, but most importantly to the policymaker. Policy-makers must be able to infer something about a group's type from the level of outside lobbying observed. Second, it must be the case that the policy-maker would take one course of action favorable to the interest group if the policymaker believed (either prior to or after the outside lobbying decision by the group) the group were a high type, and would take another course of action unfavorable to the group if the policymaker believed the group were a low type. In other words, the preferences of the players overlap when the group truly has "good news" to report about constituents' opinions. If this were not the case, the group would have no reason to use outside lobbying. Third, an informative equilibrium (separating or semipooling) is in fact played. This is a potentially troubling condition because it raises a host of concerns about what games with multiple equilibriums really tell us. I shall not address these concerns here (see Kreps 1990), but shall merely note that the model indicates that credible communication is possible under the two previously mentioned, plausible conditions.

Thus the major conclusions of this chapter are that given a set of assump-tions about what outside lobbying is intended to do and how it can be chi-canery at times, outside lobbying can influence policymakers, even in a one-shot interaction, and that the set of assumptions relied upon seems to capture nicely how policymakers and other participants view outside lobbying. Outside lobbying can communicate salience information even when a large number of groups have the ability to manufacture astroturf, or what looks a lot like grass-roots support even when it does not exist. If enough groups with enough real popular support exist and use outside lobbying some of the time, then policymakers are apt to listen to outside lobbying. Incentives may exist to discourage a vast majority of low type groups from outside lobbying, while these same incentives may encourage high type groups to undertake outside lobbying. To the extent that these incentives operate and the proposed communicative strategies are played, policymakers will be responding to sincere expressions of constituents' concerns rather than to well-funded special interests sending misleading signals.

4

Public Opinion and Mobilization

MUCH OF the discussion in the previous chapter is strictly theoretical. It says that under certain conditions, this follows from that, and then this follows that, and so in conclusion, interest groups can communicate public opinion information to policymakers through outside lobbying (costly signaling). It is another matter, of course, whether interest group lobbying relates in any way empirically to public opinion. According to the common wisdom, the average interest group works hard to create only a mirage of popular support.

A Prevailing Cynicism

For good reasons, a widespread cynicism toward interest groups and lobbying exists in the United States. Opinion polls consistently find that a vast majority of Americans regard the government as beholden to privileged, organized groups in society. The process of lobbying and pressuring politicians has always been suspect. As someone in Washington summarized his own public status, "Being a lobbyist has long been synonymous in the minds of many Americans with being a glorified pimp" (Birnbaum 1992, 7). Given what politicians, the press, and even academics say about lobbyists, the persistence of these attitudes is hardly surprising.

Politicians, even presidents, openly rail against opposing interest groups, blaming "special interests" when they do not get their way. A time-honored tradition in American politics is to claim popular support for one's own policies while tagging opponents and their allies as representing narrow, greedy interests. And the press rarely has anything good to say about interest groups or lobbying, a tradition that goes back at least as far as the Progressive Era muckraking journalists. A sample of recent newspaper headlines will attest that the tradition among contemporary journalists and editors has continued: "More and More, Lobbyists Call Shots in D.C."; "The Best Congress that Money Can Buy"; "Lobbyists Often Disguise True Colors"; "Health Care Reform: Don't Hold Your Breath, Not as Long as PACs keep Congress in Their Pay"; "When Grass-Roots Drive Actually Isn't."[1]

Some political scientists, meanwhile, have lent scholarly credence to the cynicism. Schattschneider's influential book on the Smoot-Hawley Tariff,

[1] These headlines are taken from the *Chicago Tribune*, December 6, 1992; December 7, 1992; December 10, 1992; *Washington Post Weekly Edition*, October 28, 1991; *New York Times*, March 26, 1995.

Politics, Pressures, and the Tariff (1935), captured attention precisely during the time of Roosevelt's overwhelming mandate for the New Deal. According to that book, immediately prior to one of the twentieth century's great political realignments establishing a dominant majority party, special interests held sway over such an important policy area as trade relations. His book set the tone for interest group research for decades. This kind of research even preceded the 1970s explosion in the number of interest groups active in Washington. In recent times the swarm of lobbyists in Washington, the amount of campaign money flowing into candidate coffers, and the immutability of budgetary categories favoring specific groups all seem to indicate the existence of a policymaking process where each privileged minority gets its share of the public largesse (Lowi 1979; Ferguson 1995). At least for some political scientists, the evidence of influence by undeserving, unpopular groups is unmistakable.

Presumably to overcome this common perception among the public and policymakers alike, interest group leaders spend precious resources outside lobbying. They enlist the participation of ordinary citizens in their lobbying efforts. It is surprising, nevertheless, that many contemporary observers are as cynical about outside lobbying as they are about inside lobbying and campaign contributions. The press and others often interpret outside lobbying as merely contributing to special interest politics or making an interest group appear to be something it is not.

News stories, for example, give the impression that much of outside lobbying is an attempt to mislead policymakers into thinking that policies have widespread popular support. Front page stories focus on how groups dress up their self-interested lobbying efforts in popular clothing. Advertising campaigns by interest groups are portrayed as attempts to legitimize corporate greed, and hired-gun firms like Bonner and Associates, specializing in grass-roots mobilization on behalf of corporations and their trade associations, are given unflattering publicity on the front pages of prestigious newspapers. The *Chicago Tribune*, in a typical example, profiled Bonner: "Banking officials, fearful of losing billions in profits, urgently needed Bonner's help. They wanted his 'grass roots' lobbying firm to create the appearance of a spontaneous uprising against the measure."[2]

The notion that the "appearance" of a spontaneous uprising can be purchased is so widespread in Washington that commentators are tempted to relegate all of outside lobbying to the same conceptual bin as campaign attack advertising: slick, one-sided, and misleading propaganda. Indeed, the postcard campaigns to members of Congress that are reported upon are often fraudulent.[3]

---

[2] Quoted several times in a five-part series in the *Chicago Tribune*, December 6–10, 1992.

[3] In 1995, for example, NTS Marketing from Lynchburg, Virginia, was found to have sent to Congress telegrams on telecommunications regulations that turned out to be bogus. They sent

Obviously, not all that interest groups do is unsavory. Certainly when it is your own interest group doing the lobbying, it is not so bad. Organizations representing one's own kind, or those that represent the poor, children, and the disabled, are not as nefarious as organizations representing people one distrusts or dislikes.

But this is just a kind of rooting for the home team. Even more objective observers grant that there are qualitative differences in the legitimacy of interest group claims of popular support. Implicit in much of the commentary on interest group activities, especially on outside lobbying, is an assumption that sometimes interest groups represent "true" constituent preferences, and sometimes interest groups misrepresent constituents, or mislead them or policymakers, or both. Indeed, it could be that interest groups use outside lobbying mostly as conflict expansion of a bad kind, where the salience of a policy issue is inflated artificially with propaganda. One of the best-known political science books on American interest groups in the 1980s makes the distinction explicit: "When a resourceful organization wants to be sure of winning legislators' attention to an issue, one of its best options is to try to create the semblance of a popular movement in support of the organization's cause. . . . Sometimes groups manage this task so well that they actually do create a popular movement, not merely the semblance of one" (Schlozman and Tierney 1986, 188). As Schlozman and Tierney write, outside lobbying can be loosely categorized into two kinds, a "popular movement" and a "semblance of a popular movement." The former by assumption has some basis in popular opinion whereas the latter is manufactured or phony.

Yet what is the distinction really? If two interest groups mobilize the same number of people to contact Congress, but one of them relies on volunteers and its own members and the other pays a consulting house to generate telephone calls and letters, who is to say which is real and which is artificial? Consider three underlying assumptions in the above description. First, policymakers must be easily fooled. Interest groups able to mobilize citizens can persuade members of Congress that what the interest groups want has widespread popular support and will aid reelection efforts. Second, constituents can be mobilized for nonelectoral participation, even if the group does not have much true popular support that will translate into electoral support. Interest group leaders can package almost any policy position to convince *someone* to contact Congress and lead policymakers to believe that many constituents care about the issue. And third, there is some "true" level of

---

multiple telegrams from the same constituent, or telegrams from dead people or people who had moved out of the district. They claimed to have done so unwittingly, but the episode created a stir on Capitol Hill, leading to floor speeches by party leaders denouncing the practice and public apologies by those involved. In this case, both the press and policymakers blew the whistle appropriately.

popular support that the interest group either represents or is trying to skirt. Either way, the interest group leaders can learn this true level and either keep it from policymakers or try hard to communicate it through outside lobbying. Furthermore, stating that an outside lobbying campaign is either a popular movement or a semblance of a popular movement implies that if we had the same information as the interest group leaders, we could judge the legitimacy of the lobbying efforts. And if the policymakers knew what the interest group leaders know, there would be no need for outside lobbying.

I have distinct reactions to each of these three assumptions. As for the first assumption, I consider it unlikely to be the case. Policymakers are not systematically fooled about matters so important to them. At times they are uncertain about the latent salience of policy issues because they do not have the time or resources to know this about each policy issue. If a controversial decision on a policy issue appears to be vital to a policymaker's bid for reelection, it is a safe bet he or she will go to great lengths to learn how much constituents care about it. Policymakers rely on, among other sources, interest group leaders to communicate this salience. In the previous chapter, I argued, in effect, that this first assumption is not necessary for outside lobbying to make sense as signaling. According to a signaling model, policymakers can be perfectly rational and reasonably suspicious of outside lobbying efforts, and they can still learn accurate information from outside lobbying under a wide range of outcomes.

The second assumption is more plausible. Opportunities for purchasing grass-roots support clearly exist and are exploited at times. For a price, a consulting house in Washington can deliver tens of thousands of letters to Congress next week. These letters, again for a price, may even be handwritten and signed by registered voters. Yet many people, including policymakers, know that most of these apparently manufactured outside lobbying efforts will never lead to electoral support.

The third assumption is not only plausible but absolutely central to any argument about the effectiveness or worthiness of outside lobbying. Even more, it raises questions that go to the heart of interest group politics and political representation. What is the standard by which to judge the legitimacy of claims to represent the views of constituents? In the absence of an assumption incorporating *some* version of a "true" popular mandate, we have few grounds on which to criticize any outside lobbying as astroturf. Do some interest groups represent more public interests than do other interest groups? If so, how can we tell? Given the availability of consulting firms willing to generate grass-roots support for a price, and given the willingness of interest groups to spend millions of dollars bringing about telephone calls, faxes, or telegrams to Congress, any attempt to evaluate outside lobbying requires that one establish a standard for legitimate representation. The criticisms of outside lobbying (and of interest groups in general) begin with either an explicit or an implicit standard for judgment.

This chapter provides an empirical standard to use to evaluate outside lobbying. Using published data and my own interviews with interest groups, I measure two dimensions of public opinion surrounding a policy issue: the popularity of a group's policy position and the salience of the policy issue to the constituents a group claims to represent. I then compare these measures to the outside lobbying efforts of the group. I find that evidence from recent outside lobbying campaigns casts doubt on the interpretation that outside lobbying is a routine form of chicanery. Salience information is related substantially and positively to outside lobbying. In the language used in the model from the last chapter, interest groups do "separate" by type on average, and group leaders do not usually try to fool policymakers. However, popularity information is only weakly (but positively) related to outside lobbying, suggesting that quite a few groups with intense but small numbers of supporters use outside lobbying too, though it is highly targeted. While on average outside lobbying works in concert with public opinion rather than in opposition, thus running counter to the common perception, the results from the analysis of popularity and outside lobbying are not as comforting as we would like.

Measuring the Popularity of Policies

I have made the point in the first chapter that a policymaker facing reelection and confronting a difficult policy decision must focus on both dimensions of constituents' opinions. The distinction between popularity and salience, discussed in some length in the first chapter, provides a major rationale for outside lobbying and, for that matter, for an interest group to exist in the first place. Without interest groups, policymakers would have a difficult time knowing which policies were salient among constituents. While public opinion polls give fairly accurate measures of how many constituents want a particular policy relative to another policy, interest groups can give an indication of *how much* the members of a group in society want the policy and how much these members are going to weigh policymakers' actions in deciding on electoral support.

Although interest groups are helpful in providing salience information, policymakers cannot forget about the popularity of policies. It is actually the powerful combination of supporting popular policies on salient policy issues that is the strength of organized constituents. If an interest group's policy position is long on one dimension of public opinion and short on the other, the group's influence will likely be muted. For instance, a lobbyist may represent a very small group with intense but unpopular preferences, and unless policymakers can see the connection between supporting this small group and winning over many voters (say through campaign contributions from the group), policymakers are not inclined to pay much attention. In the opposite case, a lobbyist may represent a group pursuing policies preferred by many constituents, but those policy issues may be obscure and not very salient to those constituents. Once again, policymakers may not be inclined to pay attention. The wish list of an interest group's leaders would include having many constituents of a key legislator supporting its position (high popularity) and many constituents willing to claim sincerely that their electoral support rides on the issue (high salience).

For most of us, the practice of interest groups mobilizing constituents for highly popular policies on salient issues is exactly what we would want in a democracy. Any interest group pursuing these policies high on both dimensions can be appropriately applauded. Rather, a more troubling aspect of the two dimensions of public opinion raises what Robert Dahl (1956) calls the "intensity" dilemma in democratic politics. Interest groups pursuing unpopular policies often have high salience on their policy issues. No one cares as intensely as teachers about educational reforms, and even though the teachers unions may not take the most popular positions on education policies in every case, they communicate clearly to policymakers that electoral support (and financial support) relies heavily on acting favorably to teachers. As a result, the teachers unions are considered among the most influential in Washington.[4] And each time a new set of regulations is proposed that may harm a particular industry but benefit many constituents, the industry is quick to respond with technical facts or political reasons to oppose the regulations.

How, Dahl asks, can a majoritarian system account for this dilemma? The common response for policymakers has been to bring together intense minorities on different issues to form a plurality. Yet this may mean that the overall policies of the government are a collection of unpopular policies, sort of like Lowi's interest group liberalism (1979). And few democratic theorists would suggest that policymakers *should* pay inordinate attention to intense minorities pushing for unpopular policies, even if policymakers do so in fact.

The intensity dilemma thus creates problems for policymakers and for those who want to evaluate interest group politics. An interest group may be entirely sincere in claiming that it represents constituents who care deeply about a policy issue. Such an interest group is not, strictly speaking, misrepresenting constituents' opinions. But if that organization represents a very small proportion of constituents, most of us would be inclined to suggest that

---

[4] The union leaders claim that their influence is because their members know more about education than the rest of the population does, but policymakers claim that it has more to do with the union's special status in the Democratic Party.

it would be better for policymakers to ignore the group's demands and focus on more popular policies. In the end, democracy demands that policymakers facing reelection pursue sufficient numbers of votes, each equally weighted. Ideally, many of us would say, citizens with intense preferences should not be granted any more influence over policies than should other citizens.

Group leaders representing small, intense groups must convince policymakers somehow that the group's favored policies, if pursued by the policymakers, will either win over significant numbers of voters or, more likely, will not turn off significant numbers of voters. Interest group leaders can sidestep this solution, naturally, by giving generous campaign contributions, hardly a comforting solution to democratic theorists. Yet contributions go only so far, and there are limitations, both legal and practical, on how much money one group can give. Through outside lobbying, group leaders do try to convince policymakers that their members and other constituents who agree with them care about the issue, but importantly, group leaders also need to convince policymakers that there are *enough* constituents who care about the issue to warrant the policymaker's attention. In short, policymakers pay attention to small, intense groups, but they can never forget that they need votes in bulk on election day.

Operating on the normative principle that, all things being equal, we ought to be less concerned about the salience of policy issues and more concerned about whether an interest group represents a popular policy position as opposed to an unpopular policy position, objective measures of the popularity of an interest group's policy position can aid in evaluating the actions of interest groups. (The important caveat applies: unpopular policies that protect basic civil and political rights or that are in the long run best for the sovereignty and economic health of the nation may be judged as warranted by standards other than popularity.) In tagging some outside lobbying as generating astroturf, presumably critics should have a lack of popularity, not a lack of salience, in mind, though many confuse these notions.

Reliable measures of the popularity of national policies are not hard to come by. There are hundreds of polls published each year on public policy preferences. Anyone, including of course elected officials, can usually determine the popularity of a group's policy position as measured by polling data. Furthermore, policy questions in surveys—Do you favor or oppose a law mandating seat belt use in automobiles?—provide well-defined answers, often refer to concrete proposals, and limit respondent choices. As a result, there is a great deal of consistency in measured, aggregate policy preferences over time (Page and Shapiro 1992).

Measuring the popularity of an interest group's issue position is thus straightforward. For this analysis, I simply use the percentage of respondents giving the same response as the interest group on policy questions. (Recall that I asked the interest groups the same questions asked of the public.) For example, on the following question, 33 percent of the public answered "favor" and 67 percent answered "oppose":

Do you favor or oppose a federal law which would prohibit employers from hiring permanent replacements for striking workers?

For those interest groups that answered "favor," their popularity is coded 0.33 on that issue. If they answered "opposed," their popularity is coded 0.67.

An alternative way to measure popularity is to scale the possible answers in the opinion question and calculate the hypothetical median or mean voter on the issue. For example, we could code "favor" as 0 and "oppose" as 1, and the mean response on the above question is 0.67. One could then measure the distance between the group's issue position and the mean position. This method, which is useful for questions with more than two possible answers, imbeds the public opinion and interest group information in a spatial model of voting (Downs 1957; Enelow and Hinich 1984). Of course, when the question has only two possible answers, the two measures are identical. I shall use the spatial measure briefly in an analysis of conflict expansion in chapter 5. (Using the spatial measure in the data analysis summarized later in this chapter does not alter the research conclusions in any way.)

Note that the polls used in my data consist of responses from national samples in the months prior to my interviews with group leaders. Ideally, we would have constituency-level data for each policymaker targeted by the interest groups surveyed, but this is not only impractical, it would not be much of an advantage. The interest groups surveyed are national in scope, address national policy issues, and in nearly every case claim to represent cross-constituency populations. Therefore, national polls are useful and in nearly every case appropriate in gauging the validity of group claims of popular support.

Measuring the Salience of Policy Issues

In measuring the salience of a policy issue to the constituents a group claims to represent, we are attempting to operationalize the notion of different interest group types from the signaling model. *Type* by definition means private information, and since I am claiming that information on the popularity of policies is easily discovered through polls contemporaneous to policy decisions (discovered both by policymakers and by political scientists from published polls and from private polls funded by congressional offices), popularity cannot be interpreted as measuring interest group types. Salience, in contrast, is almost never measured or reported in public opinion polls. The exceptions occur infrequently, and one of these exceptions, the American National Election Studies (ANES), provides the data that are the basis for our measure of salience.

The Gallup poll (and sometimes the CBS/*New York Times* poll) also asks American respondents to name the nation's "most important problem," but categorizations of responses by Gallup are unreliable over time and not very detailed. Policymakers certainly cannot rely on the Gallup surveys to evaluate interest group claims of high issue salience. The ANES asks respondents the same question on the most important problems, and for our purposes the ANES is more useful because it allows for three responses and codes responses into many detailed categories that are consistent over time. So in 1992, three months after my study of interest groups was completed, respondents to ANES were asked the most-important-problem question. Coded responses give a measure of the national-level salience of a policy issue. Approximately 9 percent of respondents, for example, said environmental concerns were one of the three most important problems, whereas 81 percent mentioned the general state of the economy in one of the three answers.

One possible measure for salience would be to use these numbers, 0.09 and 0.81, to estimate the salience for environmental issues and economic issues respectively. By this measure, environmental issues differ from the economy on salience by a ratio of 1 to 9 (9 percent to 81 percent). But this is not discriminating enough for our purposes. Interest groups do not want to signal to policymakers the salience of an issue to everyone. Instead, interest groups are most credible in indicating how much their members or other constituents they are familiar with (doctors, teachers, farmers, or left-handed people) care about a particular issue. The mass population can be grouped into many different categories, and these different categories may split people into more intense versus less intense groups.

For example, on the salience of abortion policies, we could compare (1) professional women without children versus stay-at-home mothers, (2) pro-life versus pro-choice women, or (3) working-class versus upper-middle-class women. The first comparison between groups divides women by life-style or career choice, the second by attitude or preference, and the third by social class. The point here is to underscore the importance of making assumptions about which subgroups of constituents matter for outside lobbying strategies. When interest group leaders are deciding over strategies and policymakers are deciding over difficult policy issues, they are concerned about the salience of an issue, but to whom? The salience of the issue to an interest group's own members? To the set of constituents that agree with the interest group? To the set of constituents sharing the interest group's overall ideological goals?

The relevant group for any situation will vary, but I shall assume that outside lobbying strategies hinge primarily on the salience of issues to the second group: the portion of the population that agrees with the interest group on the particular policy issue at hand.[5] A common question posed by policymakers is whether the people on one side of the issue—say, protectionists in debates over trade policies—are intense about the issue. In disputes over trade policy in the 1990s, a piece of lore floating around the Capitol was that the average worker, who is generally protectionist, cares a lot more about comprehensive trade treaties like NAFTA than does the average business executive, who generally favors free trade. (In my data, this seems to be true, as I discuss in chapter 6.) While constituents may be fairly evenly split on an issue as measured by popularity, the group on one side of the issue may show a willingness to participate in the debate in some way, by writing Congress, by showing up at rallies, and, most importantly, by voting for or against a politician or party based on the issue.

Thus I link policy preferences to the percentage of people saying that an issue is important. For example, an environmental group claims to represent environmentally conscientious citizens, and a trade group claims to represent the stockholders and employees of its constituent companies as well as those people in the population opposing more environmental regulations. How do these two sets of people compare on the salience of regulatory issues, such as, say, the regulation of endangered species in the Pacific Northwest? One group may have more intense supporters or members than the other does.

I partitioned respondents in ANES into those who agreed with the policy goals of an interest group and those who did not agree, by using questions about policy preferences. As an example, the following question in the 1992 ANES divides respondents by preference:

Should federal government spending be increased, decreased, or kept about the same on improving and protecting the environment?

Among those respondents who answered "increased," I measured the salience of environmental issues to them using the open-ended question on the most important problem. In this case, 84 percent of those answering "increased" mentioned the environment as one of the three most important problems facing the country. The number 0.84, is a measure of how much the group's potentially mobilizable people care about the environment. In contrast, only 15 percent of those who answered the above question "decreased" or "kept about the same" mentioned the environment as one of the three most important problems facing the country. These numbers, 0.84 and 0.15, are therefore the salience measures used for some cases in the group-issue data set involving environmental issues.

[5] We can break down the poll respondents further into attentive publics, registered voters, or other categories (Fenno 1978). I used a variety of measures, and they lead to similar results. The measure based on policy preferences captures best the salience of an issue to the audiences that interest groups seek to contact in most outside lobbying campaigns.

An alternative way to measure salience is to make it relative to the salience for other groups on the same issue. I tested a ratio measure, where I simply divide the salience measure as just described by the salience of those groups taking the opposite positions on the same policy issue. So for example, instead of 0.84 being the salience measure for environmental groups on the question above, the relative measure is $0.84/0.15 = 5.6$ (then rescaled to be between 0 and 1). The relative measure is more appropriate for a theoretical model that stresses competition between groups on the same issue, while the absolute measure is more appropriate for our model that isolates decision making within groups across issues. Nevertheless, because the measures are highly correlated, results are similar for both. The relative measure leads to coefficients for salience that are approximately 20 percent lower than coefficients for salience using the absolute measure, but there is no noticeable difference in statistical significance.[6] Results reported below are from analyses using the absolute measure first described.

There are three further things to note about the operationalization of salience. First, in using those survey respondents who agree with the policy goals of the group I am trying to capture the salience to those constituents who are potentially mobilizable by the group in an outside lobbying campaign. By potentially mobilizable, I am not exclusively referring to members (or even potential members) of the group, although such people are not excluded, of course. Rather, outside lobbying is often intended to mobilize a wider portion of the population than members of the group.[7] And for most groups, membership is not an option for the average constituent, yet outside lobbying campaigns by, say, business groups are clearly intended to mobilize sympathetic constituents beyond stockholders and employees, and many outside lobbying campaigns by labor unions are intended to stir up more than the union rank and file.

Second, one might express a reasonable concern as to why I use measures of salience recorded several months after the interest group interviews. These measures may reflect the results of interest group mobilizing (conflict expansion) as much as the causes of it. The major reason to use these measures is that they were the only reliable ones available in the chronological vicinity of my study. Moreover, three to four months is not long enough for the salience to change much, and so using the ANES is not overly damaging to the model. But even if salience does change that rapidly, recall that an

---

[6] It is interesting to note that using the relative measure bolsters the coefficient for popularity by approximately 25 percent. An explanation of these differences in results in more detail is beyond the analysis here.

[7] Besides, I cannot measure accurately the salience of an issue to group members for any interest groups save the AARP and the two political parties. These three exceptional groups are enormous, and one could adequately cull out respondents who are members of these groups from the ANES data.

interest group's type can be interpreted as its anticipated ability to increase the salience of issues. The measures could be the manifestation of conflict expansion, where the anticipation of the new level of salience is the private information known to the group alone. Furthermore, on this latter point the ANES measures may be perfectly appropriate given that they were attained during or immediately following a national election. Outside lobbying is first and foremost the attempt to signal the confidence of a group's leaders in how a set of constituents will behave in the next election in response to incumbent policymakers' actions. Data collected near Election Day capture this information nicely.

Third, the questions used in the ANES to partition respondents by preference (for the purpose of comparing the salience of issues to subsets of the population) are not identical to the ones used in my data to measure the popularity of a group's issue position. This is unfortunate and a result of the timing of the study, but little is lost, really. The ANES questions in most circumstances are very similar to the ones asked of the interest groups and of national samples prior to the interest group interviews. As a result, the marginals for the national respondents in both sets of opinion polls used are not very different.

Relating Public Opinion and Outside Lobbying

We now turn to a multivariate analysis of the group-issue data to sort out the effects of different variables on decisions to use outside lobbying. The dependent variable used is OUTSIDE, the outside lobbying index created from confirmatory factor analysis on the group-issue data reported in chapter 2. Recall that OUTSIDE measures the underlying decision of an interest group to rely on outside lobbying on an issue. It is comprised of weighted measures of the number of outside lobbying tactics used and the scope of those tactics (how many constituents are targeted).

The major independent variables of interest are the *salience* and *popularity* of the policies confronting the group leaders. There are four scenarios. First, if outside lobbying correlates positively with both popularity and salience, then outside lobbying tends to communicate public opinion information in such a way that would please any democratic theorist. Interest group activities highlight popularly supported policies that constituents care about. This result, because of correlation with salience, would also be consistent with the separating or semipooling equilibriums from the signaling model in the previous chapter. Second, if outside lobbying correlates positively only with salience, then this is consistent with the two kinds of equilibriums, but it would not be entirely good news for democratic representation. Outside lobbying then would be communicating the intensity of preferences and would not be associated with popular policies. Third, if outside lobbying correlates positively with popularity and not with salience, that is good news for democratic theorists, but it means either that our signaling story does not provide a reasonable interpretation of events or that different types of groups are pooling on common strategies. The groups are not "separating" by type, where type is the salience of policy issues to the constituents they claim to represent. Fourth and finally, if outside lobbying correlates with neither popularity or salience, then outside lobbying has little relation to public opinion and must serve alternative purposes besides communicating constituents' preferences (or all types of groups are always "pooling" on common strategies).

Of course, other things besides public opinion will influence outside lobbying decisions, and these are included in the analysis. Resources, incentives to free ride, the importance of the issue to the group's leaders, and organizational characteristics will all contribute to strategic decisions over lobbying. The material *resources* of an interest group are measured by the natural log of the number of full-time staff available for political purposes. The temptation of a group's leaders to *free ride* off the efforts of other interest groups is measured by a variable indicating whether the group is the "only group to voice these positions" (0); "one of a few groups to voice these positions" (0.5); or "one of many groups to voice these positions" (1) on important issues to the group. And the *importance* of the policy issue to the group is measured by a variable indicating whether the issue was "somewhat important" (0) or "a major concern" (1) to the group.

To control for the organizational characteristics of the interest groups, the most straightforward way to stratify groups into relevant categories is to use dummy variables for *public interest groups*, *corporations*, *trade associations*, *labor unions*, and *professional associations*. Other characteristics, such as the kinds of members allowed and the number of local chapters authorized, are important as well but are highly correlated with other variables and are not included. Each of the included variables was rescaled to range from 0 to 1 (as was OUTSIDE, but not salience and popularity, which naturally range from 0 to 1) or to be dichotomous (0, 1).

The first column of table 4.1 presents OLS coefficients and standard errors for the included variables. (The dummy variable for professional associations was zeroed out to allow for identification.) The data indicate that both popularity and salience are positively correlated with OUTSIDE. The coefficient for salience is especially significant statistically. From these data we can conclude that interest groups appear to separate by type much of the time. Moreover, outside lobbying tends to reinforce popular policies, though the coefficient for popularity is weak relative to other coefficients.

The result receives even further support in the second column. Only those cases where interest groups used any outside lobbying at all are included in

TABLE 4.1
Regression Results with OUTSIDE as Dependent Variable

	OLS	OLS	2SLS	2SLS
Constant	−0.17**	−0.26***	−0.05	0.00
	(0.07)	(0.05)	(0.05)	(0.04)
Salience	0.14**	0.12***	0.15***	0.15***
	(0.06)	(0.04)	(0.05)	(0.04)
Popularity	0.09*	0.10**	0.03	0.03
	(0.06)	(0.05)	(0.06)	(0.05)
Free riding	−0.07*	−0.01	−0.16***	−0.13***
	(0.04)	(0.03)	(0.03)	(0.03)
Resources	0.15*	0.39***		
	(0.08)	(0.07)		
Importance	0.19***	0.18***	0.17***	0.13***
	(0.02)	(0.03)	(0.04)	(0.04)
Public interest group	0.29***	0.38***		
	(0.05)	(0.04)		
Corporation	0.07*	0.03		
	(0.05)	(0.04)		
Trade association	0.10**	0.16***		
	(0.04)	(0.04)		
Labor union	0.26***	0.28*		
	(0.03)	(0.04)		
Outside lobbying tendency			0.47***	0.57***
			(0.07)	(0.06)
R^2	0.33	0.59	0.33	0.51
Adj. R^2	0.31	0.57	0.32	0.50
SE	0.24	0.15	0.23	0.16
N	299	197	276	185

Note: Shown are regression coefficients with standard errors in parentheses. Robust standard errors were used (White 1980). Variables are described in the text.
*$p < .1$, **$p < .05$, ***$p < .01$

the analysis summarized in the second column. This truncates the data, chopping off the more than one-third of the group-issue cases where OUT-SIDE = 0. Most of the coefficients become sharper in the second column, though the substantive results are similar. Salience and popularity are positively correlated with OUTSIDE and highly significant statistically. Once interest groups decide to use outside lobbying, the scale and intensity of that lobbying are sensitive to the popular support the group enjoys for its issue position, after controlling for other factors.

Coefficients for other variables conform to expectations. Public interest groups and labor unions use outside lobbying more than do other kinds of groups, a finding consistent with bivariate statistics summarized in chapter 2. And resources do matter in decisions over outside lobbying, especially as shown in the second column, when groups, having decided to use the strategies, choose the scale of those strategies. Free-riding incentives and the importance of the issue to the group have the expected effects. The coefficient for free riding is negative, and therefore the more groups that are active on the group's side of the issue, the less the group uses outside lobbying. Likewise, groups use more outside lobbying as the importance of the issue to the group increases. This last point may seem trivial, though it is important to remember that inside lobbying does not vary much across issues that the group is concerned about. But outside lobbying does vary across issues, and it varies both in accordance with how important the issue is to the group, *and* with the popularity and salience of the issue to the mass public, controlling for the importance of the issue to the group.

Because the variables are on the same scale (0 to 1), it is possible to compare the weight of one variable on outside lobbying in relation to another. Comparing coefficients, we can see that the differences in the salience of the issue are approximately as important to outside lobbying decisions as the differences in material resources, and one-half as important as whether the group is a labor union or not. Public interest groups are the keenest on outside lobbying, controlling for other factors. In short, other explanations for why groups use outside lobbying are not necessarily flouted here. Organizational characteristics, free-riding incentives, and the importance of the issue to the group are all relevant.

Even controlling for these other factors, the salience of the issue has a measurable and important effect on outside lobbying. Increasing salience by 50 percent would increase the level of outside lobbying by approximately one-fourth of one standard deviation, roughly equivalent to 1.5 units in the scale for the scope of advertising. This 50 percent increase would therefore lead an interest group to push their advertising from zero to advertising in regional newspapers like the *St. Louis Dispatch* or the *Detroit Free Press*, or from *Roll Call* or *Congressional Quarterly* to national newspapers like the *New York Times* or the *Wall Street Journal*. Similarly, the increase could lead the group to change from very small radio appeals to a nationwide television appeal. Finally, the increase could lead labor unions or public interest groups to change from very small demonstrations to larger protests at the Capitol. In contrast, an increase in popularity by 50 percent (a much less likely proposition) leads to a change in one-sixth of a standard deviation in OUTSIDE, equivalent to a small change of less than one unit in the advertising scale.

The third and the fourth columns in table 4.1 present results from a two-stage-least-squares model:

$$y_1 = \alpha_1 + \beta_1 x_1 + \beta_2 x_2 + \beta_3 x_3 + \beta_4 x_4 + \beta_5 x_5 + \epsilon_1$$

$$y_2 = \alpha_2 + \beta_6 x_6 + \beta_7 x_7 + \beta_8 x_8 + \beta_9 x_9 + \beta_{10} \hat{y}_1 + \epsilon_2$$

The variables correspond as follows:

x_1 = Public Interest Group

x_2 = Labor Union

x_3 = Corporation

x_4 = Trade Association

x_5 = Resources

x_6 = Salience

x_7 = Popularity

x_8 = Free riding

x_9 = Importance

y_1 = Outside Index for Group Data

$\hat{y}_1$ = Predicted Outside Index for Group Data

y_2 = OUTSIDE

The instrument used in the second equation is the outside lobbying index from the group data set. It was compiled from information on group strategies over all issues (see chapter 2). Then OUTSIDE (y_2) is the outside lobbying index from the group-issue data set, the same variable used as the dependent variable in all the other regressions reported in this chapter. Following standard two-stage procedures, we can regress y on all factors that do not vary across issues, in this case resources and organizational attributes (labor union, corporation, etc.). We can then regress y_2 on those factors that do change across issues, and on $\hat{y}_1$, the predicted value from the first equation. (Appropriate corrections were made for standard errors. See Kmenta 1986, 684.) The resulting coefficients from the second equation are reported in table 4.1 in column 3 for all cases and in column 4 for the cases where the groups used any outside lobbying. These columns parallel columns 1 and 2.

The purposes of this two—stage model are twofold. First, its results lend considerable support to the results for nearly all the variables presented in the first two columns, a welcome indication of robustness. Furthermore, other specifications not presented here, including an ordered probit model and models with additional variables added, lead to similar results.[8] And second, it even strengthens the conclusions drawn from the first two columns about issue salience. As expected, the coefficient for $\hat{y}_1$ is large and significant. This variable measures, as much as possible with these data, the underlying tendency of the group to use outside lobbying, without consideration for the issue-specific context. The coefficients for salience, moreover, suggest that outside lobbying decisions are influenced by issue-specific salience *over and above* the underlying tendency for an organization to use outside lobbying. This is strong evidence of issue-specific effects on decisions to use outside lobbying. It seems, unfortunately, that the popularity of policy positions does not have much of an effect in this two-stage model. Analysis of why the coefficients for popularity drop in value under the two-stage model is beyond our task here, but these lower coefficients cast a cloud over the hoped-for conclusion that outside lobbying bolsters popular policies. The most we can say at this point to summarize all the models is that popularity weakly correlates with outside lobbying (but see chapter 5).

Examples from Labor Unions

The group-issue data support the notion that across interest groups and across many policy issues, public opinion context influences the decisions of interest groups on whether or not to use outside lobbying. We can also examine strategies within a class of interest groups. The outside lobbying decisions of labor unions in 1992 are instructive. Labor unions, always skillful and eager practitioners of outside lobbying, spent more resources and time appealing to constituents on those issues for which they had popular support than on other issues. And they focused their outside lobbying only on their members when they did not have the requisite popular support.

Among others, three policy issues of concern to most national unions in the early 1990s were the legality of striker replacement workers, national health care, and trade issues.[9] On the first issue, striker replacement, the national labor unions maintained a policy position obviously favored by most union members (that replacement workers should be outlawed) but not all that popular among the mass public. Moreover, the salience of this issue was relatively small, even for those people who agreed with the unions on

---

[8] One notable robustness test involved using a single variable that combined salience and popularity. This can be interpreted as reflecting a situation where either dimension of public opinion is sufficient to encourage outside lobbying. I multiplied the two measures together to create a new variable, and included it into regressions like those reported in table 4.1. Results are as expected. The variable is in every case positive and significant, with t-statistics hovering around 3.

[9] The public opinion questions are in appendix C, numbered 2, 5, and 12.

the policy. In the group-issue data, I recorded a popularity of 0.31 and a salience of 0.42. In contrast, the unions supported national health insurance and further restrictions on trade, policies that enjoyed widespread popular support. The popularity and salience for national health insurance were 0.66 and 0.87, respectively. For further restrictions on trade, the popularity and salience were 0.69 and 0.65, respectively. In sum, we should expect that the unions used more outside lobbying on national health insurance and trade policies than on striker replacement.

The data are as expected. Nearly all the unions used extensive outside lobbying among their own members on all three issues. So the part of OUT-SIDE that consists of membership mobilization is quite high for the labor unions on the issues. For the constituents they expected to respond to the appeals—namely, their own members—the unions undertook large outside lobbying strategies.

However, for protesting and advertising, there is a marked contrast in labor union strategies between striker replacement and the other two issues. Most of the unions I surveyed paid for large advertising campaigns on trade issues (NAFTA) and on health care policies, and most held protests of some kind. On striker replacement, only one national union I surveyed protested (Amalgamated Transit Union) and only one national union I surveyed ran advertisements (Oil, Chemical, and Atomic Workers International Union). The data show that outside lobbying by unions was remarkably tame on striker replacement, one of their most important issues in years. They could not make appeals beyond their memberships, as they could with the other two issues.

Specific Tactics

While outside lobbying in general corresponds to salience and somewhat to popularity, some tactics show more correspondence than others. The measure OUTSIDE is used under the assumption that it captures group tactics that spring from the same basic intention on the part of group leaders: to appeal to constituents outside the policymaking community. In other words, the tactics are assumed to be substitutable. However, this may not be the case entirely.

When OUTSIDE is broken down into specific tactics and specific levels or ranges of those tactics, telling differences emerge in how they relate to public opinion. For example, it turns out that the use of press conferences, a part of the OUTSIDE index, does not correspond positively with salience or popularity. It seems that group leaders tend to use press conferences to explain technical material to the press or to communicate to people within the policymaking community.[10] Press conferences, especially the kinds captured in my data, are rarely used to communicate with huge audiences outside of Washington.

Figure 4.1 shows logit coefficients for selected tactics or ranges of tactics. These coefficients, indicating the marginal effect of salience and popularity on the specified outside lobbying activities, were derived from logit estimations using the same control variables as presented in table 4.1. The coefficients for the control variables are not reported in figure 4.1, and any coefficients reported to be above 1.20 are significant statistically by ordinary standards.

Results for the first two variables reveal the importance of public opinion in influencing the scale of outside lobbying. The variables for small scale outside lobbying and large scale outside lobbying summarize the data across three tactics. Small scale outside lobbying includes protests, advertisements, and membership mobilizations involving fewer than five hundred persons. These activities are correlated with salience and with popularity. Large scale outside lobbying includes massive Washington, D.C., or national protests, and advertisements and membership mobilizations targeted at one million persons or more. Both salience and popularity are more prominent for large scale outside lobbying than for small scale outside lobbying. In sum, the larger the outside lobbying campaign, the more group leaders appear to make decisions that correspond to the salience of policies and the popularity of their policy positions.

The next set of variables shows, first the negative coefficients for press conferences, as discussed previously, and that protesting is highly correlated with salience and, surprisingly, with popularity. Protesting turns out to be a means for labor unions and public interest groups with popular positions on salient issues to communicate their public opinion advantages to policymakers and others.

Continuing down the figure, a comparison among different advertising media reveals surprising results. Television is the only media that tends to carry outside lobbying messages that consistently communicate salience information. The television advertisements funded by interest groups are usually on very high profile policies, like health care, general economic policies, and taxation. These, of course, are salient policy issues to many constituents. The coefficient for popularity also shows that groups with more popular positions are the ones using television to outside lobby. In fact, measures for both television and newspaper advertising correlates with popularity. Neither radio nor magazine advertising correlate with any public opinion informa-

---

[10] Press conferences were included in the OUTSIDE index because they loaded adequately in the factor analysis summarized in chapter 2. Thus press conferences correlate with the other outside lobbying tactics but not with salience or popularity.

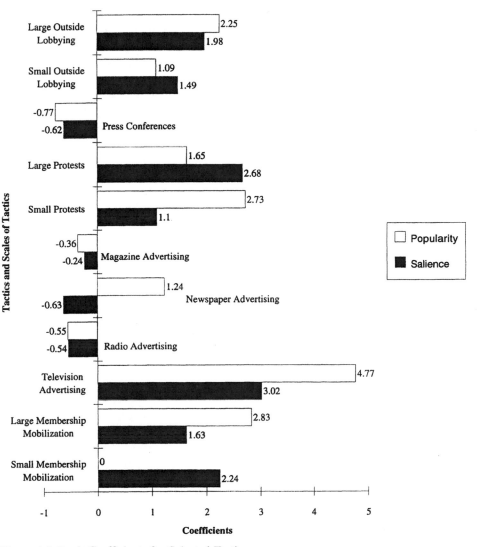

Figure 4.1. Logit Coefficients for Selected Tactics

tion. Radio and magazines target specialized audiences, and so perhaps group leaders do not feel advertisements in these media are credible signals to policymakers and therefore use the advertisements for other purposes, such as strictly for conflict expansion or membership drives focused on a specific policy issue.

The final two results presented are for variables representing distinct levels of membership mobilizations. The results indicate that small mobilizations (fewer than one hundred members) correspond to salience more than to popularity, and large mobilizations (more than one million members) correspond to popularity more than to salience. Thus, as previously discussed, small mobilizations tend to occur when a small number of members are intense about an issue, and large membership mobilizations occur more to reflect moderately salient issues and highly popular policy positions. The reversal in the ordering of the coefficients seems consistent with our intuition about the differences between salience and popularity and how groups might alter tactics in response to both. If a group of constituents is small, its leaders need to communicate to policymakers how intensely the members of that group feel about the issue. If the group of constituents is large, the leaders do not have to rely on such high levels of salience to gain the attention of policymakers. A moderate level of salience will suffice, and popularity becomes more important than for small groups. Groups supporting popular policies may need to demonstrate only a moderate level of salience on the issue. Thus while membership mobilizations are correlated with other kinds of outside lobbying and so together they load onto common factors in a factor analysis (see chap. 2), they seem to relate to public opinion information somewhat differently. Not surprisingly, membership mobilizations indicate salience information quite well, while broader outside lobbying tactics tend to be undertaken by groups pursuing popular policies.

Group Popularity

The measure of popularity used so far reflects support among constituents for policy issues, not for the interest groups themselves. For example, labor unions may not be all that popular in general, but they tend to lobby for policy programs that enjoy widespread popularity. It may be the case that outside lobbying relates more to group popularity than to the popularity of issue positions. If group popularity is important, one interpretation of outside lobbying may hold that policymakers focus attention mostly on which groups affiliate with which policies, and they take cues mostly from popular groups in their constituencies. Thus popular groups are the only ones who even bother to use outside lobbying.

This contrasts somewhat with the signaling framework as it is pursued here. By my interpretation, policymakers learn something from the outside lobbying itself, above and beyond the credibility of the groups as representatives of constituents. And my data suggest that all kinds of groups use outside lobbying. If my interpretation is more accurate, then the popularity of a group should not matter as much in outside lobbying campaigns as the popularity of the policies under consideration. Granted, policies may increase or decrease in popularity or political support due to group endorsements, but the differences between the two interpretations are matters of degree. In the former interpretation, group popularity dominates the effectiveness of out-side lobbying campaigns and therefore the tendency for groups to use out-side lobbying. In the latter interpretation, the effect of group popularity is much attenuated and mixed in with other factors on group strategies. The popularity of policies and, especially, the salience of policy issues are para-mount.

The results from my data suggest that group popularity does not matter much in decisions to use outside lobbying. To show this, I measure a group's overall popularity by averaging how "warm" or "cold" respondents to the 1992 ANES felt toward a particular group or cause in the population. These thermometer ratings range from 0 (cold) to 100 (warm), and categories in-clude unions, big business, environmentalists, and the women's movement. I use the mean response to the rating for the group category most appropriate for the groups in my own surveys. For example, all of the unions in my surveys were given a popularity rating of 53.84 because that was the mean response to the thermometer ratings for unions in 1992. This compares with 64.68 for Jews and 37.74 for homosexuals.

There is a correlation between overall group popularity and the popular support of the group's issue positions in my data. This is not surprising. Using the average popularity measure of the issues in my issue-specific data for each group, the correlation between group popularity and the popularity for the groups based on issues is 0.34, which is comfortably significant by statistical standards. In other words, by these data groups tend to be more popular the more popularly supported their issue positions are.

It turns out that a group's overall popularity corresponds with outside lobbying, although the relationship is relatively weak. Substituting group popularity for the popularity of policies in the various regression equations presented in table 4.1 shows that the coefficients for group popularity are positive but smaller than for popularity of policies. Moreover, overall group popularity does not seem to influence outside lobbying decisions when ac-counting for the popularity of groups' issue positions. Group popularity was included in the regression equations in table 4.1 (along with measures of popularity and salience), and in every case, the coefficients were close to zero, while the coefficients for the popularity of issues stayed very close to where they were in the original equations. The coefficient for salience stayed the same as well. The standard errors for the popularity of issues increased slightly, but not enough to make popularity become statistically insignificant. (Thus, because the coefficients and standard errors for popular support for issues stayed robust, the potential inefficiency from multicollinearity be-tween the two kinds of measures does not undermine our basic results.) In sum, decisions over outside lobbying reflect popular support for the issues at hand rather than the overall popularity of the groups doing the mobilizing. This is consistent with the notion that lobbying decisions do not spring auto-matically from certain kinds of organizations, but rather are a consequence at least as much of the environment facing the organizations. Public opinion on issues is an important part of that environment.

Conclusion

The empirical results in this chapter offer strong support for the idea that interest groups generally use more outside lobbying the more public opinion favors them. Public opinion has two components, popularity and salience, and both correspond to outside lobbying decisions. Salience overall has the stronger and more robust effect, and this is consistent with the separating equilibriums from chapter 3 and with the notion that groups try to communicate the part of public opinion for which they have a comparative advantage in communicating. But popularity is also (mildly) correlated with outside lobbying, so democratic theorists can take some comfort in the fact that outside lobbying, even when it can be purchased, does not spring forth only from groups pursuing unpopular policies.

But the weak relationship between popularity and outside lobbying, and the stronger relationship between salience and outside lobbying, does mean that there are some groups with intense supporters pursuing unpopular policies that use outside lobbying. In fact, with these data we can identify such groups and their strategies. In other words, we are now in a position to evaluate outside lobbying as either astroturf or real grass roots. I leave these evaluations to the final chapter.

We cannot conclude from the data that other explanations (besides signaling) for outside lobbying are not true. Organizational characteristics, resources, free-riding incentives, and the importance of the issue to a group have major effects on outside lobbying decisions. It would be hard to imagine otherwise. And as we shall see in the next chapter, there are many times when groups without the requisite public opinion support would want to expand the conflict. Consideration of the incentives underlying conflict expansion leads to potential explanations for the outliers from the regressions reported in this chapter.

Concern among critics of outside lobbying reveals a tension between the comfort of knowing that constituents are involved in policymaking decisions and the discomfort of knowing that interested elites are the ones mobilizing selected portions of the mass public. The results from this chapter suggest that in the United States there is some congruence between pressure from interest groups and the policy preferences of the mass public. Like many forms of pressure on the government, outside lobbying has the potential both for manipulation and for legitimate public involvement. Recognizing and accounting for the difference between these two possibilities is an important step in evaluating policy outcomes that result from a mixture of elite and mass participation. This chapter has provided a means to make such evaluations.

5

Outside Lobbying as Conflict Expansion

☆ based it all off on question [handwritten annotation]

THE NOTION that outside lobbying is costly signaling from interest group leaders to policymakers provides an explanation for the empirical relationship between salience information and lobbying strategies. Group leaders try to communicate information about the intensity of preferences among constituents, something that they have a comparative advantage in communicating. The basic signaling game ought to be considered a benchmark, in that it appears to explain a respectable portion of the variance of outside lobbying, controlling for other factors. Nevertheless, the coefficients for salience in the previous chapter, while they are positive and significant, are not overwhelmingly high, and there are many outliers. In other words, the relationship is rather loose. The outliers in the statistical model can have occurred for many reasons, among them the simple fact that group leaders often use outside lobbying to increase the level of salience, believing that the current level of salience is inadequate.

In my interviews I asked group leaders a deliberately ambiguous, open-ended question, and up to four responses were coded:

> Who specifically is your primary target audience in your publicity or grass-roots campaigns?

Of the groups surveyed, 56 percent of their leaders mentioned "the public" (in one of their four possible responses) or some variation of that, and 51 percent mentioned "Congress or the president." Meanwhile, 26 percent said their own group members were targeted, 23 percent said policy elites, and 18 percent said the media. In their first responses, as an indication of their major focus of attention, 41 percent of the group leaders mentioned "the public," and 41 percent mentioned "Congress or the president."

Without reading too much into these responses, we can conclude that ☆? [handwritten annotation] group leaders use outside lobbying every bit as much to influence constituents as to demonstrate grass-roots support to policymakers. In the short term, of course, group leaders intend their outside lobbying to influence constituent behavior. They want constituents to write letters, send faxes, travel to Washington, or visit the district offices of their elected representatives. That much is obvious. But outside lobbying is intended not just to bring about short term behavior changes or to cast a temporary light on members of the public for policymakers to see. Many group leaders also believe that their outside lobbying will have lasting effects on the way members of the public perceive and evaluate policies and the politicians who support those policies.

In fact, if outside lobbying is intended to change the salience of policy issues, we should not expect there to be a tight fit between the measured, *current* level of salience information and outside lobbying. Rather, the *anticipated* level of salience (which in theory will be higher than the current level) should correlate with outside lobbying.

When interest group leaders undertake outside lobbying for the additional purpose of changing the salience of an issue or the popularity of a policy position among constituents, they intend, in the memorable words of Schattschneider (1960), to expand the scope of the conflict for their advantage. Simply put, in the process of mobilizing constituents to signal to policymakers, group leaders often change the elements of public opinion they are trying to signal. Conflict expansion is an ageless strategy of politics, and takes on added value in majoritarian settings. As Tocqueville ([1835] 1966) wrote in the nineteenth century, Americans form minority associations partially to "discover the arguments most likely to make an impression on the majority, for they always hope to draw the majority over to their side and then to exercise power in its name" (178).

In this chapter I explore several aspects of outside lobbying as conflict expansion. The first part of the chapter discusses different interpretations of conflict expansion. Conflict expansion can take on a variety of meanings, and since the idea was first presented seriously in Schattschneider's research, later scholarship has introduced concepts that are strongly related to Schattschneider's idea. The second part of the chapter explains how the stages of legislation influence decisions over outside lobbying. I argue that the nature of the conflict expansion pursued, and whether an interest group benefits from signaling, depends critically on whether a group's proposed policy is an idea just introduced in the public debate or an idea already thick in the middle of the legislative process. And third, I examine an abstract model that explains the political environments under which interest groups benefit from conflict expansion. It turns out that the policy status quo plays a large role in determining decisions over outside lobbying as conflict expansion.

Ascertaining whether or not interest groups succeed in changing public opinion is beyond the scope of this study. Few scholars of interest groups would doubt that outside lobbying can have a marked effect on the salience of policies. But no one I am aware of has studied systematically the changes in salience and interest group mobilizing. Other studies that focus on the popularity of policies are revealing. Lupia (1994), in his study of referendums in California, shows that interest group endorsements can sometimes change overall levels of support for or against referendums. And Page, Shapiro, and Dempsey (1987) conclude after an exhaustive study of public opinion changes that interest group messages can have an effect on public opinion, though not as much as do television news anchors, presidents, newspaper editors, and local politicians.

Various Meanings of Conflict Expansion

Schattschneider's seminal writings on conflict expansion do not provide an adequate account of exactly what conflict expansion means and what elites do to make the conflict expand. Browne (1995) places the emphasis on ways elites increase the salience of issues, a common and reasonable interpretation, though there remains considerable ambiguity in how these changes come about. Schattschneider, Browne writes, described conflict expansion as "a fight breaks out and public attention converts low-salience policy problems to ones of high salience" (11).

Let us consider three interpretations of conflict expansion that are consistent with recent literature on group mobilizations and collective action. First, conflict expansion can mean the transmission of new information to the public about the consequences of public policies. This interpretation may lead to the conclusion that conflict expansion means influencing popularity as well as increasing the salience of an issue. Berry (1989), for one, sees much of grass-roots lobbying, especially advocacy advertising, as attempts to educate the public. And Baumgartner and Jones (1993) refer to "Schattschneider mobilization" as the efforts of opponents of the status quo to undermine existing institutions by spreading bad news about their consequences. By this account, conflict expansion is a method of costly signaling that differs from the signaling described in chapter 3. Instead of interest group leaders signaling information about constituents' preferences to policymakers, conflict expansion means interest group leaders try to signal to constituents the policy consequences of actions taken by policymakers. The intention is to change how constituents think about a policy, which can result in increasing or decreasing the popularity of a policy or in increasing the salience of a policy issue. (As I argue shortly, this is most common early in the policymaking process.)

This kind of conflict expansion also refers to elite attempts to highlight alternative aspects of a policy for subsets of constituents. Often called framing, it really boils down to the strategic use of information to make constituents put more or less weight on specific consequences associated with a policy. For example, an interest group opposing an environmental regulation can highlight to working-class constituents the job losses associated with the policy, and alternatively, to business executives the high costs of conforming to the regulations. A tax on fossil fuels can be framed as an issue about the environment (to gain support), about unfair taxation on Western states, truckers, or commuters (to bolster the opposition), or about deficit reduction (again, to gain support). Many issues can be alternatively framed to take on entirely different meanings and subsequently acquire different levels of salience, or particular policies can become more or less popular (Jones 1994; Edelman 1964; Bosso 1987).

The second interpretation of conflict expansion is that group leaders try to underwrite the costs of collective action for specific sets of constituents; this is generally intended to increase the salience of a policy issue, though in some circumstances it could change popularity. Group leaders essentially offer selective incentives, in Olson's terminology, for constituents to participate in the group's lobbying effort. They can make it very easy for constituents to write letters to Congress, call their representatives, travel to Washington, D.C., or show up at a local rally (Berry 1989, chap. 5). For example, one national insurance company in 1992 called its most influential business customers and dictated a letter on health care policy so that their customers could send a detailed letter on company stationery to members of the Senate Committee on Labor and Human Resources. The assumption behind this strategy (and this interpretation) is that the latent preferences of enough constituents are favorable for the interest group to use outside lobbying, but constituents are initially unwilling to pay the costs to participate at a level that will influence policymakers. Outside lobbying simultaneously focuses the attention of constituents on a particular course of action, makes that action less costly for constituents to undertake, signals to policymakers that the group represents angry constituents, and demonstrates that the group's leaders *can* mobilize constituents.

There is a tension in this second interpretation having to do with the visibility of the interest group leaders' costs of mobilizing constituents. Recall from the discussion in chapter 3 that policymakers are most impressed by large-scale grass-roots activities spawned by low-cost interest group mobilizations. An interest group can try to expand the conflict by subsidizing constituents' participation, but to the extent that policymakers detect the subsidization, policy influence becomes diluted. Group leaders have to strike a middle ground where they expand the conflict enough without inducing accusations from policymakers or the media of purchasing grass-roots support.

The third interpretation of conflict expansion is that interest group leaders provide cues to coordinate the actions of constituents. Constituents do not need to be subsidized; they need to know what to do. It is assumed, once again, that enough constituents have latent preferences that are favorable to the group, and these constituents are willing to participate in an outside lobbying campaign. However, they rely on cues from interest group leaders to tell them what activities to participate in, whom to contact, in what manner, and when. Coordination is a public good for the group of constituents.

In using game theory models with multiple equilibriums, oftentimes theorists who apply models to specific social situations rely on Schelling's notion of *focal points* to make predictions about outcomes. An equilibrium may be focal (that is, more noticeable or prominent than other equilibriums) because each player thinks the other players are going to play the strategies induced by the focal equilibrium. Especially in coordination games, focal points can be very important, as experimental evidence has made clear (Schelling 1978; Kreps 1990).

Therefore, an interest group's advertising campaign, its membership mobilization, or a press conference, can be a way for the group's leaders to say, "OK, now everyone who agrees with us on this policy, march to the right and throw your hands up in disgust." Of all the possible actions that constituents can do, the fact that they coordinate on an interest group's signal means that they are listening to what the interest group leaders are saying. The successful coordination in turn signals something to policymakers about the now increased unity of a group of constituents. So once again, the outside lobbying both increases the salience of the policy issue and signals to policymakers.

To summarize the three interpretations, conflict expansion can be intended as constituent education, the provision of selective incentives, and coordination of constituents on a common action. Of course, these interpretations overlap, and real outside lobbying can accomplish all three (plus signaling to policymakers), but they emphasize different purposes. Susanne Lohmann (1993), for one, has combined in a single game theory model of grass-roots participation the ideas of coordination on a focal equilibrium and information transmission from constituents to elites. Ainsworth and Sened (1993) also describe a game theory model of lobbying that combines coordination of constituents and signaling of policymakers.

The Stages of Legislation

It was useful earlier to assume in the signaling model in chapter 3 that the function of outside lobbying is more or less the same for all interest groups in all situations. However, when we consider the additional purpose of conflict expansion, the policy context facing an interest group takes on additional importance. The context will shape both the incentives for the group to use outside lobbying and the opportunities for the group to undertake different kinds of conflict expansion. More specifically, the requisite levels of salience and popularity for a group to benefit from outside lobbying might change over the different stages of legislation.

By stage of legislation I mean the position of a policy idea along a time line from a new proposal brought forth from many possible sources—parties, candidates, journalists, interest groups, social movements, think tanks, or campaign contributors—to a final bill voted upon in the House and Senate and signed by the president. The time line might even extend into implementation by an executive branch agency. All but a few policy ideas die before reaching the end of the line. The notable ones that survive typically have long and tortuous histories. For example, serious safety regulations of automobiles made it into law in the early 1970s after nearly a decade of strenuous conflict expansion, savvy inside lobbying, and signaling of grassroots power by public interest advocates like Ralph Nader. A set of rather nebulous ideas put forth in the mid-1960s became law only after proponents, both inside and outside the government, overcame opposition in congressional committees and then on the floors of the chambers of Congress (Gorey 1975).

Kingdon's ideas of agendas and alternatives are useful as they relate to the following description of the stages of legislation. For Kingdon (1984), agendas are the policy problems the government can consider, like the trade deficit, rising health care costs, or famine in Africa. Alternatives are specific policies being debated by policymakers, among which they must make decisions. In my formulation, the early stages are where interest groups want to push ideas onto the government's agenda, whereas the latter stages are when interest groups want to convince policymakers that one alternative has more support among constituents than another alternative has.[1]

I consider three stages of legislation from the perspective of interest group leaders deciding over lobbying strategies. The first, the *need for action* stage, happens when some set of persons (interest group leaders, the media, a set of politicians, think tanks) is trying to get a policy problem on the government's agenda. In the second, *agenda-shaping* stage, the policy problem has been recognized by enough policymakers as requiring attention, but they are deliberating over which policy alternatives to set. For example, competing bills are sent to one or several congressional committees to be hashed out. Policymakers usually alter a policy idea many times during this stage. The third stage, *debate and voting*, occurs when a very small number (usually two) of concrete policy proposals face up or down votes by the legislature,

---

[1] Likewise, in the earlier stages salience can refer more to the policy problems that constituents want addressed, while in later stages salience refers more to solutions to policy issues as they have been defined and articulated by competing elites. The distinction here is not always clear-cut. The ANES measures of salience used in this book refer to policy problems literally, but separating policy problems from the solutions offered by the major political parties is not straightforward. For example, there are many possible solutions to declining wages (a problem constituents want addressed), including more trade protection (policy issue: foreign trade), more generous social welfare policies (policy issue: social welfare policies), an increase in the minimum wage (policy issue: employment), and attempts to lower or raise the deficit (policy issue: economic planning or budgetary politics). Which issues are more salient than others, especially for issues later in the policy process, and how those issues are defined, depend on how issues and the solutions offered over those issues are presented to voters in electoral competition. See Kingdon 1984.

the citizens (a referendum), or an executive. For each of these three stages, the goals of those interest groups deciding to use outside lobbying can be different.

Need for Action Stage

In general, policy ideas become better formulated and better understood by policymakers as time goes on. Early in the process, when policymakers are not yet confronted with explicit choices, and when many interest groups merely want to present or float ideas that are a long way off from being introduced into law, the constraints of current public opinion (especially popularity) on lobbying efforts may be quite low. Group leaders want to convince constituents that certain issues deserve government attention. They want to expand the scope of the conflict (influencing popularity *and* increasing salience) through educating constituents. This is most important for groups without ready access to mainstream or powerful policymakers. Leaders of groups without a lot of apparent support among constituents may not be able to place items on the agenda through inside lobbying alone.

Consider a group that is a counterexample first. The National Education Association (NEA), representing tens of thousands of educators nationwide and a long-standing ally of the Democratic Party, can gain the audience of members of Congress easily. They are granted legitimacy on education issues (at least among Democrats) almost automatically because of their organizational history. Thus, through inside lobbying alone, the NEA can present ideas and new proposals to policymakers. There is no need to use outside lobbying to educate teachers on the importance of many of their pet issues, nor does the NEA need to establish legitimacy among policymakers as the representatives of large numbers of constituents.

In contrast, groups not so well established may need to use outside lobbying to get their ideas on the agenda. Animal rights groups, gay activists, right wing groups, or ethnic groups demanding new levels of foreign aid for their homeland outside lobbied in the 1990s to demonstrate the seriousness of their issue or the need for immediate action. Many of the outliers from the regressions reported in table 4.1 are from these kinds of groups (National Gay and Lesbian Task Force Policy Institute, Liberty Lobby, Zero Population Growth, Rainbow Lobby). Outside lobbying for these groups involves attempts to legitimize particular viewpoints that may not have widespread acceptance. Confident that their ideas deserve to be heard by policymakers, they emphasize bases of legitimacy beyond public support, like human or civil rights, natural law, respect for life, nationalism, or constitutional protection. And empirically, they use a great deal of outside lobbying even when their positions have relatively low popularity and salience. According to statements from group leaders, they hope to change public opinion. A lobbyist for the National Organization for Women spoke about her organization as "not afraid of taking unpopular positions," and noted that her organization was usually "ahead of our time." Public legitimacy for policies her group proposes, she implied, will *follow* the group's activities rather than *precede* them.

Leaders of these groups also know that perceptible and meaningful changes in public opinion take time. They need to have patience. Robin Kane, a gay civil rights activist, told me that her group cannot hope to convince a majority of Americans that same-sex marriages should be given legal status, at least not in the short term. Rather, her group wants to soften the opposition by making the idea familiar and less threatening. Gradually it will gain acceptance. And as Dan Weiss of the Sierra Club put it, "We usually can't, and nor can the other side, push a button. It doesn't work like that. We think of many [*sic*] of our grass-roots campaigning as a long-term educational process." Likewise, one interest group veteran of the Great Society era spoke of the animal rights movement with admiration: "They have started a public debate which is becoming increasingly difficult for policymakers to ignore. If you begin to get people to accept the concept that animals have some rights, then someday you may be able to get them to believe that animals have equal rights. And then what you're talking about is closing down zoos, banning circuses, prohibiting the sale of leather, on and on, which is their ultimate goal."

Therefore, this first stage of policymaking presents a diverse set of incentives for interest groups. For some groups, the conflict may be automatically expanded by events out of their control, and they may be ready to signal constituents' salience right away. For other groups, many public appeals during this stage are meant to expand the range of legitimate policy and to place controversial ideas on the crowded public agenda. These ideas will not necessarily have much popular support, at least not at that time. Group leaders want to influence the popularity of policies, something that is much easier to do in this first stage of legislation than in the later stages of legislation.[2] Finally, for some groups like the NEA, outside lobbying is not necessary because they already have access to powerful policymakers. So groups with considerable popular support may not need to outside lobby at this stage. All in all, we should expect considerable variance in the relationship between both dimensions of public opinion and outside lobbying strategies during the need for action stage.

---

[2] Indeed, in Page and Shapiro (1992), the claim is made repeatedly that in the initial stages of problem definition and public awareness of a policy problem, public opinion (popularity) on particular policies fluctuates. Later on, after the public has had time to digest information, public opinion (popularity) on policies stabilizes.

Agenda-Shaping Stage

Once an idea is on the agenda, the incentives for interest groups change, at first slightly and then more completely. The most common situation comprising the second stage is when a bill is in congressional committee. Congressional committees are more often than not given the authority to amend, defeat, strengthen, or otherwise emasculate a given bill. On controversial policies, intense bargaining takes place among policymakers, legislative chambers, branches of government, and of course, interest groups. For many interest groups and many policy issues, the agenda-shaping stage is when the real action takes place. A prominent example in 1992 of an issue in this stage was health care policy. There were numerous bills floating around committees on the means to control health care costs and guarantee coverage for the poor.

Hundreds of major interest groups wanted access to these deliberations over health care. They pursued specific committee members' attention with vigor, and if they could get in the door to speak with the members, they would have accomplished at least half their goal. Access to the agenda setters is a valuable commodity, and groups use both inside and outside lobbying to attain it. Sometimes, they pay for it, literally. Campaign contributions, as one handy inside lobbying strategy, can induce access (Austen-Smith 1995). They can signal to policymakers that interest groups have worthwhile information. Even beyond access, contributions may influence committee behavior. Hall and Wayman (1990) demonstrate that interest groups contributing to legislators' campaigns usually get committee members to work on behalf of the group (or avoid working against the group).

Beyond the value of inside lobbying to interest groups as means of access and to policymakers as means of acquiring useful information about policies or constituents, outside lobbying has its distinct advantages during this stage. First, interest groups can continue to expand the scope of the conflict to help their side of the cause. Framing issues properly can be especially helpful, as many groups and policymakers are trying to figure out which constituents will pay attention to which versions of the potential legislation. For health care, already in 1992, two years prior to the infamous debacle over the Clinton health care plan, interest groups competed to frame the issue as a matter of (1) adequate choice over doctors, (2) controlling taxes used for Medicare, (3) guaranteed coverage for all, and (4) the high costs of benefits borne by businesses.

And second, signaling from interest groups about constituent opinion becomes increasingly useful to elected officials as policy alternatives take shape and as these alternatives gain public attention. Hansen (1991) shows how groups that are perceived to represent constituents of committee members usually get access to committee deliberations. Outside lobbying as signaling can be a means for interest groups to signal and gain access during the agenda-shaping stage. Also, outside lobbying during this stage will be both highly targeted at a few members of key committees and widely targeted to keep public pressure on and continue the momentum during committee deliberations. And group leaders who are not so confident in their existing public support or not confident in the public support they anticipate being able to induce through conflict expansion will likely want to avoid raising public awareness of the issue lest they provoke a backlash. In short, outside lobbying will be plentiful by those groups confident in their public support, and we should expect there to be a tight relationship between salience (and perhaps popularity) and outside lobbying.

Debate and Voting Stage

If policy ideas survive the agenda-shaping stage, they emerge as concrete policy proposals to be debated and then voted upon. These ideas, often in the form of legislative bills but sometimes in the form of referendums (at the state level) or constitutional amendments, enter the third stage. At this point, policymakers (or voters in the case of referendums) are asked to consider a small set of possibilities, usually two, the status quo and the most prominent alternative. Among the three stages, the debate and voting stage would seem to approximate best the game theory model from chapter 3. Most people have heard of the policy and have formed opinions, and it is up to interest group leaders to communicate to policymakers the salience of the issue among favorable constituents.

At the same time, however, two factors may dampen the enthusiasm of popularly supported groups for using outside lobbying. For one, the salience of a policy issue may already have been increased to its limit and may already be known to policymakers by this stage. And two, politicians tend to take over many of the functions that interest groups perform in earlier stages. Prior to floor votes on controversial issues, congressional leaders and the president typically undertake their own outside lobbying campaigns on the issues. They try to convince fellow lawmakers of the same things that interest groups were trying to convince them of during the committee stages: that constituents care about the issue and that enough constituents will vote on the issue.

For these reasons, salience may not be as much of a constraint on interest group strategies as it was in earlier stages. Interest groups begin to follow the lead of politicians, who themselves coordinate and mobilize groups of constituents (both organized and not) to convince colleagues in the government. So we should expect a mixed result for outside lobbying during this stage. Salience may be mildly correlated with outside lobbying, but is is likely to be a weak relationship.

As an example, the balanced budget amendment was a policy idea that made it to the debate and voting stage in 1992. The amendment was finally voted down on the floor of the House in June, after failing to achieve the two-thirds vote necessary for passage. On an issue even that large in scope, interest groups became involved. They communicated their positions forcefully to policymakers through inside lobbying, and some groups undertook outside lobbying campaigns on the proposed amendment. Outside lobbying in the spring of 1992 was, as might be expected, selectively applied. Groups lobbying for popularly supported programs or tax provisions subject to changes under the balanced budget amendment, such as the Association of Private Pensions and Welfare Plans, the National Association of Investment Companies, and the National Committee to Preserve Social Security and Medicare, used outside lobbying much more than did groups supporting the proposed amendment.

However, as the final floor vote approached, politicians, especially President Bush, took over the coordination of constituent communications, and then even the groups supporting the amendment began to mobilize their members (U.S. Chamber of Commerce, for example). In general, when the White House weighs in heavily in any policy battle, many aspects of the game between interest groups and Congress change. The implications of presidential involvement are discussed in more detail in the next chapter.

Testing for Differences across Stages

The various policy issues included in my data, such as health care, striker replacement, environmental policies, and foreign aid, were categorized as existing in one of the three stages of policymaking by the middle of June 1992, when my study was underway. A policy idea was classified as in the need for action stage if it was not presented as a bill to a congressional committee by June. A policy idea undergoing congressional committee markup, testimony, or committee debate was classified as in the agenda-setting stage. Finally, if a bill was reported from a committee in either the House or Senate, debated on the floor of either chamber, or voted upon on the floor of either chamber, the policy issue was classified as in the debate and voting stage. An issue was classified in reference to the latest stage reached by the time of the study.

Several examples can help to illustrate these categorizations. The policy idea of allowing openly homosexual men and women in the military was in the need for action stage in 1992. Some interest groups strongly in favor of this idea worked hard to pressure policymakers to put the issue on the agenda. Gay and lesbian organizations and civil rights organizations in that year were actively seeking the commitments of several presidential candidates to allow, should these candidates win office, openly gay soldiers and officers in the military. Bill Clinton, for one, committed to the policy. The groups undertook extensive, though fairly targeted, outside lobbying campaigns on the issue. For example, the National Gay and Lesbian Task Force Policy Institute measured a 0.69 on OUTSIDE, a solid 1.4 deviations above the mean value of the index, even though the popularity of the policy was 0.46 and the salience of the issue was 0.41, both average measures of popular support. At the same time, the American Psychiatric Association and the Rainbow Lobby, both supporters of the policy, used no outside lobbying on the issue.

Another issue in the need for action stage was minimum wage. This issue is somewhat different from gays in the military because, for the minimum wage, the issue of raising it or abolishing it comes up once every few years. However, there were no bills reported to committee on changing the minimum wage in early 1992. Meanwhile, the Amalgamated Transit Union used extensive outside lobbying on the issue, gaining a measure of 0.66 on OUTSIDE, while the Teamsters did no outside lobbying on the issue. The Teamster's chief lobbyist told me it "wasn't the right year to push for minimum wage" increases. The policy of raising the minimum wage was very popular (0.75) and wage issues of average salience (0.42) to those in the population who supported it.

As previously mentioned, an issue squarely in the agenda-shaping stage was health care policy. Several committees in both chambers, especially Senate Labor and Human Resources, bandied about different proposals to mandate government control over health care provision, financing, or regulation. At the time, President Bush adamantly opposed any bills the Democrat-controlled Congress favored, and Congress had little chance of passing the bills over presidential veto. Consequently, the issue was largely moot in the short term. No serious proposals made it out of committee by June. But health care trade associations, public interest groups, labor unions, and peak business associations all weighed in heavily with inside and outside lobbying over health care during this period. As predicted by the signaling model, those groups with more intense supporters on health care used more outside lobbying. Unions and groups representing the elderly conducted advertising and membership mobilizations that dwarfed those used by business and trade groups. And the president did not use his own outside lobbying on health care at the time.

Finally, the idea of banning replacements for striking workers was in the debate and voting stage in early 1992. This policy idea passed the House in 1991 and was subject to a lengthy Republican filibuster in the Senate in the summer of 1992. Democratic sponsors never mustered the sixty votes needed to break the filibuster, and the bill was pulled from the Senate floor by Democratic leaders in June 1992. I argued in chapter 4 that public opinion was a surprising constraint on labor union lobbying over striker replacement. Despite the fact that labor unions found the issue to be their most important in years, they were relatively quiet on the issue outside of their memberships because public opinion was not all that favorable. Indeed, a significant portion of the outside lobbying on this bill came from business associations. For example, the U.S. Chamber of Commerce and the International Mass Retail Association undertook relatively vigorous outside lobbying campaigns on the issue.

However, it may have been the case that not only was public opinion a constraint on labor unions, but so were the actions of politicians. Democratic members of Congress, it is reasonable to conclude, took over the outside lobbying for the unions on striker replacement. Once the Democratic leadership of the House took the issue on as one of the priorities for 1992, labor unions perhaps did not feel as though they needed to expend the resources to demonstrate popular support. They let the House leadership try to convince enough Republicans that constituents cared about the issue. (They failed, as very few Republicans voted for it.)

Given these categorizations, testing for differences across stages is fairly straightforward. Figure 5.1 shows the various policy issues included in my data set.[3] The stage of legislation is noted for the issues, plus the mean outside lobbying undertaken by liberal and conservative groups. It is immediately apparent that liberal groups use more outside lobbying on every issue than do conservative groups. This is consistent with our findings from chapter 2 about the variation in outside lobbying across different kinds of groups. Labor unions and public interest groups (who *tend* to be liberal) outside lobby more than business and professional groups do.

However, conservative groups use outside lobbying relatively more on issues in the third stage of legislation than during the other stages, especially compared with the second stage. And given the fact that conservative groups on average have lower public support for their issue positions than liberal groups do, this foreshadows the conclusion made shortly that public opinion is a more imposing constraint during the second stage than during the other stages because in the second stage the conservative groups stay relatively quiet. Especially in the third stage, both conservative and liberal groups jump into the fray.[4]

---

[3] Several issues were left out because I was not able to interview groups on more than one side of the issue.

[4] As an aside, we also concluded from the model in chapter 3 that the levels of outside lobbying observed on a given issue should decrease for higher type groups as the lower type groups on the same issues represent constituents with very low salience. This is because, by the logic of the signaling model, higher type groups on those issues do not have to use much outside lobbying to distinguish themselves from lower type groups. Figure 5.1, plus additional information in my data, provides little evidence for this effect. Take, for example, the difference between outside lobbying on trade issues between conservative groups and liberal groups ($0.45-0.12 = 0.33$) and between the salience levels of the two sides of the issue, using average salience levels across all the trade questions used in the data ($0.65 - 0.22 = 0.43$). We can calculate the same numbers for all the issues shown in figure 5.1. These two sets of numbers should be negatively correlated when using the issues as cases, but unfortunately they are not. However, the salience differences are somewhat negatively correlated ($r = -0.22$, $p = 0.24$) with the level of outside lobbying among the lower type groups, and this has a nice interpretation. (So on trade issues, instead of using 0.33 and 0.43, we would use 0.12 and 0.43.) When the salience differences across sides of an issue are large, lower type groups do not even bother to

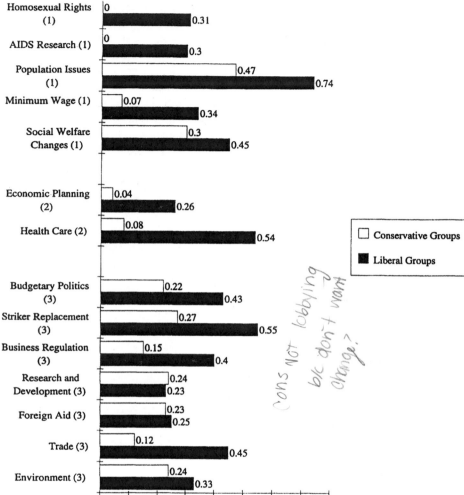

Figure 5.1. Outside Lobbying by Liberals and Conservatives across Policy Issues (stage of legis-lation in parentheses)

A multivariate analysis reveals further that the different stages lead to different levels of constraint imposed by public opinion. We can include new variables in the regression equations analyzed in the previous chapter. I cre-

try to "mix in" with higher type groups. Policymakers can detect large differences in salience, and so there is little point in groups supported by low salience to try to convince legislators to support their side of the issue through outside lobbying.

ated nine new variables for inclusion in the regression equations summarized in table 4.1. First, three dummy variables representing the three stages of legislation were created for the group-issue data set. So a case was coded 1 for *Stage 1* if it represented an issue in the first stage, and zero otherwise (likewise for variables *Stage 2* and *Stage 3*). Then interaction terms were created for the stages and the two public opinion variables, salience and popularity. For example, the interaction between *Stage 1* and salience is simply *Stage 1 * Salience*. Then I included six of the new variables in the regression equations (three must be left out to identify the model).

In figure 5.2, coefficients for the interaction terms are displayed. (The coefficients are derived from an equation where *Stage 3* and the two interactions terms for the third stage were left out for identification). These coefficients represent the marginal effects of popular support on outside lobbying decisions for the three categories of issues. The coefficients for the controlling variables are not reported, but none of them changed much in these new calculations. And the coefficients for the dummy variables were insignificant statistically. Coefficients reported for the interaction terms were significant statistically when they exceeded a value of 0.1.

These results are quite revealing. First, they make it clear that a good portion of the relationship between public opinion and outside lobbying is based on issues in the agenda-shaping stage. Outside lobbying is a better signal about salience among constituents during this all-important stage than during the other two.

Second, the patterns for salience and popularity over the three stages shed light on the different incentives for groups to emphasize signaling, influencing popularity, and increasing salience. For the first stage, need for action, the relationship between public opinion and outside lobbying is weak, as expected. In fact, the coefficient for popularity is negative. Evidently, group leaders facing the first stage do not have much concern for whether their policy positions are popularly supported at that time. They probably use outside lobbying almost purely for conflict expansion, where conflict expansion means increasing salience among supporters *and* increasing the number of supporters. All types of groups use outside lobbying.

The second stage, agenda shaping, conforms very well to the predictions of the separation scenario in the signaling game. Thus, according to these data, groups facing this second stage undertake strategies in much greater correspondence with salience than they do in the first stage. In addition, groups pursuing popular policies use outside lobbying more than their counterparts do. Outside lobbying seems to be almost purely signaling of salience among popularly supported groups in this stage.

For the last stage, debate and voting, outside lobbying does not correspond very much to salience, a finding that was anticipated; the coefficient is small but positive. It turns out, however, that outside lobbying is related substantially to the popularity of policies in this stage. Outside lobbying

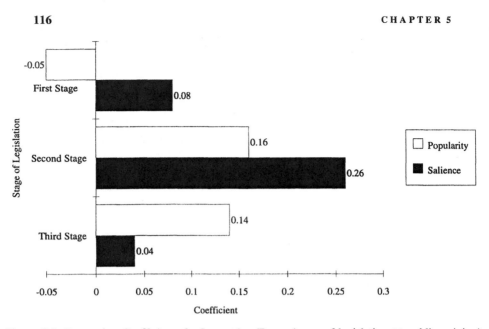

Figure 5.2. Regression Coefficients for Interaction Terms (stage of legislation × public opinion)

settles into a certain pattern where all that is left for interest groups to do is to try to increase the salience of the issue to their supporters as much as possible, although groups with very low popular support do not even bother.[5]

The first and second stages, meanwhile, exhibit highly targeted outside lobbying, as might be predicted. In data not shown, groups facing policies in the first and second stage, compared with interest groups facing the third stage, advertised in magazines and newspapers targeted specifically at policymakers in particular regional areas (as well as at national audiences in the second stage). In contrast, broadly targeted advertising becomes more common in the third stage, but in the absence of other kinds of more highly targeted outside lobbying. Clearly what is happening is that interest group leaders facing the third stage feel they can communicate to policymakers with broad brush strokes, whereas in earlier stages group leaders feel they need to target specific policymakers. This has a nice institutional interpretation. Outside lobbying in the first stage is intended to induce a small number of policymakers to introduce the idea in the form of a bill, and in the second stage is intended to pressure key, selected committee members in Congress.

---

[5] Incidentally, the free-riding variable takes on a very large coefficient for those cases in the third stage. Interest group leaders answering my survey perhaps had politicians in mind as much as other groups when they reported that they were not the only groups active on this issue. Indeed, many politicians begin to weigh in with outside lobbying campaigns when the issue is finally being decided. The free-riding among groups increases the errors of the estimates for salience and biases the coefficients downward for the third stage.

Finally, in the third stage the whole set of policymakers is targeted to try to shift momentum on the policy one way or another.

A third observation is that because popularity is correlated with outside lobbying during the second and third stages, we can amend our results from the previous chapter somewhat. The regression results in figure 4.1 led to the conclusion that popularity was weakly correlated to outside lobbying, and therefore many groups supporting unpopular policies used outside lobbying. However, most of the groups supporting unpopular policies that used outside lobbying did so during the need for action stage. We can reasonably assume that many of these groups use outside lobbying to educate constituents and to try to influence the popularity of policies. In later stages, this kind of conflict expansion will not be as successful because popularity has become stable (see Page and Shapiro 1992). The focus of attention in the second and third stages is on salience, either signaling salience (mostly in the second stage) or increasing salience (mostly in the third stage).

The third finding raises an interesting alternative explanation for these data. To understand the difference between this explanation and my own, let us focus on the contrast in coefficients between the first and second stages. It may be the case that the second stage exhibits a stronger relationship between salience or popularity and outside lobbying than the first stage does, simply because more popularly supported policies survive to the second stage. Proponents of all kinds of policies will outside lobby early, and this will depress the relationship between public support and outside lobbying in the need for action stage. But then since surviving policies tend to have more popular support relative to those policies that die along the time line, proponents of policies later are the only ones around to outside lobby. This could be why the relationship is stronger in the agenda-shaping stage. The cause of the relationship may not be interest group decision making, but rather the natural effect of more popularly supported policies surviving in a democracy.

This plausible explanation falls short, however. The key difference between this explanation and my own is that my explanation asserts that groups in the second stage are careful not to try to signal something that does not exist to policymakers (public opinion is a real constraint on outside lobbying), while the alternative explanation asserts that the process of moving legislation forward weeds out unpopular proposals, so all that is left by the second stage are relatively popular proposals supported by their proponents. In other words, the alternative explanation presumes that issues in my study have only proponents. In fact, many groups using outside lobbying in later stages are reacting to proposals brought forth by other interests. So it is not the case that proponents of the popular policies are the only ones around in the second stage because the less popularly supported policies (and their supporters) "fell away." The opponents step in too, though selectively in relation to their confidence in popular support.

To summarize this section, interest groups using outside lobbying in the need for action stage try to get their issues onto the agenda. Their leaders emphasize a particular kind of conflict expansion—educating constituents— in order to influence the popularity of particular policies and the salience of particular policy problems. Interest groups in the agenda-shaping stage use outside lobbying mostly to signal their current level of salience to selected policymakers. By the debate and voting stage, many types of groups use outside lobbying to increase the salience of the policy issue among their supporters, though the unpopularity of policies seems to be a real constraint. Indeed, for both the second and third stages, there is a tendency for groups supporting popular policy positions to use outside lobbying and for groups supporting unpopular policies to avoid outside lobbying.

Changing Salience and the Importance of the Status Quo

We now turn to another contextual factor influencing interest group decisions over conflict expansion: the relative popularity of the choices confronting policymakers. When interest groups expand the scope of the conflict, regardless of whether they are spreading information about the consequences of a policy, offering selective incentives to constituents to participate in collective action, or coordinating constituents' behavior, they are essentially putting increased pressure on policymakers to adopt a certain policy or act on a certain policy problem. From the perspective of policymakers, it all looks the same. Interest group leaders mobilize a select group of constituents, hoping to influence how constituents evaluate policymakers, and ultimately making it harder for policymakers to cross those constituents (and interest group leaders).

To formalize this process, it will be convenient to depict conflict expansion as increasing the salience of a policy issue in a spatial modeling framework and to use pictures to illustrate various scenarios. A spatial voting model represents policies as positions along a line or in a space where one side of the line or space represents one extreme and the other side represents the other extreme (Hotelling 1929; Downs 1957). For example, one side of a line might represent new regulations on business and vigorous enforcement of existing regulations, while the other side might represent a drastic rolling back of existing regulations of business. Moderate policies are between the extremes. Preferences of voters, policymakers, or interest groups then can be represented as ideal points along the line, where an ideal point is the most preferred policy of a given actor. Policies are valued in direct proportion to the proximity of a policy to an actor's ideal point. The spatial model is general enough to represent virtually any possible set of collective choices and preferences.

Let us consider that along a hypothetical issue line there exists a policy that is the "most popularly supported," or the most desirable policy for a policymaker's constituents. (y can be interpreted as the policy position of the median voter).[6] This policy y exists under relatively innocuous assumptions. Namely, a most preferred policy exists if all constituents have single-peaked preferences along a single dimension.[7] Let us further assume that policy preferences among constituents are fixed, but salience for policies is not. Interest groups can increase the salience of selected issues through outside lobbying.

For a variety of reasons, let us say, the policy status quo is not y, but rather q, where q is some distance from y. The distance $|q - y|$ represents the aggregate costs to the constituents from the status quo, where the costs to constituents from y are normalized to zero. By one view, the government in a pure democracy would adopt y if it were the perfect agent of its constituents and had perfect information or were not influenced by campaign contributions or other inducements. Instead, q has been chosen because of inducements m, which can be interpreted as the sum total of whatever it is policymakers gain in value when they grant special privileges to interest groups. More specifically, m can be the value gained by policymakers from inside lobbying by interest groups. It could be money, insider information about policy consequences, administrative assistance, or even friendship. Furthermore, the salience of the issue to the public is θ, where as θ increases, it raises the pressure on the government to adopt y as policy. For example, if conflict expansion is information transmission from interest group leaders to constituents, then θ can be interpreted as information among constituents. The more information constituents have about the issue, the more pressure there is for policymakers to adopt this most popularly supported policy y. Also, as mentioned, interest groups can increase θ through their public appeals.

Putting these together, the government receives

$$-\theta(q - y) + m$$

which should equal something near zero. The sum of the nonpublic opinion-based inducements m is just enough to make the government want to choose q as opposed to y. Figure 5.3 represents a policy issue graphically. The diagonal lines dropping from y are the losses by the public associated with

---

[6] If conflict expansion is intended to influence popularity, as it appears to be in the need for action stage, then y may not be stable or known with much certainty. Consequently, we can assume for this section that most of the insights apply to legislation in the second or third stages.

[7] Another way to say this is that there is a core, or a Condorcet winner, for that policy.

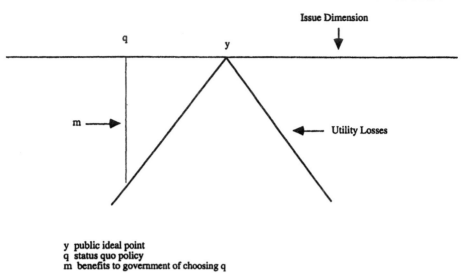

y public ideal point
q status quo policy
m benefits to government of choosing q

Figure 5.3. Hypothetical Policy Space

alternative policies.[8] The farther policies are from y, the worse off constituents are in the aggregate. If the government's reelection chances drop in a corresponding manner, then m compensates the government for adopting a policy with less popular support than y. Note that losses for constituents *and* the government become steeper the larger θ is. Or, conversely, it takes more m to convince the government to adopt a policy away from y. Steeper losses mean that policies away from y are more costly to the public and therefore to the government.

Interest groups form a constellation of ideal points around y. In figure 5.3, q is to the left of y, so the interest groups to the left of y had more influence through inside lobbying during the adoption of q than did groups to the right of y. Yet every so often, the status quo policy is challenged by an alternative policy, x. Interest groups, which are assumed here only to react to policy alternatives, can inside lobby, outside lobby, or both. If they inside lobby, they contribute to m, where the sum total of m from groups on all sides will pressure the government either toward q or toward x. If groups outside lobby, they can increase θ. Whether increasing θ will add pressure to adopt q or x depends on the relative proximity of the alternatives to y. Proponents of whichever alternative, q or x, is closer to y will benefit more from increasing θ. (The assumption is that increasing θ pressures the government equally from both sides of y. The assumption is not necessary for this analysis, but it makes exposition easier. Of course, we can think of interest groups trying,

---

[8] For ease of exposition, losses are linear. Conclusions do not rely on this assumption.

through targeted outside lobbying, to increase pressure on *one* side of *y* if it is to their advantage.)

A tentative conclusion, therefore, is that interest groups with ideal points near *y* will, all else being equal, prefer the issue to be salient to voters. In other words, the more popular support a group's position has on an issue, holding *m* fixed, the more the group will prefer θ to be high, and the more it will tend to want to use outside lobbying as conflict expansion on the issue. This conclusion is comforting for democratic theorists. Popular policies lead interest groups to use outside lobbying to make those popular policies more salient to constituents and, consequently, to policymakers. Let us call this the *Comforting Hypothesis* because it means that outside lobbying as conflict expansion reinforces popular pressures on policymakers.[9]

Scenarios for Conflict Expansion

Upon closer inspection, however, the Comforting Hypothesis does not account for various spatial patterns of the policy status quo, alternative policies, and interest group ideal points.[10] Under different configurations or scenarios, interest groups have incentives to behave in ways directly contradictory to the Comforting Hypothesis.

Without loss of generality, let us assume that the status quo *q* is to the left of the most popularly supported policy *y*, as in figure 5.3. And let the aggregate inside lobbying benefits *m* stay fixed for the moment. Interest groups are deciding solely on whether to outside lobby. (Groups may have exhausted their reservoirs of *m*.) Four scenarios regarding the placement of *q*, *y*, the alternative *x*, and an interest group's ideal point *IG* exhaust the possibilities.

In the first scenario, *IG* is to the left of *q*. The interest group always prefers the status quo *q* to the most popularly supported policy *y*, and furthermore, the group is on the side of the policy space with the advantage (so far) and is more extreme than *q*. This is because *q* is on the group's side of *y*, and *IG* < *q*. Figure 5.4 demonstrates this first scenario. The areas along the

---

[9] Incidentally, Snyder (1991) finds further theoretical support for this conclusion. In his model of legislative "bribes," or contributions, lobbyists within a spatial voting framework collude among themselves to buy off legislative votes. Equilibrium prices of bribes depend on the degree to which lobbyists can discriminate among legislators. And fitting the argument so far, he finds that the more salient an issue is to legislators, the more lobbyists with moderate (or popular) ideal points benefit. In our terms, Snyder focuses on *m* and ignores the influence of interest groups on salience. He does not explore the possibility that interest groups can increase salience. But if lobbyists in his model could influence salience, they would follow the argument here rather closely. Those nearer the median voter will want to increase salience.

[10] Of course, it also ignores the ability of interest groups to increase pressure in other ways. Here, I do not explore the possibility of increasing *m*, for example.

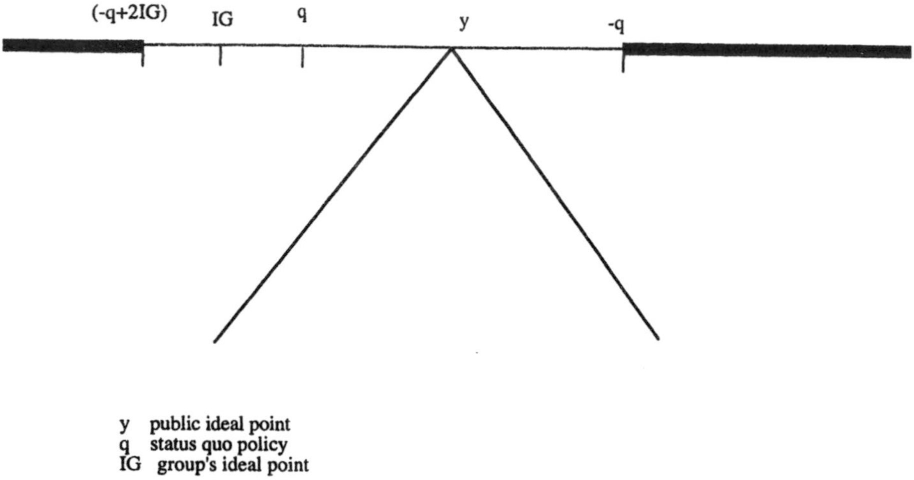

y   public ideal point
q   status quo policy
IG group's ideal point

Figure 5.4. Scenario 1

thick part of the policy line represent the set of alternatives x for which the group benefits from increased θ. Note that the set of policies that are more preferred than q by the group and more preferred by the public than q is empty. The public and the group agree only on what alternatives to q they do not want.

As an example, consider that most mainstream Jewish lobbying groups in the United States in the early 1990s were reasonably content with current levels of foreign aid to Israel, but they preferred slightly more aid. In fact, they lobbied hard for more loan guarantees in 1992. The public in the aggregate, judging from surveys, was relatively happy with the status quo, but appeared to prefer less foreign aid overall in the federal budget.[11] It is reasonable to assume that the status quo policy on aid to Israel was somewhere between the ideal points of most Jewish lobbying groups and the mass public. Under this scenario, if alternatives are proposed that involve much lower levels of foreign aid than the status quo, Jewish groups might be quick to engage in outside lobbying. In figure 5.4, alternatives off to the right of $-q$ would induce outside lobbying by Jewish groups, even though the groups are more extreme than the status quo policy relative to the most popularly supported policy. These groups might raise fears of instability in the Middle East if aid were to fall too low. In general, interest groups in this kind of situation will appeal to citizens' fears about the consequences of allowing policy to stray too far from q or y. However, alternatives not under the thick line would induce inside lobbying intended to obstruct proposals perhaps

---

[11] See, for example, public opinion question 53 in appendix.

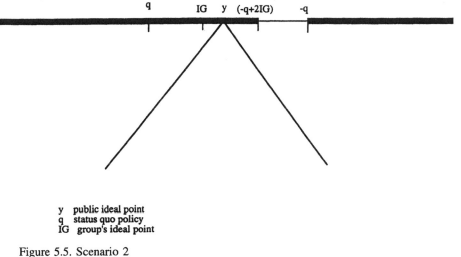

y   public ideal point
q   status quo policy
IG group's ideal point

Figure 5.5. Scenario 2

more popularly supported. Groups would want (quietly) to undermine other groups' outside lobbying.

In the second scenario, depicted in figure 5.5, *IG* is between *q* and *y*. The interest group's most preferred policy is more popularly supported than the status quo. For many alternatives, those on the thick lines, this group has incentives to outside lobby. The patch of alternatives not on the thick lines would induce only inside lobbying. That patch will include *y* if *IG* is closer to *q* than to *y*. As in the figure, it will not include *y* if *IG* is closer to *y* than to *q*.

This scenario is not all that common relative to other scenarios. Most interest groups, I believe, are found on one side or the other of the status quo and the most popularly supported policy. One example that illustrates this second scenario, however, is welfare policy, specifically Aid to Families with Dependent Children (AFDC) in the mid-1990s, before welfare was changed dramatically in 1996. Many moderate organizations, including peak business groups and centrist policy think tanks, preferred welfare programs to be changed, either cut down in size or altered to require recipients to work or go to school. Many governors, and even President Clinton, supported these changes as well. Polls indicated that a vast majority of the public preferred to see AFDC slashed, probably far more than the moderate groups would like to have seen. The status quo was not acceptable to either the public or to these groups, but the groups preferred policies slightly more generous than the majority of the public. The groups felt comfortable outside lobbying for many policy changes because the public supported the changes. Hypothetically, for many alternatives on the far side of *y* from *IG*, the groups would not outside lobby because the public might support policies too extreme for the groups. Outside lobbying campaigns by *IG* for alternatives within q and $-q$ $(q < x < -q)$ would stress the need for reasonable revisions in welfare policy, while outside lobbying campaigns by *IG*, when faced with alternatives on the extremes of the policy line, would stress the need for moderation in welfare policies, perhaps emphasizing the need to stick with the status quo.

The third and fourth scenarios are closely related. In both, $IG > y$, which means the interest group's most preferred policy is on the far side of y from q. Or to put it another way, the interest group is on the less privileged side of the policy issue relative to the most popularly supported policy. In the third scenario, $y < IG - q$ as in figure 5.6, and the interest group wants to outside lobby for all alternatives between q and $-q$ $(q < x < -q)$, plus policies on the relative extremes of the policy line. I think of groups favoring campaign finance reform, such as Common Cause or Public Citizen, as currently falling under this scenario. The status quo policy is clearly far away from these groups' preferred policies, while the public generally does not favor reforms proposed by many of these groups. Public financing of campaigns is an example of a reform the public does not favor, but these groups do favor. The most popularly supported policy can be said to be between what the groups want and the status quo. At the same time, the groups do prefer some relatively popular policies. For most alternatives that arise, save those alternatives granting the government too much discretion to fund particular candidates (the region on the thin part of the line), these groups want to outside lobby, and their messages often emphasize the need for widespread mobilization. Unfortunately for a majority of the mass public who favor reforms, these groups typically face real resource constraints, and their issues have relatively low salience among the public (Rothenberg 1992; Sorauf 1992).

The fourth scenario, described by $IG > -q$ and depicted in figure 5.7, includes a great many interest groups. The groups want policy to swing the other way from the status quo, and yet their most preferred policies have low popular support. Many business groups prior to 1994 might be considered to have existed in this scenario on issues of regulation and labor relations. Other groups, more on the fringes of politics than business groups are, might be in this scenario as well. Even these groups have large regions of the space where alternatives within those regions will induce some outside lobbying. As discussed in more detail in the next section, groups with low popular support in this scenario sometimes outside lobby because prominent alternatives are favorable to them and to the mass public.

These latter two scenarios offer support for Schattschneider's maxim that losers in conflicts often want to expand the scope of the conflict. When groups are on the far side of y from q, they are less privileged by the government relative to groups on the other side of the policy line in the previous

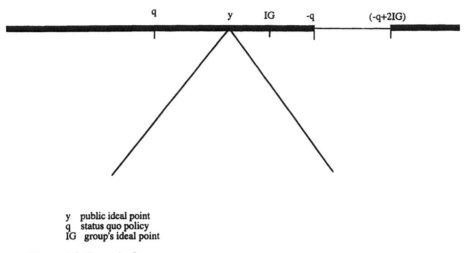

y   public ideal point
q   status quo policy
IG group's ideal point

Figure 5.6. Scenario 3

round of policy battles on the issue. Further, there is a whole swath of poli-cies between q and $-q$, a likely region for alternatives to appear in, where such groups prefer to increase the salience of the issue. It is not necessarily because groups to the right of y in figures 5.6 and 5.7 have less access to the government; they might have a great deal of access. Instead, they can benefit from favorable public opinion to a greater extent than can groups in scenario one, simply because a larger number of serious alternatives will fall between q and $-q$ than beyond q and $-q$.

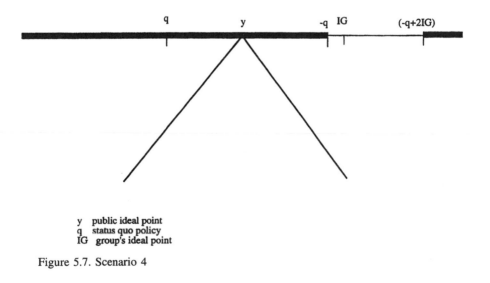

y   public ideal point
q   status quo policy
IG group's ideal point

Figure 5.7. Scenario 4

When Groups Supporting Unpopular Policies Outside Lobby

Two of the scenarios just described can be combined to provide a counterexample to the Comforting Hypothesis, that more popularity for the policy should lead to more outside lobbying by groups supporting the policy. They also highlight the importance of the policy status quo in lobbying decisions. Figure 5.8 depicts an issue where one group, *IG*, lives under the second scenario, and another group, *ig*, lives under the fourth scenario. A prominent alternative policy *x* is between *q* and $-q$ and thus has more popular support than the status quo policy does. According to the Comforting Hypothesis, *IG* wants to use outside lobbying and *ig* does not because *IG* has more popular support (is closer to *y*). By the logic used so far, however, this conclusion is wrong.

To see that it is wrong, note that while *ig* is farther from *y* than is *IG*, *ig* prefers the alternative *x*, which is more popularly supported than the status quo *q*, and *IG* prefers the status quo *q*. Therefore, *ig* prefers to outside lobby and *IG* does not, even though *IG*'s ideal point has more popular support. This example demonstrates that outside lobbying should relate to the popular support of alternative policies relative to popular support of the status quo policy, rather than the absolute popular support of the ideal points of interest groups. Groups use outside lobbying when the mass public agrees with them about the desirability or undesirability of alternative policies, not strictly whether the public agrees with the ultimate goals of the groups.

This point may seem rather obvious, but many observers, in evaluating outside lobbying campaigns, make the common mistake of confusing the messenger and the message. Insurance companies using outside lobbying to scuttle health care reform in 1994 were criticized because they appeared to be defending a status quo policy that time and again in polls proved to be less popular than Clinton's plan. However, the insurance companies in general were actually using outside lobbying on the least popular parts of the Clinton plan (for example, reduced doctor choice) and suggesting in their advertisements that the companies supported a modified Clinton-style plan that would be more popular than the Clinton plan and the status quo. In fact, in my interviews with lobbyists for the Health Insurance Association of America, they made it clear that their advertisements were partially in support of an alternative bill in Congress (the Chaffee plan) that was closer to the Clinton proposal than to the Republican plans.

Another prominent example, this time from the early 1980s, concerns President Reagan's professed ideas about business regulation, government spending on social programs, and defense spending, which were criticized by political opponents and academics as too extreme. Respected books were published demonstrating with public opinion data that the public supported

Group ig is further than group IG from the most popular policy y, yet ig prefers outside
lobbying and IG does not

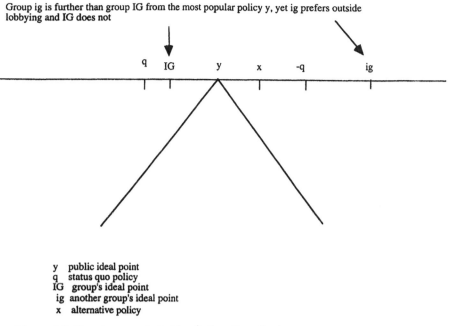

y   public ideal point
q   status quo policy
IG group's ideal point
ig another group's ideal point
x   alternative policy

Figure 5.8. Counterexample to Comforting Hypothesis

the policies Reagan vociferously attacked (see Ferguson and Rogers 1986).
How, they wondered, could Reagan win by "going public" when his ideas
were not very popular? Personal popularity of the president could not fully
explain the anomaly.

Indeed, Reagan's position on the issue of government regulation, to lower
dramatically the regulatory burden on businesses, did not have tremendous
popular appeal. Public opinion polls throughout the 1970s and 1980s consistently showed popular support for environmental and safety regulations
(Page and Shapiro 1992, 155–59; Ferguson and Rogers 1986, 14). Some
portion of the public, especially those most vehement on the issue, like business executives, considered the regulatory burden on businesses to be too
intrusive. Other citizens had more liberal positions. On average, one might
say, citizens wanted regulatory burdens to be lighter than they were at the
time (or at least more coherent), but not as light as Reagan and most business executives wanted them.

Figure 5.9 offers a graphical representation of this example. Reagan preferred policies far to the right, and the status quo was on the left side of the
most popularly supported policy from Reagan's position. By this interpretation, Reagan was able to appeal to the public to pressure Congress to slow
the rate of regulations, but he could not get the public to agree to his most

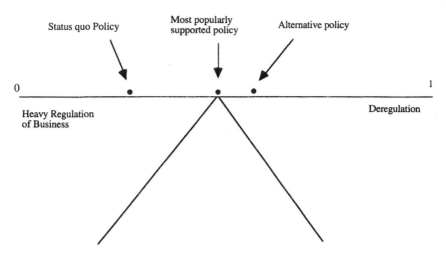

Hypothetical: Ronald Reagan prefers a relatively unpopular policy (near 1), and has stated so publicly, but he can propose an alternative that is more popular than the status quo and then appeal to the public to move policy towards 1.

Figure 5.9. Reagan Example

preferred alternatives. By increasing the salience of the issue (and by having some measure of control over the agenda), he could pressure other policy-makers to bring about regulations more in line with what the average citizen wanted and more in the direction of what he wanted, but not quite at his ideal point. In sum, if an alternative arises that is closer to a group's ideal point than to the status quo, if the alternative has more popular support than the status quo, and if the group does not expect other, better alternatives to arise any time soon, then the group benefits from outside lobbying even if its ideal point is relatively unpopular.

If my data on outside lobbying contained precise measurements of status quo policies and alternative policies, I could examine the frequency of this kind of scenario. However, I simply cannot be confident enough in coding policies in these public opinion questions to warrant quantitative analysis.[12] An illustrative example from the data is useful, however.

[12] Furthermore, because most of the public opinion questions used in the data analysis have only two answers, the measures used for popularity are appropriate and this argument does not run counter to the results found in chapter 4. If we could code status quo policies and alternative policies, if there were many public opinion questions used with more than two answers, and if we could account for relative popularity in questions with more than two answers, then the analysis in chapter 4 would have to be changed to allow for relative versus absolute popularity measures.

Policy Question: Which of these two statements comes closer to your own point of view? Protection of the environment should be given priority, even if it means a loss of jobs in some industries, or the availability of jobs should be given priority, even if the environment suffers.

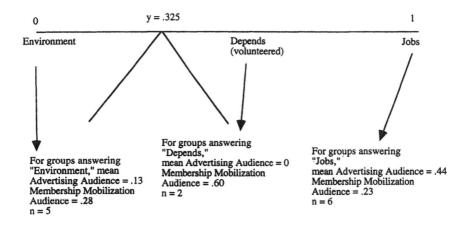

0                              $y = .325$ 1

Environment   Depends   Jobs
                                                  (volunteered)

For groups answering   For groups answering   For groups answering
"Environment," mean   "Depends,"   "Jobs,"
Advertising Audience = .13   mean Advertising Audience = 0   mean Advertising Audience = .44
Membership Mobilization   Membership Mobilization   Membership Mobilization
Audience = .28   Audience = .60   Audience = .23
n = 5   n = 2   n = 6

Common wisdom (and the Comforting Hypothesis) would predict that groups answering "environment" would outside lobby more than groups answering "jobs" because public opinion is "closer" to "environment." However, groups answering "jobs" outside lobby, especially advertising, because they know the alternative policy, near 0, is less popular than the status quo, near y.

Figure 5.10. Environment versus Jobs Example

To begin, consider that public opinion questions overstate the discreteness, or "lumpiness," of public preferences. The question in figure 5.10 forces respondents, both the mass public in the original survey and interest groups in my own survey, to choose one of two categories, environment and jobs. But most individual respondents have ideal points that fall somewhere between these two end points. Interest groups also have more finely tuned preferences. For the moment, let us assume that interest groups on this issue represent relatively extreme points, so group leaders bunch around the end points more so than the public. Finally, I use the mean public response to the question to measure the most popularly supported position. In this case, $y = 0.325$ represents a policy on the environmental side of the issue, but that is not completely neglectful of the impact of regulations on jobs.

According to the Comforting Hypothesis, given the position of y in this example, 0.325, groups on the left side of this issue ought to outside lobby more than groups on the right. In fact, the opposite is true, especially with regard to advertising for wide audiences. Membership mobilizations were nearly the same, but groups on the right side used extensive advertising more than did groups on the left side. Why? I offer the following hypothesis. Democrats in Congress in 1992 had inserted into a massive energy bill several environmental regulations that were vigorously opposed by many business groups and unions. These opposition groups claimed that the new regulations would cost many jobs. Also, these groups were not all that pleased with the policy status quo, which they considered already too onerous. If the policy status quo can be coded as anywhere between 0 and 0.650, and the alternative policy can be coded as 0, then the above logic holds.[13] Groups near 1 ($ig > -q$) in the figure want to outside lobby to pressure Congress to maintain the status quo. Groups near 0 want to avoid getting the public involved. In other words, while many interest groups on this issue preferred policies less popularly supported than the alternative, their immediate goal was to bring popular pressure on Congress to vote against the alternative and in favor of the status quo because the status quo was both more popularly supported than the alternative and in the policy direction of the groups' ideal points.

The rhetoric of the opposition groups and the actions of the proponent groups support this depiction. In their outside lobbying campaigns, the opponents, among them the Foodservice and Packaging Institute, the United Brotherhood of Carpenters and Joiners, the Interstate Natural Gas Association, and the Teamsters, emphasized in widespread advertising the extremism of the proposed regulations on energy producers. They heralded the current regulations as "reasonable" and "balanced." On the other side, however, environmental organizations, among them Alliance for Acid Rain Control and Energy Policy, Zero Population Growth, and the Environmental Defense Fund, not normally a passive lot in terms of outside lobbying, kept relatively quiet on these proposed regulations. They seemed to know that their opponents who were fighting to keep the status quo had the attentive public focusing on job losses. So even though the environmental groups had more popularly supported ideal points than their opponents, given the two choices facing Congress, the environmentalists were supporting the less popularly supported choice. They chose to focus on localized membership mobilizations rather than on wider advertising campaigns.

As another brief example, consider tort reform in 1996. The business community's preferences on limiting tort damages was surely less popular than the status quo policy at the time. The first bill in 1996 backed by the business community, to limit damages in a wide range of torts, was opposed even by most Republicans in the Senate and received considerable negative attention. But when a compromise bill was proposed, one that was described

---

[13] This result holds for other reasonable codings as well. If the alternative x is to the left of y, then as long as the status quo is between x and $x + y$, the result stands.

as a "half-a-loaf" bill by supporters of the original bill, the business community started a medium-size outside lobbying campaign, confident that this new bill was now more popular than the status quo. Comparing the various sides of the issue, the pro–tort reform side, including business and nonprofit organizations like schools, hospitals, and churches, outside lobbied a decent amount while the anti–tort reform side, including trial lawyers and a majority of public interest groups, was relatively quiet. One might be tempted to explain the difference in strategies as a result of the differential popularity of the groups involved. Trial lawyers do not have a great deal of popular support in general. But much the same could be said for many of the business corporations funding the pro-reform side. Rather, the pro–tort reform side was supporting the more popular policy relative to the status quo, rather than the more popular policy position overall.

Conclusion

This chapter has presented several arguments about how matters of context besides raw public opinion—the current stage of legislation of a policy idea and the relative popular support enjoyed by the status quo policy—can be expected to influence outside lobbying strategies. These arguments mostly concern the changing incentives for conflict expansion over a variety of contexts. In short, when group leaders want to expand the conflict, they have to consider whether the agenda is set already and if their group's preferred policies are more popularly supported than the policy status quo is.

These contextual considerations operate over and above the incentives for group leaders to adopt rational strategies in a signaling game with policymakers. For many situations, the two purposes for outside lobbying are complementary, in that the ability to expand the conflict can usually help an organization trying to convince policymakers of its electoral strength. But there are times when a group's leaders are confident they can benefit from signaling information about its members to policymakers, but to do so on a large scale would expand the conflict in ways not beneficial to the group. So, for example, a group's leaders representing a sizable membership that is intense on an issue may feel that they can demonstrate to policymakers that its members will follow policymakers' actions very closely on a bill. However, the same set of leaders may feel that if they expand the conflict too far, opponents of the policy may weigh in and swing momentum the other way. In other words, signaling the current state of salience among a small set of constituents (when it is to your advantage) is a rather conservative strategy, but conflict expansion beyond the group's own members brings with it further risks of bringing in people opposed to the group.

In the next chapter, I demonstrate how the incentives, risks, costs, and opportunities associated with outside lobbying operated on one important area of policy in the 1990s, trade relations with foreign countries. We shall observe two patterns in the case study on NAFTA that are consistent with the ideas in this chapter. The incentives for outside lobbying change over the course of legislation, and policymakers can do their own brand of outside lobbying. Indeed, when the president becomes involved, it can have a profound effect on interest group strategies and policymakers' reactions to those strategies.

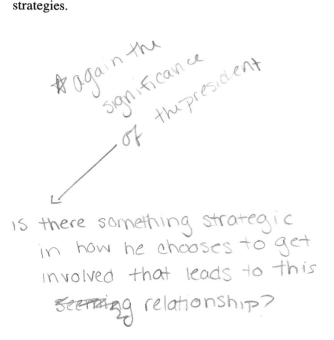

※ again the significance of the president

is there something strategic in how he chooses to get involved that leads to this ~~seeming~~ relationship?

6

Lobbying over Trade Policy

ON NOVEMBER 17, 1993, the House of Representatives approved the North American Free Trade Agreement (NAFTA), 234–200, giving President Bill Clinton one of the most significant legislative victories of his first term in office.[1] NAFTA lowered tariffs and other barriers to trade between Mexico, Canada, and United States, and set up the world's largest free-trade zone. The floor vote, on which 40 percent of Democrats and 75 percent of Republicans voted for NAFTA, followed a huge volume of outside lobbying by labor unions, business groups, environmental groups, and Ross Perot's upstart political party, then called United We Stand. Scores of legislators from both major parties remained publicly undecided until right before the vote. Many observers at the time felt that the overall sentiment in Congress was to approve NAFTA, but outside lobbying pressure from the national labor unions and other anti-treaty groups kept members of Congress nervous about voting for the treaty. There was a great deal of uncertainty in Congress over how much the business community cared about the issue and over how much business groups were willing to help defend votes for the treaty in the upcoming 1994 election campaigns. It was not until business interest groups expanded the conflict sufficiently enough among the business community (with help from the president) and signaled the increased salience credibly that the tide turned and NAFTA was no longer headed for defeat.

In this chapter I tell the story of outside lobbying over NAFTA, highlighting many of the points made throughout this book so far. The story helps to illustrate the incentives for interest group leaders to try to signal to policymakers and expand the conflict among constituents, as well as to describe how those incentives change across different stages of legislation. The political struggle over NAFTA is also an interesting story in its own right, and so it justifies a telling in some detail.

Background and a Brief History

Issues of foreign trade inevitably invite vigorous interest group participation in the United States. For one, the Tariff, as it was known in earlier times, has

---

[1] Information in this chapter came from scores of interviews with interest group leaders, consultants, Clinton administration officials, and congressional staff, and from press accounts of events. A list of persons interviewed (and who agreed to being identified) is in appendix A.

always been seen to have concentrated benefits and dispersed costs, encouraging potential beneficiaries to seek tariff protection for their pet industries. For another, coalitions over trade rarely form along party lines, as both the Democratic and Republican parties each has in its constituency industries and sectors that benefit from foreign trade, and industries and sectors that lose against foreign competition. Neither party can be united solely around trade policies, and thus party leaders cannot enforce much party discipline on controversial trade votes. Only three out of four House Republicans voted for NAFTA, even though they were members of the supposed party of free trade. And 60 percent of Democrats voted against it, ignoring the president of their own party. In short, members of Congress on average pay more attention to the effects of foreign trade on the local economies in their districts than to general nostrums from party leaders about the virtues of free trade or protection. Constituent communications will count for a lot on trade issues. Not surprisingly, quite a few famous studies of interest group activities center around controversial trade policies (Schattschneider 1935; Bauer, Pool, and Dexter 1963). On important trade issues, there are always many lobbyists and many wavering legislators from both parties receiving pressure from all sides.

Societal divisions over trade have shifted over time. From the 1970s to the early 1990s, trade policy changed from an issue of concern mostly to business lobbyists of specific industries to an explosive political issue seen to affect the environment, health and safety standards, wages, profits, immigration, and taxes of every community and business in the country. Trade issues therefore make strange bedfellows in the 1990s. Anti–free trade coalitions have included environmental groups, labor unions, many religious groups, nativists, small business owners, and those supporting more restricted immigration. When Patrick Buchanan brought his protectionist message into the 1996 Republican presidential primaries, his campaign found support among conservative Republicans, Perot supporters, and some Democrats.

The various elements of the loose coalition opposing NAFTA in 1993 reflected this great political diversity. The Citizen's Trade Campaign (CTC), funded by unions and environmentalists, represented the more Democratic, liberal side of the protectionist cause. United We Stand, funded by Perot, represented the more conservative, nativist side. These organizations did not cooperate openly, but collectively they mobilized hundreds of thousands of citizens for the same purpose, to defeat NAFTA.

The pro-NAFTA side was more homogenous. By and large the coalition consisted of business firms and trade associations, with a smattering of other kinds of organizations. USA-NAFTA, the major pro-NAFTA organization created by the U.S. Chamber of Commerce and the Business Roundtable, had four thousand business firms and associations as nominal members, though only several hundred firms contributed resources to the coalition.

While business leaders pronounced themselves united over NAFTA, one of the leaders of USA-NAFTA admitted to me that only 70 percent of Chamber members supported NAFTA. At least on trade issues, business is considered united when 70 percent of firms are on board.

The pro-NAFTA side had a crucial proponent, of course. In the 1992 presidential campaign, candidate Clinton assailed the NAFTA his opponent, George Bush, had negotiated. Upon taking office in 1993, Clinton nevertheless renegotiated several provisions with Mexico and threw his full support behind NAFTA. In fact, he claimed in early 1993 that NAFTA was one of the most important policies sought by his administration. Congressional Democrats, who held majorities in both legislative chambers, were bitterly divided over NAFTA, but Clinton had the support of Thomas Foley, the Speaker of the House. The crucial House vote on NAFTA was scheduled for mid-November, and Clinton staked a large part of his presidency on its approval.

As a Democrat, Clinton's relationships with House Republicans and with business in general were rocky at best, especially following tense budget negotiations in the summer of 1993. Yet Clinton in the fall appealed openly to business leaders and Republicans to join with a minority of Democrats to approve the treaty. He and other members of his administration met regularly with USA-NAFTA leaders to coordinate inside and outside lobbying. He spent much of October and November mobilizing the business community to sway wavering Democrats, to ensure Republican support, and to defeat a majority of his own party in the House.

By the time Clinton's efforts were underway, he and his allies had a lot of ground to make up. For most of 1993, the anti-NAFTA side clearly had the upper hand. Local and national organizations opposed to NAFTA, especially unions and United We Stand, had undertaken massive outside lobbying campaigns for more than a year, and they were winning. They used every outside lobbying tactic they could to oppose NAFTA, expanding the conflict and signaling loudly and clearly the salience of the issue to working class and environmentally conscientious constituents. They ran advertisements in most major newspapers, sent mailings with postcard inserts for members to send to Congress, published 800 numbers for people to call and donate to the cause, held rallies all over the country, marched in Washington, and visited members of Congress in groups of constituents. As of mid-October, Congress had received several million pieces of mail from the anti-NAFTA side. NAFTA appeared headed for defeat, largely because enough members of Congress were convinced that the only constituents who really cared about the issue were on the anti side. Mail and phone calls to Congress were running 100–1 against NAFTA through mid-October, and even the White House conceded that they were losing the public debate to Ross Perot and other anti-NAFTA spokespersons.

As the number of undecided members of Congress declined through late October and early November, however, the pro-NAFTA side made up for lost time. Business corporations altogether spent nearly $8 million in the final weeks of the pro-NAFTA lobbying campaign, not to mention the millions of dollars in Washington spent by the Mexican government to promote the pact through inside lobbying and funding of research that (unsurprisingly) showed the positive effects of free trade. Members of Congress began to hear from business leaders mobilized by USA-NAFTA. Clinton personally met with undecided members of Congress, and he enlisted his cabinet to go directly to districts of undecided legislators and mobilize business executives. His trade representative, Mickey Kantor, met with business leaders on a regular basis to coordinate strategies and to provide support for businesses in the districts of undecided legislators when those businesses had trade disputes with foreign countries.

Within weeks of the massive business/White House outside lobbying effort in late October, mail to Congress was running even, and more previously undecided members of Congress were falling into the pro-NAFTA camp than the anti-NAFTA camp. The tide swung quickly, but it brought the issue only to the point where both sides were uncertain over the outcome of the vote. Clinton and his temporary business allies were several dozen votes short ten days before the vote.

Clinton began to deal more seriously for the remaining congressional votes in the final weeks. He promised Florida citrus growers that they could continue to use a controversial pesticide until the year 2000. He promised a Maryland Democrat the administration would investigate alleged unfair trade practices by a Canadian firm that competed with a major Maryland chemical plant. He set up personal campaign visits to districts of vulnerable Democrats in California, Ohio, and Maryland. He ordered the government to build a plutonium laboratory in Texas. And he secured a commitment from the Mexican government to extradite to Florida an accused rapist, following a personal appeal from a member of the Florida delegation in Congress. Finally, he personally lobbied dozens of undecided legislators, inviting them and their spouses to White House dinners and musical venues at the Kennedy Center.

The final outcome of the vote was uncertain until the last day, but the outside lobbying by the business coalition and the inside deals offered by Clinton eventually paid off. So did a gamble by the White House to agree to debate Ross Perot on national television. Perot debated Vice President Al Gore on *Larry King Live* the week before the vote, and his performance made the White House guardedly confident of victory. Perot faltered badly, and the anti-NAFTA forces conceded that, according to one anti-NAFTA lobbyist, Perot made their cause look "like the politics of the past, while Gore successfully projected NAFTA as the policy of the future."

When it was all over, Clinton claimed a substantial victory, labor vowed retribution on Democrats who had crossed them, and Clinton and peak business organizations were once again adversaries. Media attention turned from NAFTA to Clinton's health care plan. A period of extraordinarily intense outside lobbying had given way briefly to a more ordinary period of selective outside lobbying, only to be followed months later by another period of intense outside lobbying on all sides. During the health care debate, however, as during much of his term, Clinton and business organizations could not find enough common ground to join forces. NAFTA, consistent with a lot of trade politics in the United States, created temporary coalitions only weakly correlated with party divisions.

Outside Lobbying over Two Stages of Legislation

The history of outside lobbying in the ten months prior to the vote on NAFTA can really be broken into two periods. One period, from Clinton's inauguration in January until about early October, corresponds readily to the second stage of legislation, the agenda-shaping stage. During this time, as in the data analyzed in the last chapter, there appears to have been a fairly tight correspondence between salience information and outside lobbying by groups. The next period, from early October until the vote in mid-November, marked the debate and voting stage, and saw outside lobbying from all kinds of groups on both sides of the issue. It also saw the vigorous participation of the White House, something that changed the dynamics among all the groups deciding over lobbying strategies. (The first, need for action stage had occurred long before, when free traders in business, think tanks, and the Reagan administration in the mid-1980s began to coalesce around the idea of a North American free trade zone.)

During the second stage of legislation on NAFTA (until October 1993), attention among interest groups was focused on the side agreements being negotiated by the Clinton White House and the Mexican government. Interest groups on the anti-NAFTA side were doing nearly all the outside lobbying during this stage. They certainly undertook a fair bit of conflict expansion, trying to highlight to constituents what was at stake in these negotiations and in the treaty as a whole. The national unions held anti-NAFTA seminars and pushed the message that NAFTA meant job losses. Many environmental groups sent out scathing letters to their own members complaining of the detrimental effects that were going to come about on the Mexican border on account of the side agreements the Clinton administration was negotiating. At the same time, these outside lobbying efforts sent strong signals to members of Congress.

For example, in Detroit throughout the summer, members of the United

Auto Workers (UAW) hung pamphlets on doorknobs in working-class neighborhoods. The pamphlets read in large, bold letters, "Will your paycheck go south? 12 reasons to say: Not This NAFTA." A cutout postcard was attached to the pamphlet for people to send to their members of Congress. At least 250,000 of these pamphlets were distributed nationwide, and this was only a small fraction of the UAW's efforts, which was only a fraction of all union efforts. The UAW and other unions handed out anti-NAFTA pamphlets at shopping malls, state fairs, and auto trade shows throughout the summer. They even handed them out at the 1993 Baseball All-Star Game in San Diego in July. Nearly every major union published special newsletters on NAFTA and sent them to all union members.

The environmental groups, especially the Sierra Club and Friends of the Earth, were also generating letters and telephone calls from their members. Even the Doris Day Animal League sent out anti-NAFTA postcards to its members during the summer.

Indeed, constituents that unions represent (and to a lesser extent the ones that environmental groups represent) *may* have been the only sizable group that really did care enough about NAFTA to condition their votes on the issue. In my data for 1992, a full year before the NAFTA vote, trade issues received very high scores for salience among anti–free traders (0.65, for example), while the same issues received only small scores of salience among free traders (0.22 on the same question). And judging from mail, visits, and telephone calls, members of Congress could easily be forgiven for thinking in the summer that the union members (and a few thousand environmentalists) were the only ones who cared about NAFTA. (I present more data on public opinion surrounding NAFTA below.)

The agenda-shaping stage ended with grim prospects for passage of NAFTA in the House. The anti-NAFTA side, by all accounts the groups representing constituents for which trade issues were more salient, dominated the attention of many members of Congress (especially Democrats), thanks largely to successful outside lobbying by the group leaders. Using the terminology from chapter 3, the anti-NAFTA side represented very "high type" interest groups. They could credibly claim that they had increased the scope of the conflict on their side of the issue, and they had communicated loudly and clearly that many constituents were going to remember their representative's vote in the 1994 elections.

After the side agreements were completed, and especially after the White House began to devote full attention to NAFTA in late September, the issue entered the debate and voting stage. Outside lobbying on the issue changed. The most important change that occurred was the waking up of the pro-NAFTA side, represented mostly by USA-NAFTA. Business leaders undertook a massive outside lobbying effort, intending both to expand the conflict by making business executives all over the country recognize the seriousness of the impending defeat of NAFTA, and to signal to policymakers that business people really did care about the issue. It was not easy to make business executives pay attention, and likewise it was difficult to make the signals from USA-NAFTA appear credible. It took substantial resources, both money and staff donated from the world's largest corporations. They had a long way to go.

The labor unions and environmental groups did not back off from outside lobbying, but now they had to compete for the attention of members of Congress on the issue. Throughout October and November, members of Congress received unprecedented numbers of mail pieces, telephone calls, faxes, and visits from leaders of interest groups and constituents on both sides. Quite a few of them remarked that they felt more pressure on NAFTA than on any issue in recent memory.

The intense interest group activity and pressure from colleagues and from the president made many members of Congress skittish about their upcoming NAFTA votes. In October, over one hundred members of Congress were still publicly undecided. A dozen members were publicly undecided the day before the vote. "It was, by a considerable margin, the toughest decision I've ever had to make in public life," said Tom Sawyer in Michael Wines's article "The Free Trade Accord," in the *New York Times*, November 17, 1993. Sawyer, a Democrat from Akron, Ohio, reflected the sentiment of several dozen Democrats from unionized districts.

With so many votes up for grabs immediately preceding the floor vote, interest groups and politicians on both sides of the issue mobilized hundreds of thousands of citizens for direct political action up to the final day. For example, on November 10, a professional grass-roots lobbying firm in Washington, D.C., contacted several hundred people from upper-middle-class neighborhoods in districts of undecided legislators. The firm's client was an association of insurance companies. Callers, typically former staff members of Congress, had scripts that ran as follows:

> Hello, this is [name]. I'm calling you tonight from Washington on behalf of your insurance company to talk to you about NAFTA, the North American Free Trade Agreement. Have you heard of it? How do you feel about it? We're generally in favor of NAFTA because it will lower trade barriers with Mexico and Canada, leading to more jobs and lower prices for Americans. Are you willing to write a letter to your congressman, telling him you support NAFTA? I can send you information about NAFTA by fax.

Likewise, the 150,000 members of Public Citizen, the public interest group founded by Ralph Nader, received the bimonthly magazine of the organization in early November. The issue was devoted to NAFTA. "Help Stop NAFTA," read one headline. A 900 number followed, whereby for three dollars the caller could stimulate an automatic postcard to be sent to his or her member of Congress. The postcard read, "I am working against

NAFTA. NAFTA jeopardizes our country's environmental, consumer, and labor laws and undermines family farmers. Vote against NAFTA and please inform me of the basis of your position."

And over the course of seven days prior to the vote on the floor of the House there were anti-NAFTA rallies in twenty-two cities organized by the CTC. For example, in Dalton, Georgia, two representatives from local environmental groups mobilized fifty or so people to picket the office of Nathan Deal, a Democrat who had pledged to support NAFTA. The pickets read, Not This NAFTA, and NAFTA Is a Bad Deal for Deal. In Wisconsin, two thousand labor union members and members of Perot's United We Stand organization attended a rally where a parade of speakers talked of the environmental degradation, declining wages and safety standards, and loss of jobs resulting from NAFTA and similar trade policies.

Thus outside lobbying had changed, in the course of moving from agenda-shaping to debate and voting, from a one-sided to a two-sided affair. Business groups decided to enter the fray and try to expand the conflict. They actually succeeded in large measure because they had resources, because there probably was a decent amount of latent salience on the issue among business executives, and mostly because of the efforts of the president.

The changes in outside lobbying over NAFTA are consistent with the findings in the last chapter. During the agenda-shaping stage, outside lobbying correlated strongly with the salience at the current time. Groups representing constituents with intense preferences on the issue felt the need to signal that intensity through outside lobbying, while groups without the requisite support could not signal credibly and had not yet tried to expand the conflict. Then during the debate and voting stage, many groups used outside lobbying, diminishing any correlation between salience and outside lobbying. Up to the final vote, there were vigorous efforts at conflict expansion and signaling by both sides.

The Players

Let us return once again to the major players in outside lobbying as they responded to the issue of NAFTA. In the first chapter, I listed the players as interest groups, policymakers, and constituents. One more player is very important in the NAFTA story—the president—and he acted somewhat like a hugely wealthy interest group (with the ability to make massive campaign contributions and do personal favors). His involvement swung the tide in favor of the treaty.[2]

---

[2] Certainly the mass media were crucial, though more to transmit information among these other four sets of actors than as an independent force. Mass media companies, in contrast, were important interest group players, as they saw the Mexican market as a potentially lucrative one.

Interest Groups

LABOR UNIONS

When it was nearly over, an AFL-CIO lobbyist remarked, "We probably sent out more material on NAFTA than on any other issue, ever."[3] Much of that material was sent before the business interest groups paid any attention to the issue. By the spring of 1993, labor unions members were already stirred up over NAFTA. The conflict had been expanded for them. The main goal of labor union leaders throughout the summer was to convince undecided Democrats (and a few Republicans) that voting for NAFTA would be costly in both financial and electoral terms. As one Teamster lobbyist put it, "If they vote for NAFTA, they shouldn't come to us for contributions or campaign help, or to pass out literature door to door." The enthusiastic response among union members to the outside lobbying by their leadership offered strong support for this threat.

The Teamsters were the most adamantly opposed to NAFTA. Benjamin Cardin, Democrat from Maryland, for example, received over five hundred letters from one Teamsters local. Many unions publicly expressed support for free trade in general, just not for this NAFTA. The Teamsters were dead set against NAFTA and did not even want to discuss amendments or side agreements. NAFTA, according to the Teamsters, would allow Mexican truck drivers, with lower accreditation and safety standards than U.S. drivers, to compete for loads in the United States. This was seen as the most serious threat to Teamster jobs since the deregulation of trucking in the late 1970s. In fact, Teamsters in Michigan opposed NAFTA so intensely, their leaders privately approached several Republican lawmakers in the state and promised electoral support in the primary season if the representatives voted against NAFTA. Nothing ever came of this promise, as all Michigan Republicans voted in favor of the treaty. Teamsters also carried out selective strikes in November 1993 to protest the treaty.

Much of the funding for the anti-NAFTA coalition, however, came from the UAW. The auto union spent about $3.5 million on NAFTA, with more than $250,000 going to the CTC. Compared to the Teamsters, the UAW leaders devoted more attention to convincing people outside their union to oppose NAFTA. They ran television and radio advertisements in Michigan, California, and Illinois, and they helped organize rallies with United We Stand and other organizations. They were at the very center of CTC's decision making, placing the UAW in direct alliance with environmentalists and good-government activists, some of their regular opponents in politics. According to UAW lobbyists and their environmental allies, there was room for negotiations over NAFTA, but the existing treaty was unacceptable.

---

[3] Quoted in the Peter Kilborn, "Little Voices Roar in the Chorus of Trade-Pact Foes," *New York Times*, November 13, 1993, A8.

There was a good deal of educating of union members over NAFTA. Following the NAFTA vote, many union officials were upbeat about the prospects for future union mobilizing. In terms of the response among their members to their outside lobbying, their campaign was a huge success. The UAW lobbyists, for example, felt that the NAFTA debate gave union members reasons to care about trade issues beyond simple nativist sentiments. One UAW publicist put it this way:

> A guy wants to go out and take a sledgehammer to a Toyota. That is his gut level instinct on trade. So our job in part is to take that gut level understanding and that emotion, and give expression to it in a way that is constructive to him and can impact policy in a realistic fashion. All of that is a part of the lobbying process. I do think we were very effective on that.

The union leaders, however, were realistic about the prospects for winning votes in Congress when a Democratic president opposes the union cause on an issue. They responded with resignation and anger after the vote. Along with the optimism on the part of union leadership about the future was a vow to get even with the Democrats who crossed them. I shall examine the credibility of this vow later.

It was never a serious option for national labor unions *not* to outside lobby on NAFTA. They had all the benefits of public opinion on their side. Union leaders were firmly convinced, and rightly so it turns out, that their membership would respond in force to outside lobbying. Furthermore, the leaders were convinced that members of Congress would notice pressure from union locals and working-class constituents, and would be forced to justify carefully any pro-NAFTA position.

In one important respect, the unions may have miscalculated in their efforts at framing the issue to expand the conflict beyond their memberships. A CTC leader after the House vote told me that in retrospect the focus of the anti-NAFTA coalition's message on job losses was a mistake. The pro-NAFTA forces had credible counterarguments that the American economy overall would benefit from trade, and that companies would eventually have to hire more workers to take advantage of new export markets. This leader thought that focusing on unfair trade issues, the environment, or safety standards would have been better in the long run for those opposed to the treaty. Evidently, the unions were caught in a dilemma. To mobilize their members and other sympathizers, they needed to emphasize job losses resulting from NAFTA. But to convince members of Congress to oppose NAFTA, they perhaps should have emphasized other messages about NAFTA that did not have ready retorts from the business side. Since unions members were the ones contacting members of Congress, union leaders could not make one appeal to members and another appeal to members of Congress.

Nevertheless, the outside lobbying by unions, effective in many ways, brought the issue great attention and scrutiny by the public, the press, and many pro-free trade members of Congress. Even ardent pro-NAFTA leaders were impressed. One member of the Clinton administration remarked, "The unions had no case on the issue. They carried one of their weakest cases, and damn near won. They almost took it across the goal line. We [on the pro-NAFTA side] had all the editorial pages controlled, the economists, the think tanks, the intelligentsia all over this town was on the pro side, and they almost won!"

ENVIRONMENTALISTS

While unions were united and vigilant over NAFTA, the fifteen most prominent environmental organizations split on the issue, and this hurt the anti-NAFTA cause. The six mainstream groups, such as the Environmental Defense Fund and the Audobon Society, supported Clinton's NAFTA as the only way for the United States to gain leverage over Mexico on environmental issues. Nine other groups, such as Greenpeace U.S.A., the Sierra Club, and Friends of the Earth, opposed Clinton's negotiated version of the treaty for its lack of regulatory teeth against Mexican companies.

The environmental split on NAFTA hurt the anti-NAFTA cause because it gave pro-environmental Democrats from California and Texas an excuse to vote for the treaty. No one, including potential electoral opponents or editorial writers, could claim that environmentalists completely opposed the treaty. Significantly, the anti-NAFTA environmental groups outside lobbied on NAFTA while the pro NAFTA environmental groups did not. This pattern occurred for two reasons, consistent with our story. First, the environmental groups that did oppose the treaty were much more likely than their counterparts to mobilize voters and stir up public controversy. Second, and related, the kinds of people the two sets of groups represent differed in precisely the ways that correlated at the time with opposition or support for NAFTA. The anti-NAFTA groups tended to represent antiestablishment persons, while the pro-NAFTA groups tended to represent professionals and those sympathetic to business causes. In short, the groups that outside lobbied on NAFTA could be fairly confident that their members would oppose NAFTA and would be willing to participate in some way against it.

Two groups in particular are worth comparing. The Environmental Defense Fund struggled internally over whether to support or oppose Clinton's version of NAFTA. The organization ended up supporting NAFTA but deciding not to outside lobby. It does not specialize in outside lobbying, but the leaders had recently used extensive outside lobbying over the Endangered Species Act and over some issues involving the Arctic wilderness. Why not outside lobby on NAFTA? One of their chief lobbyists gave me four reasons, none of which make much sense: the timing was bad, the group does not do grass roots, the leaders did not want to overload members, and it was redundant because of their inside lobbying. In marked contrast, the Sierra Club opposed NAFTA, and its leaders outside lobbied extensively. According to lobbyists at the organization, Sierra Club members, especially California and Texas members, were deeply concerned about environmental conditions at the United States-Mexican borders. Conditions at the borders had been campaign issues for several congressional races in 1990 and 1992, partially as a result of Sierra Club publicity. The Sierra Club could make credible claims to some members of Congress that the people the club represented cared about aspects of NAFTA and would act on it. The Environmental Defense Fund could not feel confident making such claims. They were seriously constrained by opinion among their members.

Given their split over NAFTA, though, environmental groups were not all that important to the final NAFTA outcome, according to most observers. They gave a boost to the anti-NAFTA side, and they played a large role organizationally in the CTC. But certainly unions dominated most anti-NAFTA efforts, and the pro-NAFTA environmental groups were silent both in inside and outside lobbying. Far more important to the pro-NAFTA side were business organizations.

BUSINESS GROUPS

By all appearances the coalition brought together to represent the pro-NAFTA position for the business community was impressive and almost certainly unprecedented. Business mobilized quickly and massively in October and November, and by the time of the House vote USA-NAFTA had over four thousand firms, local chambers, and associations as members. All fifty states had organizational captains (CEOs of Fortune 500 companies), and dozens of staff members in Washington, on hire from consulting firms, business associations, and corporations, worked full time on NAFTA. The coalition sent out millions of mail pieces, not to mention the pieces sent out by individual corporations to stockholders and employees, and generated tens of thousands of letters and telephone calls to Congress in October and November. USA-NAFTA even organized rallies in many cities (though these rallies were considerably more sedate than the rallies organized by the CTC). And in the last few weeks before the House vote there were daily meetings over lobbying strategies among the heads of Allied-Signal, Eastman Kodak, AT&T, TRW, 3M, and other giant corporations.

Organizing the business community was not easy, however. State captains complained to the Washington offices of USA-NAFTA in September that NAFTA was not a salient issue among businesses. Most firms were not even taking the time to join the coalition. All it took to join was to fax a form to the Washington offices. Minnesotans for NAFTA, organized by 3M, sent out forty-five hundred letters to Minnesota companies and had received one hundred membership forms two months later. Another lobbyist reported back to Washington, "We've been approaching a great variety of small and medium-size businesses, trying to get them to support NAFTA. It's been very, very hard." Even after the vote, a number of White House officials and members of Congress expressed views that the business effort was "a joke," "a failure." One White House official was almost apologetic on behalf of the business community: "Corporations and trade associations are very bad at grass roots. They can do very well at tax cuts, and against tax increases, but on major policy issues, they're not good at all at getting their employees to contact Congress. The employees just don't care enough."

Prior to October, the business effort *was* a joke. Members of Congress had heard virtually nothing from the pro-NAFTA side. Robert Matsui, a Democrat from California, warned the USA-NAFTA leadership in September, "The NAFTA vote will be won or lost by the amount of grass-roots support we are able to gain across the country." Clinton complained publicly in September that business was not doing enough to win passage of NAFTA. Public debate over NAFTA was dominated by labor unions well into October.

The business community could eventually turn around and deliver as much mail to Congress and as many visits from business owners and executives to congressional offices as it did in November because it had ample resources. Businesses all over the country did not suddenly wake up to NAFTA. Rather, with logistical help from the White House, several large corporations donated money and staff to USA-NAFTA, and USA-NAFTA used the money to generate grass roots results. USA-NAFTA spent $8 million in the last few months and generated approximately half a million pieces of mail, faxes, and tens of thousands of telephone calls to Congress. Count in a few hundred office visits to members of Congress, and congressional contacts (mail, telephone, visits) come out to about $30 apiece for USA-NAFTA. If my figures are correct, this was an expensive outside lobbying campaign given the results it generated *in terms of contacts to Congress*. In terms of policy influence, of course, it may have turned the tide in favor of NAFTA and been a small price to pay compared with the benefits to American businesses. Nevertheless, the key point is that business had the resources to spend on the outside lobbying campaign, and because they were a relatively "low type" interest group, they needed to spend those resources.

Business leaders believed that most members of Congress were inclined to be free traders, and if given a credible reason to oppose their union constituents—like local business support for NAFTA or editorial support in local newspapers—they would support the treaty. As I will discuss below, the efforts of USA-NAFTA gave many members of Congress political "cover" to follow their own free-trade instincts. In sum, business had good reasons to outside lobby, even though they were not entirely supported by the preferences of the public and especially since the salience of the issue was low to the citizens they claimed to represent.

THE PRESIDENT AS OUTSIDE LOBBYIST

Relations between the White House and business leaders in Washington were strained from the beginning of the NAFTA debate. The White House staff originally wanted USA-NAFTA to craft a lobbying campaign with the Democratic Leadership Council (DLC), a core party caucus with close ties to Clinton. Several White House officials even suggested to the leaders of USA-NAFTA that corporations give money to the DLC and let the DLC run the campaign. The USA-NAFTA leaders refused, and only when Clinton stepped into the NAFTA debate personally in October did the tension die down.

The White House needed to be careful about how it proceeded. Federal law stipulates that the executive branch cannot use federal money to get private persons or organizations to lobby Congress. The law perhaps would not survive a court challenge, but even absent a reason to sue, every presidential administration since its enactment has adhered to the letter of the law. The executive branch can, however, share information with private groups, and significantly, the president and vice president are exempt from the law. On NAFTA, Clinton broadened the scope of what it means to "share information." He sent each member of his cabinet on a tour of congressional districts to stir up business support for the treaty. The week of the House vote, for example, Bruce Babbitt, the secretary of the interior, spoke at pro-NAFTA rallies in Charlotte and Greensboro, North Carolina, and in Atlanta. Janet Reno, the attorney general, spoke at a "workers rally" in Miami, though the rally was attended mostly by white-collar workers. And Mickey Kantor, his trade representative, met continuously with business executives from the districts of undecided congressional members to iron out trade problems. Nearly the entire administration spent weeks mobilizing citizens who supported NAFTA to contact their members of Congress and attend rallies. The president himself spoke eighteen times on NAFTA to groups of business leaders in October.

The White House played an even broader outside strategy than sending out cabinet members to attend rallies and organizing presidential speeches. It openly shared information and coordinated tactics with USA-NAFTA, sending schedules of official appearances, talking regularly with the leaders of the coalition, and even urging pro-NAFTA members of Congress to get local businesses to join.

Much like any set of interest group leaders, the president and his advisers decided on outside lobbying because they wanted to demonstrate support for the proposition that important constituents, in this case the business commu-

does th PREZ PLAY THIS ROLE ALL THE TIME

nity, really did care about this policy issue. The effort by the business community was languishing, and the pro-NAFTA side was losing badly as a result of vigorous outside lobbying by the opposition.[4] The White House, according to one member of the administration, had to "equalize pressure by getting the mail and the phone calls approximately even." They knew many Democrats were free traders but were feeling considerable pressure from labor unions. The administration therefore wanted to make it easier for these Democrats to claim to newspaper editors, potential campaign donors, and general opinion leaders in the districts that since pressure from the district was relatively even, the member could vote his or her conscience. In Washington, this kind of lobbying by the White House is often referred to as "granting the member political cover."

Once this kind of political cover—granted by mail, telephone calls, and visits from business leaders in the district—existed for some undecided members, the president sought to win the remaining votes with various pork barrel projects and personal attention. Concurrent with its outside lobbying, the White House played a strategy of intense inside lobbying and a legal form of bribery. Undecided members like Benjamin Cardin received daily telephone calls from the highest officials in the administration, including the president. "Never overestimate the power of the presidency," one former member of Congress remarked to me. "The tickets to the Kennedy Center with the president, the White House dinners, calls from the president to local campaign donors. Those things mean a hell of a lot." Likewise, the president won over many members with regulatory relief for local industries, promises to campaign for the members, money for local law enforcement, museums, and the repair of the infrastructure. Roundly criticized for these dealings, the president and his advisers made no apologies.

Opponents of NAFTA, of course, were very bitter. Their successful outside lobbying was thwarted, not so much in their minds by the outside lobbying by business but rather by the massive resources at the president's disposal. Said one official at the UAW, "I don't think they won it fair and square. We had the votes and we won the issue, but then they started buying and selling. We don't have bridges, roads, and airports to give away."

The narrow White House victory on NAFTA makes it hard to point to any one single tactic by the administration that won the vote. Undecided members of Congress had different reasons for voting the way they did. Some

---

[4] Such games between two sides of an issue are clearly beyond the theory proposed in chapter 3. However, it is easy to incorporate into an interest group's decision calculus, albeit in reduced form, the other side's actions. An alternative depiction may be that over NAFTA the two sides were in a form of prisoner's dilemma, where both labor and business, given the outcome, would have been better off spending no resources on outside lobbying. I doubt labor leaders ever saw their decision this way. They tended to see an opportunity to win and did not expect business to react the way business ultimately did.

decided after receiving tangible benefits from the White House, some decided after hearing from business leaders in their districts that NAFTA would add jobs, and some just decided to follow their intuition and risk opposing their union supporters. Washington observers and participants had plenty of hypotheses about crucial congressional votes. What is not in dispute by nearly anyone involved in the NAFTA battle, though, is that the treaty surely would have been defeated on that day in November had not the president stepped in and lobbied the Congress using both inside and outside strategies.

Policymakers

When Clinton became directly involved in persuading Congress to support NAFTA in the fall, 1993, he appointed two men, William Daley, brother of the mayor of Chicago, and William Frenzel, a former member of Congress, as his chief lobbyists. Daley, a Democrat, was to lobby Democrats, and Frenzel, a Republican, was to lobby Republicans. Daley and Frenzel quickly settled on a ranking of members of Congress according to whether the member was definitely pro-NAFTA, definitely anti-NAFTA, or some measure of undecided. They both agreed to focus on the members from their respective parties leaning one way or another but not definite and on the clearly undecided members.

There were good reasons for members of Congress from both parties to remain undecided until late. First, they could raise campaign funds from both sides. According to the staffs of several undecided members, fundraising during the NAFTA battle was unusually successful for an off-election year. Second, they could gain concessions from other members of Congress and especially from the president while they held out. As one member remarked at a USA-NAFTA meeting, "Once the Florida delegation demanded and got what they wanted, some outrageous demands [from other members] have been made." Finally, they could gather a lot of information from interest groups about the electoral and economic consequences of NAFTA. Undecided members were hungry for information. The undecided Democrats had heard plenty from union members about the evils of NAFTA, but they repeatedly expressed frustration at not hearing enough from business about the proposed benefits. Said one staff member of an undecided member, "For a long time, business was inept. We had to pull teeth to get anything concrete from them about job creation after NAFTA."

For other members of Congress, pressure from constituents or their own policy preferences made the option of remaining undecided impossible. Democrats from the strongest union districts voted against the treaty almost without exception. Regardless of personal views on free trade, the electoral costs of supporting NAFTA for these members were too dear. Some Democrats and majority of Republicans supported the pact wholeheartedly for philosophical reasons. Free trade was the key to prosperity, the wave of the future, the only way to help Mexico economically, or some combination of these ideas. Clinton liked to claim that in a blind vote, NAFTA would win hands down because most members of Congress supported free trade. If so, Republicans and Democrats in the South and Mountain West could support NAFTA openly, since organized labor was not a factor in their districts.

The decision was most agonizing for Democrats from unionized but economically diverse districts. Democrats from California, Illinois, Maryland, Missouri, and Texas were targeted heavily by both sides. For example, Cardin from Maryland committed to support NAFTA several days before the final vote. Cardin's office was deluged by mail almost solely from local Teamsters throughout the year, until October. Then he began to receive mail from the pro-NAFTA side. With mail running even in November, he eventually traveled around his district, interviewing business executives. He calculated, according to his staff, that he might lose support from unions in the short run for voting for NAFTA, but that in the long run, his district would benefit economically. As one of his staff members put it, "The congressman's decision came down to the fact that NAFTA would add jobs in his district, and he decided this after talking to the business leaders." Also, he admitted, Cardin simply felt that the unions could not make good on their threats to bounce him from office.

In Chicago, two undecided Democrats, Mel Reynolds and Luis Gutierrez, were the focus of outside lobbying efforts by unions and business groups. Both received personal White House invitations to meet with Clinton on NAFTA, and both remained neutral until the final days before the House vote. Yet Reynolds voted for NAFTA and Gutierrez voted against NAFTA. Reynolds, an African-American, expressed the view that his mostly African-American constituency, while generally opposed to NAFTA, did not consider the issue very important. Vague promises from Clinton to campaign in his district seemed to put Reynolds over the edge and into the pro-NAFTA side. Gutierrez said that he could not betray his mostly Latino and mostly unionized constituents. Personal appeals from Clinton, in the end, did not work to sway him.

One way to think about the decisions of the undecided members is to consider that by the debate and voting stage, they were in pooling equilibriums with each interest group side. In this case, the interest groups pooled on high levels of outside lobbying. Members of Congress sought to use information from outside lobbying to determine which decision (yea or nay on NAFTA) would cost the least in electoral support. But since outside lobbying was coming from both sides of the debate, this determination was difficult merely from the outside lobbying. In these situations, legislators had to rely on their intuition or on other sources of information than on evidence from outside lobbying. Cardin was likely pro-business in this case, and Reynolds found Clinton's appeals decisive. Gutierrez, in contrast, was not swayed from a strong prior inclination to support union causes. I shall have more to say below about the decisions of legislators on NAFTA.

Constituents

Ordinary constituents responded to the NAFTA debate in several measurable ways worth exploring. A significant portion of the public participated directly in the NAFTA debate by attending rallies and demonstrations, calling members of Congress, sending mail to Congress, visiting members' offices, and talking about NAFTA with pollsters and in public forums. A conservative estimate is that several million Americans participated, judging from the volume of mail and telephone calls, attendance at events, and the claims about mobilization made by interest groups. Also, those who did participate seemed overwhelmingly to be members of labor unions. A smaller proportion of participants were business managers, environmentalists, and community political activists. Without survey evidence on participation from the fall 1993, it is impossible to provide systematic support for these estimates, but several political and interest group leaders involved in the debate agreed that my estimates were reasonable.

NAFTA was a relatively salient issue to many Americans. Almost one-half of survey respondents said in November that they followed the news on NAFTA either very closely or somewhat closely. And less than one-sixth of respondents in most surveys on NAFTA had no opinion on the matter, much lower than for many other controversial political issues.

Throughout this book, however, the applicable notion of salience has been the importance of the issue to subgroups in the population deemed mobilizable by interest groups, rather than the salience of the issue to the entire population. The available evidence on this score is thin but revealing. I have already reported in this chapter the salience measures for trade issues in 1992 and how they differed on the two sides. Table 6.1 reports further results following survey questions from November 1993. As the vote in Congress approached, one-fourth of those surveyed said that they would be less likely to vote for their congressional representative if the representative voted in favor of NAFTA, while somewhere around one-sixth of those surveyed said they would be more likely to vote for their representative under these conditions. Comparing the marginals of the two responses, some of the Washington lore surrounding NAFTA at the time is supported. The common wisdom was that constituents who opposed NAFTA were more willing to use the NAFTA vote as a basis for electoral support than were constituents in favor

TABLE 6.1
Public Opinion on NAFTA (percentages)

If your representative in Congress votes in favor of NAFTA, will that make you more likely to support your representative for re-election, less likely, or won't it make much difference in your vote?

	More Likely	Less Likely	No Difference	No Opinion
ABC News, 11/9/93	20	24	53	3
ABC News, 11/11/93	16	25	53	6
ABC News, 11/14/93	15	25	57	3

of NAFTA because many of NAFTA's opponents, especially members of labor unions, saw NAFTA as the most important vote of the congressional session. In contrast, constituents in favor in NAFTA, especially business managers and owners, considered NAFTA to be one of several relevant issues.

The surprising fact about public opinion throughout the NAFTA debate, however, is that mass preferences remained largely unchanged throughout the entire struggle in Washington, D.C. Amid all the outside lobbying that took place over NAFTA—and it was huge in scope and intensity from both sides—and amid all the media attention, aggregate public support for NAFTA remained fairly constant. Table 6.2 shows a time series of public preferences regarding NAFTA. More Americans in polls opposed NAFTA rather than supported NAFTA, but the differences were not large in any national surveys. When people in the samples were asked the same questions at different points during 1993, roughly 30 percent expressed support for NAFTA under one poll giving people the overt option of "Haven't heard enough," and roughly 41 percent expressed support for NAFTA when such an option is not overtly given. Moreover, on average, 32 percent and 43 percent opposed NAFTA in these respective surveys. As the chief lobbyist for the Teamsters admitted to me, public opinion (he meant popularity) on NAFTA was virtually dead even before the House vote.

This stability is perfectly consistent with one of the major assumptions throughout this book. Public preferences remain largely unchanged in the short run, and interest groups seek to increase salience (especially in the second and third stages of legislation).

In sum, the mass public participated in much higher numbers in the NAFTA debate in comparison with that of most other controversial policy issues, though that participation, not surprisingly, corresponded closely to certain occupational and demographic categories. Further, this participation followed vigorous interest group mobilization. Moreover, public opinion re-

TABLE 6.2

Public Opinion on NAFTA over Time (percentages)

Pollster/Date	Favor	Oppose	Haven't Heard Enough	Not Sure
Hart & Teeter[a]				
1/23/93	28	31	36	5
4/17/93	27	25	44	4
7/24/93	31	29	36	4
9/10/93	25	36	34	5
10/22/93	29	33	34	4
ABC News[b]	Approve	Reject		No Opinion
11/9/93	40	45		15
11/11/93	38	46		17
11/14/93	42	42		16

[a]Do you favor or oppose the North American Free Trade Agreement with Mexico and Canada that eliminates nearly all restrictions on imports, exports, and business investment between the United States, Mexico, and Canada? If you feel you have not heard enough about this issue yet to have an opinion, please just say so.

[b]Do you think Congress should approve or reject the NAFTA?

mained a relatively fixed landscape upon which interest groups and legislators made strategic decisions. Legislators, like those studying the history of NAFTA today, could only guess at the salience of the issue to subsets of their constituencies.[5] Interest groups, of course, were perfectly willing to provide evidence that their supporters considered NAFTA to be very important to them.

Outside Lobbying and the Final Outcome over NAFTA

After the House vote, interest group leaders and legislators on both sides also agreed that outside lobbying by interest groups was a major factor in the outcome. The anti-side had the early advantage because it had successfully communicated many constituents' fears of free trade with Mexico. Their outside lobbying effort was massive by any measure. The business effort, while not decisive, brought the treaty from a point of certain defeat to a point where the president could win the remaining congressional votes. This same business effort, moreover, was helped considerably by the White House.

Why did the pro-NAFTA side win? Several reasons have been offered by participants in the conflict. The White House liked to tell anyone who would

[5] For my purposes, without the existence of an ANES survey in 1993, I cannot estimate for NAFTA the kind of salience I estimate on other issues in chapter 4.

listen that members of Congress on average felt that NAFTA was good public policy, but that union muscle prevented many Democrats from voting their underlying preferences. Thus, once outside lobbying by the pro-side made the lobbying pressure a wash, the pro-side ultimately won on its merits. The more cynical version of this hypothesis is that there exists a decidedly pro-business bias in Congress and in Washington in general. Labor union officials certainly believe this, especially since the early 1980s, when the national Democratic Party began openly courting business money for congressional campaigns. One anti-NAFTA activist with graduate training in political science remarked, "I can't think of a case where the united forces of capital and the national state worked together and didn't win against their opponents."

The organizers of USA-NAFTA liked to credit the efforts of the business community, claiming that the outside lobbying by business was the most effective in its history. The outside lobbying by business may have been relatively remarkable by the standards of the Business Roundtable, but no one in any congressional office I spoke with, nor in the White House, gave the business community credit for passing NAFTA. And some offer as an explanation the diminution of Perot during the debate with Gore. After the debate, supposedly, the anti side lost its clothes like the emperor in the children's fable.

I believe that two aspects of the NAFTA case ought to figure into any causal story about the final floor vote. The first is quite obvious to all participants. Clinton's direct involvement in mobilizing business and in persuading members of Congress to vote for NAFTA was crucial to the outcome. He did in fact provide a lot of "cover" for undecided members; not so much cover from unions but cover from district opinion leaders—like newspaper editors and local politicians—who generally want members of Congress to be responsive to sentiment in their districts. It provides a boost to a member of Congress when he or she can respond to attacks from an opponent with news about pork barrel projects delivered by the president, or with "I heard from a lot of business people that NAFTA would add jobs in this district." Just reporting that opinion is divided in the district gives a member more freedom to decide on his or her own than having to report that mail is running a hundred to one against NAFTA. According to Bianco (1994), members of Congress are granted "leeway" or "trust" by some voters when the members can build reputations of reliable sensitivity to constituent concerns.

The second aspect is that the implicit threat from labor unions to punish supporters of NAFTA at the polls was not credible in many cases and did not materialize in 1994 *because Clinton countered them.* Labor unions were not as "high" in type as they claimed or as even their leaders thought at the time, but it was not because they had the wrong information. The context changed when Clinton started dealing for votes. By one plausible interpretation of events, many undecided members who voted for NAFTA changed their evaluations of the labor threat after the White House stepped in. Further, the White House was confident that labor's hostility would be short-lived. They knew that unions would work hard for the president's health care plan, the next item on the president's agenda. As it turns out, the AFL-CIO suspended contributions to the Democratic National Committee for three months after the NAFTA vote, but then resumed contributions in February 1994 with a $10 million pledge toward Clinton's health care plan.

While national labor unions publicly vowed retribution against pro-NAFTA Democrats in the House, these legislators largely went unscathed when Clinton worked to counteract union efforts. One major target was David Mann, a Democrat from Ohio. Local labor leaders promised to punish Mann, who had won his primary in 1992 by 416 votes. In the 1994 primary, local unions backed his opponent, William Bowen, and mobilized heavily against Mann. However, Clinton fulfilled a promise to Mann and campaigned in his district prior to the primary. Mann won the 1994 primary by 667 votes.[6] Likewise, the Illinois Federation of Labor did not endorse Dan Rostenkowski, Mel Reynolds, and Richard Durbin in the 1994 primaries, three Democrats who voted for the treaty. All three won their primaries.[7] There was not one case in 1994 where labor unions could follow through on their threat to defeat a pro-NAFTA Democrat in the primaries. Clinton had made it a personal commitment to change the "high" type group into a "low" type group.

[6] Mann subsequently lost the general election to Steve Chabot, a Republican. Perhaps labor unions had the last laugh when Mann lost, but they certainly would not have favored the Republican sweep in 1994 that Chabot benefited from. Regardless, labor backed Mann in the general election.

[7] Rostenkowski lost in the general election, Reynolds won but was convicted of a felony in 1995, and Durbin won his general election.

[handwritten marginalia: "(1) Clinton was the more credible threat?"]

7

Conclusion

THE EMPIRICAL RESULTS from chapters 4 and 5 and the case study from chapter 6 suggest that outside lobbying by interest groups often communicates real content about public opinion to policymakers in the United States. These strategies appear to be related systematically to the salience and popularity of policy issues and therefore can be credible signals of public opinion information and, by inference, future electoral behavior. This is especially true in the stages of legislation when alternatives are being bandied about and policymakers tend to know which constituents might be affected by a given policy. The standard pattern is intuitive: interest groups use outside lobbying more often and on greater scale if they are pursuing policies with intense support among constituents instead of policies with more diffuse support. One lobbyist for a trade association expressed his confidence in outside lobbying:

> Politicians use grass-roots contacts as sort of a hyper-concentrated version of what people are thinking back home. A lot of members of Congress are nervous, and they know that anyone who's going to pick up the phone, or take the time to write a letter, is not only going to be a knowledgeable voter, and an active voter, but an active person who's going to go out and change people's minds.

This describes the standard pattern, anyway. In some ways, however, the exceptions to the standard pattern are every bit as interesting to study. When are we likely to observe outside lobbying among groups who do not have much popular support for their positions on issues? I have suggested several answers. First, group leaders may not feel that the constituents they represent are sufficiently informed or mobilized on an issue, and therefore the group leaders use outside lobbying to expand the conflict and increase the salience of an issue.[1] This is especially likely when a group is trying to get a policy problem onto the government's agenda. Second, group leaders understand that the policies they are pursuing, while not altogether popular, are relatively more popular than prominent alternatives, including the status quo policy. And third, interest group leaders are themselves mobilized by one set of policymakers to outside lobby another set of policymakers, as in the case

---

[1] It may be case that interest groups leaders systematically overestimate their popular support. There is some evidence for this in chapter 1. Group leaders have an overall hubris (at least in answering survey questions) that leads them to express the belief that they have majority support for some policies when in fact they do not even have plurality support.

of the president on NAFTA. Finally, as the date of a policy decision approaches, we often observe interest groups on all sides using outside lobbying, trying to squeeze out the last bit of latent salience among their supporters and to signal their support to policymakers.

For all of the different scenarios and contexts, the policy preferences of constituents play an extremely important role in structuring incentives for interest group strategies. Public opinion constrains the behavior not only of policymakers, but of interest groups as well. The two "forces" on government, interest groups and public opinion, certainly interact and reinforce each other. Figure 7.1 contrasts two views of policymaking. The top picture reflects a common depiction, where scholars pit public opinion against interest groups as influences on the government. Arnold (1990) puts the question starkly: "Why does Congress frequently approve proposals that serve organized interests or that deliver narrowly targeted geographic benefits? Why does Congress sometimes break free of parochial concerns and enact bills that serve more diffuse, general, or unorganized interests?" (3).

By Arnold's formulation, when explaining a specific policy outcome, one is led to conclude that either interest groups influence the government or public opinion influences the government. Another scholar concludes his book in a way reflecting a similar dichotomy: "More often than not political change in the U.S. has come about because of changes in public opinion rather than pressure from special interest groups" (Miller 1983, 137). And Page and Shapiro (1992) stress the role that interest groups sometimes play in circumventing public opinion.[2]

The bottom picture in figure 7.1 is a more accurate depiction and suggests that the top picture is misleading. Public opinion constrains the behavior of interest groups, and interest groups influence public opinion, especially through increasing the salience of issues. This is the main conclusion from our empirical results.

One might want to go further and stress the difficulty in separating the two concepts. Constituency opinion is communicated and transmitted through interest groups, and therefore it does not in any meaningful sense interact with groups. I do not wish to go that far. Policymakers receive information from opinion polls and other methods to discern the popular support for proposals and candidates among the entire mass public. And at times, constituency opinion seems to overwhelm policymakers and influence policy independently of any interest groups. As one lobbyist for the homeless remarked:

> Sometimes public opinion just sort of rears up. If it's something so big, it clearly is beyond the interest groups, whoever they are, corporate, education, labor, what-

---

[2] Page and Shapiro also emphasize that interest groups often operate to mislead or manipulate the public. Thus they recognize an aspect of the interaction between public opinion and interest groups.

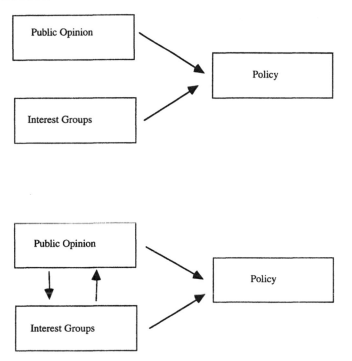

Figure 7.1. Public Opinion and Interest Groups

ever. And when members of Congress become aware of that, a sort of paralysis or mania sets in. Am I making it clear? That kind of phenomena is sort of like tornadoes and hurricanes. You just sort of dive for cover or find a safe place to stand because the whole ground and skies are shaking. There's not a whole lot you can do about it, except to find a safe place to stand.

The point of this is to say that interest groups are organized groups of constituents, but they, even in the aggregate, are not synonymous with what policymakers consider their constituencies or public opinion in their districts. To say that public opinion and interest groups cannot be separated is like saying that members of Congress cannot be separated from their constituents. Members of Congress give voice to their constituencies in the national government. Their representation, however, is uneven, imperfect, and reflects in some measure their own individual interests. The same can be said for interest group leaders.

Astroturf versus Real Grass Roots

Yet for all the evidence we can muster to demonstrate that the use of outside lobbying is *on average* a good indication of popular support, few will deny that it can mislead policymakers, constituents, or both. Outside lobbying is especially troublesome when constituents are given false information about policies or about problems in their neighborhoods or towns. All we can hope for is that others—the media, other interest groups, competing candidates, policymakers—present more accurate information eventually. (Alas, sometimes the damage is done before better information is made public.)

For this book, much of the focus is on true or false information presented to policymakers about their constituents' preferences. How can we tell the difference between real grass-roots strength and astroturf? Observers in Washington may not be much help. Opponents in Washington are inclined to deride each other's efforts as phony. The national press is quick to jump on hired guns because they are paid to generate evidence of grass-roots support. And policymakers, meanwhile, whose livelihoods depend on reading the public mood accurately, take very seriously many of the constituency contacts generated by outside lobbying; they tend to play it safe and try to placate small groups of angry constituents.

In fact, we can devise a method of evaluating outside lobbying as either astroturf or the real thing. With our measures of salience and popularity for a policy issue and the outside lobbying that occurred on the issue, it is possible to categorize the different opinion scenarios facing interest group leaders. Figure 7.2 shows a simplified typology. (Note that as in chapters 4 and 5, salience refers to the salience of the policy issue to those constituents who agree with the group's policy goals on the issue.) In the cells are numbers representing the group-issue cases in that category, and the mean value on OUTSIDE for those cases. High and low salience and popularity were measured as above or below the mean value for the respective measures.

If the popularity of a policy is low and the salience of the policy issue is low, then groups have few incentives to use outside lobbying as signaling, and elitist politics take place. According to our systematic data summarized in chapter 4, outside lobbying under these conditions is relatively rare. However, if a group's leaders decide to use outside lobbying, they typically want to increase the salience of the issue temporarily among a small group, and signal that increased salience while it remains high. Because this salience has little basis in popularity and the group will be unlikely to influence the reelection prospects of the policymaker based on this issue, we can legitimately consider these attempts astroturf. The outside lobbying not only does not signal high salience (salience may increase to respectable levels, however), but it also does not correlate in any way with popular policies.

As an example, the Association of Private Pensions and Welfare Plans used a moderate level of outside lobbying on health care policies in 1992. Their preferred policy on employer mandates (they opposed any plan where employers might be required to offer health insurance to employees) mea-

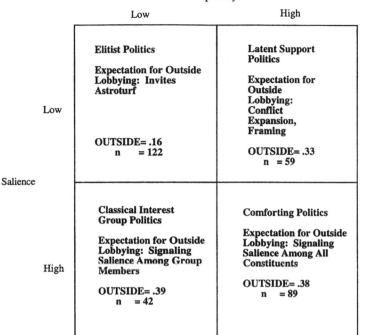

Figure 7.2. Incentives for Interest Groups to Use Outside Lobbying

sured a 0.30 on popularity and 0.09 on salience. They directed a telephone and letter-writing campaign on health care policy among their members and held press conferences to publicize their opposition. On the same issue, a major insurance company hired a public relations company to stir up phone calls from elderly constituents opposing any kind of national health care system organized from Washington that might (as they put it) undermine Medicare. Their position measured 0.29 in popularity and 0.09 in salience on the issue. These campaigns were pursuing relatively unpopular policies, with little hope that they would ever be majority supported. Finally, in a more typical pattern, Abbott Laboratories opposed any kind of national health insurance, but used no outside lobbying on the issue.

If the popularity of a policy is high and the salience of a policy issue is low, then interest groups will be inclined to try to expand the conflict among many constituents. Public opinion is ripe for exploitation, but it will take skill in framing issues properly and outwitting the opposition. The National Restaurant Association, for example, undertook a fairly high profile letter-writing campaign in 1992 opposing legislation outlawing striker replacements. They tried to make the issue one of fairness to small business owners and the avoidance of higher prices at restaurants. This policy was actually majority supported by my measures (0.67 in popularity), but it was low in salience among business executives and managers (0.36 in salience). The mean level of outside lobbying for these groups (0.33, from figure 7.2) comes about mostly from national, broadly targeted campaigns.

If the popularity of a policy issue is low and the salience of a policy issue is high, then interest groups often want to use limited, targeted outside lobbying aimed at their members and to take care to avoid expanding the conflict too much to spark the opposition. This is typical interest group politics, and the signaling for policymakers is strictly about the intensity of the issue among favorable constituents. Every bit of increased popularity counts in a group's favor, but it is unlikely the group itself can increase popularity measurably. The National Gay and Lesbian Task Force Policy Institute pursued a vigorous outside lobbying campaign in 1992 on a relatively unpopular policy (0.39) but with high salience (0.73) among constituents sympathetic to gays and lesbians: keeping immigration open to persons with AIDS. They advertised in the gay press, protested in selected cities, and generated thousands of letters from its members to Congress on the issue. In general, groups using outside lobbying in this category (mean = 0.39) used many tactics, but the tactics had limited scope.

Finally, if a policy is highly popular and the issue highly salient, interest groups want to signal both of these facts as loudly and clearly as possible. Outside lobbying under these conditions provides welcome support for the Comforting Hypothesis. If this were the only kind of outside lobbying taking place in American politics, we could take comfort in knowing that interest groups reinforce majority supported policies through their outside lobbying and we could go back to wringing our hands about quieter actions like campaign contributions. As an example, the National Committee to Preserve Social Security and Medicare, a group vilified in the press, should be applauded for at least some of its work on health care. In my data, it received the maximum value on OUTSIDE (1.00), and pursued health care policies of popularity and salience measuring 0.71 and 0.87, respectively. The mean for these groups (0.38) results mostly from group leaders choosing a few tactics with very large scope (like advertising in national newspapers or massive letter-writing campaigns).

In sum, critics of outside lobbying should reserve their vitriol for interest group leaders who are seeking to expand the conflict temporarily (with no basis in electoral support) in pursuit of unpopular policies. If either aspect of public opinion is high, and especially if popularity is at least respectable, then interest group leaders can reasonably claim to be representing some part of constituency opinion accurately, and critics should not be so concerned.

Unequal Representation and Outside Lobbying

While interest groups and policymakers are very sensitive to the views of many constituents, it would certainly be a mistake to believe that money and other resources do not bolster the influence of some constituents and some interest groups, even through outside lobbying. In the story on NAFTA, the business community could launch its massive outside lobbying campaign quickly because it had the resources and just needed to marshal them. For any group, outside lobbying has costs, and some groups can absorb these costs more readily. And while in the signaling model in chapter 3 I assumed that groups without popular support pay more for the same level of outside lobbying as groups with popular support, on average groups without popular support are the ones who can afford it.

Moreover, some constituents will always count more than others. Outside lobbying cannot systematically correct for that, and in many cases it can exacerbate the problem. When policymakers are led to believe through outside lobbying that "the people" have spoken when really only several hundred doctors, CEOs, or millionaire investors have written or called, then representative democracy may not be well served. It would be small comfort if the only citizens being mobilized through outside lobbying were those already privileged by the campaign finance system and the unequal patterns of participation that give disproportionate power to the wealthy.

Policymakers therefore have a responsibility to try to cull the wheat from the chaff. First, and obviously, they should pay more attention to large groups of ordinary citizens rather than to small groups of well-placed citizens. (Cleaning up our campaign finance system will help in this regard.) And second, they ought to try to detect astroturf, and one way to do so is to factor in the costs associated with outside lobbying. On controversial, important policies, they should rely on multiple sources of information, including public opinion polls if possible, to determine whether the constituents they are hearing from were mobilized easily with little prompting or whether an interest group had to expend large resources to generate a few small, well-placed contacts.

Of course, it is hard to justify any limitation or discouragement of outside lobbying by interest groups. To regulate it heavily would raise serious concerns about the rights of free speech and certainly violate current interpretations of the First Amendment. But even more, in many cases outside lobbying means that interest groups can potentially communicate the wishes of large subsets of the public, perhaps even the wishes of a majority. Because it can involve thousands or even millions of people, outside lobbying entails one important element of democratic control, mass participation in decision making. The goals should be to develop institutions to help elected officials to distinguish more effectively between groups with real popular support and groups without real popular support, and for the press and elected officials to be wary of astroturf. Laws requiring lobbyists to disclose funding sources and grass-roots consulting firms to verify the authenticity of letters and telephone calls can only help.

Outside lobbying exists precisely on the fine line between pressure from public opinion and pressure from interest groups, and therefore it is hard to evaluate using a well-accepted standard of democracy. Our system of government encourages interest groups to form and press their demands on government. It should be seen as a good sign that our system of government also encourages groups to try to demonstrate that their efforts have widespread popular support. Policymakers *should* pay close attention to the citizens mobilized by outside lobbying. But if large segments of society, especially the poor, are rarely mobilized by interest groups or do not participate when groups try to mobilize them, then even groups representing them will have little clout in our system. And in the face of improving technological means to generate phony grass roots, it is vitally important that we come to terms with the ways groups can lead policymakers away from popular policies or policies that will benefit most citizens. Research on outside lobbying can help. If we want our government to respond more to the mass public and less to privileged minorities, then it is helpful to be able to define, understand, and recognize the difference.

APPENDIXES

A

Groups and Persons Interviewed

I AM GRATEFUL to those persons who agreed to be interviewed for this book. Leaders of the following groups were interviewed to create the systematic data set of 50 groups and 323 group-issue cases:

Abbott Laboratories
Alliance for Acid Rain Control and Energy Policy
Allied-Signal
Amalgamated Clothing and Textile Workers
Amalgamated Transit Union
American College of Surgeons
American Conservative Union
American Group Practice Association
American Jewish Congress
American Nurses Association
American Petroleum Institute
American Psychiatric Association
Americans for Democratic Action
American Society of Association Executives
Association of Private Pensions and Welfare Plans
Bankers Association for Foreign Trade
Bechtel Corporation
Chemical Specialties Manufacturers Association
Common Cause
Competitive Enterprise Institute
Consumers for World Trade
Environmental Defense Fund
Foodservice and Packaging Institute
Health Industry Manufacturers Association
International Brotherhood of Teamsters
International Mass Retailers Association
Interstate Natural Gas Association of America
Liberty Lobby
National Association of Chain Drug Stores
National Association of Investment Companies
National Association of Letter Carriers
National Coalition for the Homeless

National Committee to Preserve Social Security and Medicare
National Cooperative Business Association
National Environmental Development Association
National Gay and Lesbian Task Force Policy Institute
National Ocean Industries Association
National Restaurant Association
Oil, Chemical, and Atomic Workers International Union
Rainbow Lobby
Savings and Community Bankers of America
Southern Company
United Brotherhood of Carpenters and Joiners of America
U.S. Chamber of Commerce
Waste Management
Zero Population Growth
A corporation (confidential)
A corporation (confidential)
A large insurance corporation (confidential)
A trade association (confidential)

Leaders of the following groups were also interviewed about their special outside lobbying campaigns, but data from the interviews are not included in the two data sets used in the book because they were not randomly chosen from a large list of interest groups:

American Federation of Teachers
American Jewish Committee
Association of American Railroads
Chevron Corporation
Citizens Trade Campaign
Health Insurance Association of America
Illinois State Council of Senior Citizens
National Committee for an Effective Congress
National Education Association
National Low Income Housing Coalition
National Organization for Women
Public Citizen
Recreation Vehicle Dealers Association of North America
Sierra Club
United Auto Workers
USA-NAFTA

Besides the interest group leaders, the following individuals were interviewed in depth for information in this book. Others were interviewed but preferred to remain anonymous.

Jeffrey Birnbaum, journalist
Jack Bonner, political consultant
William Frenzel, White House consultant, Brookings Institution
Gail Harrison, political consultant
James Jaffee, staff of House Ways and Means Committee
Leona Kozien, private citizen
Christopher Lynch, aid to Representative Benjamin Cardin
Claire Martin, political consultant
Jim McAvoy, political consultant
Jan Schakowsky, Illinois State representative
Don Weiner, anti-NAFTA activist

B

Questionnaire for Interest Groups

THIS INTERVIEW is solely for my own research. You will find that none of my questions will be sensitive, although you have the option at any time of indicating statements or portions of the interview you do not want to be associated with your organization. If you so request, your name or the name of your organization will not be used in my research to identify you or the organization in any way.

1. What is the full name of your organization?

2. What is the total membership of your organization?

3. How many full-time staff work exclusively for your organization?

4. What is the approximate annual budget for your organization?

   a. [If no answer] Does the annual budget of this organization exceed:

$ 500,000?	Yes	No
1 million?	Yes	No
5 million?	Yes	No
10 million?	Yes	No
50 million?	Yes	No
100 million?	Yes	No
500 million?	Yes	No

5. Are the members of your organization part of a particular industry in the economy?

   Yes No
          [if yes, question 7] [if no, question 8]

6. [Optional] Which of the following best describes how the members of your organization are tied to a particular industry?

   a. Members are mostly employees or organizations that represent employees of a particular industry.

   b. Members are mostly firms or organizations representing firms in a particular industry.

   c. Members are professionals or organizations that represent professionals in a particular industry.

7. [If not apparent] Which of the following labels most accurately describes your organization?

    a. Professional association
    b. Public interest group
    c. Corporation
    d. Trade association
    e. Labor union

8. Does your organization have local offices or chapters besides this central headquarters?

    Yes   No

9. Do you have a PAC?

    Yes   No

    9a. [If yes] What is the name of your PAC?

Now I would like to ask some questions about your organization's political activity.

10. How would you describe your organization's concern with the following issues?
    (Issue 1)

    a. One of your major concerns
    b. A somewhat important concern
    c. Not a very important concern
   etc.

Now I would like to ask some very simple questions about your organization's positions on policy issues. These questions may seem vague or too simple, but for comparability with public opinion questions, it helps me if you can answer them in regards to the official positions of your organization.

11. [The policy questions linked to topics that were of concern to the group, taken directly from opinion polls. See the next section for a listing of public opinion questions.]

Organizations use many different techniques to try to influence the government and public policy. For each of the following techniques (questions 12 through 36), I am going to ask you if you use it:

regularly   occasionally   never

12. Making financial contributions to electoral campaigns

13. Testifying at Congressional hearings

14. Testifying at agency hearings

15. Direct personal contact with members of Congress or their staffs

16. Direct personal contact with members of the executive branch or their staffs

17. Filing suit or engaging in some sort of litigation

18. Contributing personnel to political campaigns

19. Talking with people from the press and media

20. Running advertisements in the media about your positions on policy issues

21. Running advertisements in the media to attract members

22. Hiring a public relations firm to assist in your political activities

23. Polling the general public on policy issues of concern to you

24. Polling your members on policy issues

25. Entering into coalitions with other organizations to advance your policy goals

26. Presenting research results or technical information to policymakers

27. Presenting research results to the media

28. Holding press conferences to announce research results or policy positions

29. Inspiring letter-writing or telegram campaigns to public officials

30. Sending letters to members to inform them of organizational activities

31. Engaging in direct mail fund-raising for your organization

32. Urging influential members, other than staff, to lobby public officials directly

33. Protesting or demonstrating

34. Making public endorsements of candidates

35. Publicizing voting records of lawmakers

36. Serving on governmental advisory commissions or boards

37. [Open-ended] What are the main factors that determine which techniques your organization uses?

38. How significant a role does opinion-polling information play in the techniques you use?

    a.   A major role
    b.   Somewhat of a role
    c.   No role at all

39.   How significant a role does opinion polling information play in your positions on issues?

    a.   A major role
    b.   Somewhat of a role
    c.   No role at all

Now I'm going to ask about some details of the techniques you said you use.

40.   For which issues did you protest or demonstrate over the past year?

41.   For which specific issues did you advertise in the media over the past year?

42.   Where did your advertisements appear? In what publications, networks, or media were they?

43.   For which specific issues did you hire a public relations firm over the past year?

44.   For which specific issues did you urge members, other than staff, to lobby or write public officials over the past year?

45.   For which specific issues did you hold press conferences over the past year?

46.   Thinking about the policy issue of ——— once again, do you think your organization takes a position that the majority of the public agrees with, or do you think a majority of the public disagrees with your position on this issue?

    a.   A majority of Americans agree with your position on this issue.
    b.   The public is evenly divided on this issue
    c.   A majority of Americans disagree with your position on this issue.
    d.   Don't know/No answer.

[repeat for each issue]

47.   Once again, taking the issue of ——— how much conflict do you perceive over this issue?

    a.   A great deal of conflict
    b.   A fair amount of conflict
    c.   Not much conflict

[repeat for each issue]

48. Some organizations occasionally try to appeal to the general public, either through mass advertising or publicity campaigns. In general, how would you rate the effectiveness of these campaigns?

   a. Very effective
   b. Somewhat effective
   c. Not effective

49. [If appropriate] How would you rate the effectiveness of your campaigns?

   a. Very effective
   b. Somewhat effective
   c. Not effective

50. [If appropriate] Who specifically is your primary target audience in your advertising or publicity campaigns?
   [open-ended, then code] [if necessary, prompt randomly]

   a. Congress
   b. President
   c. The general public
   d. Specific members of the public
   e. The media
   f. Members of your organization
   g. Policy elites
   h. Your opposition
   i. Government in general

51. On the issues most important to your organization, which of the following statements would apply to you?

   a. You are the only group to voice these positions.
   b. You are one of a few groups to voice these positions.
   c. You are one of many groups to voice these positions.

52. Which three government agencies, committees, or officials do you devote most of your resources to influencing?

53. Are there any comments you would like to make about some of the topics we've discussed today?

54. And what is your position in the organization?

   Thanks for your help with these questions.

C

Opinion Questions

THE FOLLOWING questions were asked of the mass public and of interest group leaders. The date of the poll and the name of the polling organization for each question follow the results. The group leaders were requested to give the official positions of their organizations.

1. Here are some things that can be done to deal with the problem of America's ability to compete economically in the world. For each one, please tell me whether you feel it would help a lot, would help some, would not really help, or would go too far and be a step in the wrong direction: . . . Reduce government safety and environmental regulations that make it harder for American businesses to compete against countries that don't have these regulations.

Help a lot	12%
Help some	22
Not really help	19
Go too far/Step in wrong direction	40
Not sure	7
N	1,003

   September 1991
   Peter Hart

2. Do you favor or oppose a federal law which would prohibit employers from hiring permanent replacements for striking workers?

Favor	29%
Oppose	60
Not sure	11
N	1,250

   April 1992
   Yankelovich Clancy Shuman

3. Which of the following three approaches to financing health care would you favor: A health care plan that requires businesses either to provide coverage for all their employees or contribute to a federal fund that would cover all employees; a national health care plan run by the government, financed by the taxpayers, which would cover all Americans . . . Maintain the current system of private insurance, Medicare, and Medicaid.

Plan that requires businesses either to provide coverage for all employees or contribute to federal fund	32%
National health care plan run by the government	44
Maintain the current system	20
Don't know/No opinion	3
N	1,512

December 1991
ABC News/Washington Post

4. Do you favor or oppose national health insurance, which would be financed by tax money, paying for most forms of health care?

Favor	65%
Oppose	26
Don't know/No answer	9
N	1,281

January 1992
CBS News/New York Times

5. Do you think the government should require employers to make health insurance available to all their workers, or is this something that should be left up to the individual employer?

Require	64%
Left to employer	29
Depends (volunteered)	4
Don't know/No answer	3
N	1,424

June 1991
CBS News/New York Times

6. If it's a choice between the federal government or the state governments, which do you think should take the lead in changing the health care system?

Federal	62%
State	30
Both	3
Neither	1
Not sure/Refused	4
N	2,000

February 1992
Louis Harris and Associates

7. Recently there has been a controversy in the Northwest over whether to protect the spotted owl, an endangered species, which would result in the loss of jobs in the area. In general, which do you think is more important—protecting an endangered species or protecting jobs?

Protecting endangered species	34%
Protecting jobs	51
Both equally important (volunteered)	8
Neither is important (volunteered)	1
Not sure	6
N	1,004

July 1991
Hart and Teeter Research Companies

8. Would you approve or disapprove of building more nuclear power plants to generate electricity?

Approve	41%
Disapprove	48
Don't know/No answer	11
N	1,424

June 1991
CBS News/New York Times

9. Some people think we should build more nuclear power plants because they don't burn coal or oil, which create air pollution. Others

think that we should not build any more nuclear power plants because of the threat of accident or radiation. Which do you agree with?

Should build	35%
Should not build	57
Not sure	8
N	1,004

July 1991
Hart and Teeter Research Companies

10. Do you think the U.S. government is doing too much, too little, or about the right amount in terms of protecting the environment?

Too much	4%
Too little	68
About right	26
Don't know/Refused	2
N	1,222

April 1992
Gallup Organization

11. There are two statements which people sometimes make when discussing the relationship between the environment and the economy. Which of these statements comes closer to your own point of view? Protection of the environment should be given priority, even if it means a loss of jobs in some industries, or the availability of jobs should be given priority, even if the environment suffers.

Environment	62%
Jobs	29
It depends (volunteered)	5
Don't know/Refused	3
N	1,222

April 1992
Gallup Organization

12. In general, do you think markets in the United States are too open to foreign products, too closed to foreign products, or does the United States strike about the right balance with its markets?

Too open to foreign products	66%
Too closed to foreign products	5
U.S. strikes about the right balance	24
Not sure	5

N   1,004

November 1991
Peter Hart and Associates

13. Let me read you a number of products. For each one I mention, please tell me whether you think this product should or should not be protected from foreign competition. Do you think beef should or should not be protected from foreign competition?

Should be protected	61%
Should not be protected	33
Not sure	6

N   1,004

November 1991
Peter Hart and Associates

14. Do you think rice should or should not be protected from foreign competition?

Should be protected	34%
Should not be protected	57
Not sure	9

N   1,004

November 1991
Peter Hart and Associates

15. Do you think automobiles should or should not be protected from foreign competition?

Should be protected	54%
Should not be protected	42
Not sure	4

N   1,004

November 1991
Peter Hart and Associates

16. Do you think the United States should place more restrictions on the sale of Japanese products in this country, even if it means these products would cost more, or do you think the United States should not place any more restrictions on the sale of Japanese products here?

Should place more restrictions	59%
Should not place any more restrictions	35
Not sure	6
N	1,001

November 1991
Marttila and Kiley

17. Here is a list of changes many people would like to make in the current welfare system. Do you favor or oppose that change? Eliminate all welfare programs entirely.

Favor	6%
Oppose	93
Not sure	1
N	1,250

May 1992
Yankelovich Clancy Shulman

18. Cut the amount of money given to all people on welfare.

Favor	18%
Oppose	75
Not sure	7
N	1,250

May 1992
Yankelovich Clancy Shulman

19. End increases in welfare payments to women who give birth to children while on welfare.

Favor	36%
Oppose	59
Not sure	5
N	1,250

May 1992
Yankelovich Clancy Shulman

20. Replace welfare with a system of guaranteed public jobs.

Favor	70%
Oppose	25
Not sure	5
N	1,250

May 1992
Yankelovich Clancy Shulman

21. Require all able-bodied people on welfare, including women with small children, to work or learn a job skill.

Favor	87%
Oppose	11
Not sure	2
N	1,250

May 1992
Yankelovich Clancy Shulman

22. Spend extra money to provide free day care to allow poor mothers to work or take classes during the day.

Favor	92%
Oppose	7
Not sure	1
N	1,250

May 1992
Yankelovich Clancy Shulman

23. Increase the minimum wage to make work a more attractive alternative to welfare.

Favor	74%
Oppose	24
Not sure	2
N	1,250

May 1992
Yankelovich Clancy Shulman

24. Generally speaking, do you think the federal government should spend a great deal more money on poverty programs, or somewhat more, or somewhat less, or do you think the federal government should spend a great deal less money on poverty programs?

Great deal more	26%
Somewhat more	43
Somewhat less	18
Great deal less	6
Not sure	6
Refused	1
N	1,776

February 1992
Los Angeles Times

25. Here are several ways people have suggested would help conditions for minorities in urban areas. Do you favor or oppose each of these? Automatically increase the minimum wage each year to keep pace with inflation.

Favor	75%
Oppose	22
Don't know/Refused	3
N	1,015

May 1992
Gallup Organization

26. Please tell me if you agree or disagree with each of these things. The government should require that people who have AIDS notify their doctors and dentists.

Agree	96%
Disagree	4
Don't know/No opinion	.5
N	1,205

July 1991
ABC News

27. The government should require that doctors and dentists who have AIDS notify their patients.

    Agree   96%

    Disagree   3

    Don't know/No opinion   1

    N   1,205

    July 1991
    ABC News

28. Should the United States keep people who have tested positive for exposure to the AIDS virus from entering the country to live here permanently, or not?

    Yes   57%

    No   36

    Don't know/No answer   7

    N   1,424

    June 1991
    CBS News/New York Times

29. The government should require AIDS tests for doctors who perform surgery.

    Agree   92%

    Disagree   8

    Don't know/No opinion   5

    N   1,205

    July 1991
    ABC News

30. Do you think public education efforts to reduce the spread of AIDS among young people should focus more on encouraging them to practice safe sex or encouraging them to abstain from sex?

    Safe sex   53%

    Abstinence   42

Both equally   4

Don't know/Refused   1

N   1,002

November 1991
Gallup Organization

31. If you had a say in making up the federal budget, would you increase spending for the following medical research, decrease spending, or keep spending at about the same level?
AIDS research

Increase   70%

Same   23

Decrease   5

No opinion   2

N   1,004

March 1992
Gallup Organization

32. I will read a list of things some people say the government should do to prevent the spread of AIDS. Please tell me whether you approve or disapprove of each. Make condoms available to high school students as part of an AIDS prevention program.

Approve   63%

Disapprove   35

No opinion   2

N   1,004

March 1992
Gallup Organization

33. Begin teaching children about AIDS and other sexually transmitted diseases in early grades.

Approve   87%

Disapprove   12

No opinion   1

N   1,004

March 1992
Gallup Organization

34. Do you favor or oppose . . . allowing schoolchildren to spend a moment of silent meditation in public schools?

Favor	89%
Oppose	9
Not sure	2
N	500

October 1991
Yankelovich Clancy Shulman

35. Do you favor or oppose . . . allowing schoolchildren to say prayers in public schools?

Favor	78%
Oppose	18
Not sure	4
N	500

October 1991
Yankelovich Clancy Shulman

36. The Bush administration says that employers should be allowed to impose educational requirements greater than the job really requires—like a high school diploma for a janitor—in order to encourage young people to finish high school. Critics say this would result in discrimination against older workers who didn't finish high school. Do you think employers should or should not be allowed to impose educational requirements that do not relate to the duties of the job?

Should	31%
Should not	64
Don't know/No answer	5
N	1,519

September 1991
CBS News/New York Times

37. Do you approve or disapprove of school courses on sex education?

Approve	87%

Disapprove   10

Don't know/Refused   3

N   1,216

September 1991
Gallup Organization

38. Here are several ways people have suggested would help conditions for minorities in urban areas. Do you favor or oppose each of these? Offer parents vouchers to help pay the cost of private or parochial school education.

Favor   42%

Oppose   53

Don't know/Refused   5

N   1,015

May 1992
Gallup Organization

39. Here are some things that can be done to deal with the problem of America's ability to compete economically in the world. For each one, please tell me whether you feel it would help a lot, would help some, would not really help, or would go too far and be a step in the wrong direction. Restrict foreign ownership of American property and companies.

Help a lot   48%

Help some   25

Not really help   13

Go too far/Step in wrong direction   12

Not Sure   2

N   1,003

September 1991
Peter Hart and Associates

40. Here are several ways people have suggested would help improve the situation of blacks in American society today. Do you favor or oppose each of these changes? Spending more federal funds on job training programs.

Favor   72%

Oppose   24

Don't know   4

N   990

June 1991
Gallup Organization

41. Which would be a more effective way for the government to get the economy moving again—cutting taxes to encourage spending and investment, or spending more money to create jobs?

Cutting taxes   28%

Government spending   59

Both (volunteered)   4

Neither (volunteered)   5

Don't know/No answer   4

N   1,281

January 1992
CBS News/New York Times

42. The federal government now supports about four thousand domestic programs. Would you favor or oppose abolishing . . . small business subsidies?

Favor   24%

Oppose   73

Not sure   3

N   1,258

November 1991
Louis Harris and Associates

43. Some people have suggested that the U.S. government should issue an annual economic plan, in consultation with business and labor, with a strategy for promoting America's economic strength. Other people say that this would allow government too much of a role in economic affairs. Do you think it would be a good idea or a bad idea for the U.S. government to issue an annual economic plan for promoting America's economic strength?

Good idea   54%

Bad idea   31

Some of both (volunteered)   5

Not sure   10

N   1,003

September 1991
Peter Hart

44. Generally speaking, do you think the federal government should
    spend a great deal more money for domestic programs, or somewhat
    more, or somewhat less, or do you think the federal government
    should spend a great deal less money for domestic programs?

    Great deal more   22%

    Somewhat more   45

    Somewhat less   18

    Great deal less   8

    Not sure   6

    Refused   1

    N   1,776

    February 1992
    Los Angeles Times

45. If the United States makes big cuts in its military spending, should
    the money be spent mainly to cut taxes, mainly to reduce the federal
    deficit, or mainly on domestic problems?

    Cut taxes   18%

    Reduce the federal deficit   25

    Domestic problems   50

    All three   2

    Two or three (volunteered)   4

    Don't know/No opinion   1

    N   1,512

    February 1992
    ABC News/Washington Post

46. Here are several ways people have suggested would help conditions
    for minorities in urban areas. Do you favor or oppose each of these?

Fund public works projects to improve housing and streets in minority neighborhoods.

Favor	81%
Oppose	17
Don't know/Refused	3
N	1,015

May 1992
Gallup Organization

47. Give federal tax incentives to encourage businesses to invest in minority neighborhoods.

Favor	71%
Oppose	25
Don't know/Refused	4
N	1,015

May 1992
Gallup Organization

48. I will read you a list of different types of scientific research. Please say for each one if you feel this country should spend a lot more, a little more, a little less or a lot less on it. Space research on space exploration and development.

A lot more	11%
Little more	24
Little less	35
A lot less	22
No change	7
N	1,255

March 1992
Louis Harris and Associates

49. Do you favor or oppose each of the following measures to spur on the economy? Subsidizing research and development for businesses.

Favor	42%
Oppose	50

Not sure   8

N   500

January 1992
Yankelovich Clancy Shulman

50. President Bush recently announced that the United States will join six other nations in providing financial aid and loans, as well as food and humanitarian and technical assistance to the former Soviet Union. Generally speaking, do you favor or oppose this plan?

    Favor   53%

    Oppose   44

    No opinion   4

    N   1,002

    April 1992
    Gallup Organization

51. Do you think the United States is doing too much, not enough, or about the right amount to help the former Soviet Republics in their current economic crisis?

    Too much   36%

    Not enough   21

    About the right amount   39

    No opinion   4

    N   1,002

    April 1992
    Gallup Organization

52. Recently President Bush announced his support for a $24 billion international aid program for the republics of the former Soviet Union, which would include $4 billion provided by the United States. Do you favor or oppose the United States providing this aid?

    Favor   43%

    Oppose   51

    Not sure   6

    N   1,001

    April 1992
    Peter Hart and Research/Strategy/Management

53. Do you think that the United States should increase or decrease the amount of military and economic aid it gives to Israel, or do you think it should remain about the same?

Increase	6%
Decrease	32
Should remain about the same	59
Don't know/No opinion	3
N	1,233

September 1991
ABC News

54. Do you favor or oppose the United States providing $10 billion dollars in loan guarantees to Israel in order for them to refinance the resettlement of Jewish immigrants from the former Soviet Union?

Favor	18%
Oppose	73
Not sure	9
N	1,502

January 1992
Peter Hart and Research/Strategy/Management

55. Do you think the U.S. should give additional money and technology to foreign countries if it is earmarked for improving the environment?

Yes	47%
No	49
Don't know	3
Refused	5
N	1,000

May 1992
Gordon S. Black Corporation

56. Which of the following is more important to protect the environment in Africa and Asia? Industrialized nations should provide aid for the African and Asian nations or African and Asian nations should make independent efforts to protect their own environment.

Industrialized nations should provide aid	27%

African and Asian nations should make   66
    independent efforts

Don't know   6

Refused   1

N   1,000

May 1992
Gordon S. Black Corporation

57. Do you think it should be the policy of the country to restrict foreign imports in order to protect jobs and domestic industries, or do you think there should be no restrictions on the sale of foreign products in order to permit the widest choice and the lowest prices for the consumer?

Restrict   70%

No restrictions   23

Not sure   6

Refused   1

N   1,776

February 1992
Los Angeles Times

58. Do you favor or oppose the U.S. government allocating more health dollars to the research, development, and testing of new or improved methods of birth control?

Favor   60%

Oppose   38

Don't know/Refused   2

N   1,222

April 1992
Gallup Organization

59. I am going to read some ways that have been proposed to control the population growth in developing nations. Please tell me whether you generally favor or generally oppose each one as I read the list: Making birth control information widely available.

Favor   95%

Oppose   4

Don't know/Refused   1

N   1,002

April 1992
Gallup Organization

60. Would you favor or oppose an increase in U.S. economic aid and
technical assistance to help developing countries slow their
population growth?

Favor increase economic aid	54%
Oppose it	39
It depends (volunteered)	4
Don't know/Refused	4

N   1,002

April 1992
Gallup Organization

61. I am going to read some ways that have been proposed to control the
population growth in developing nations. Please tell me whether you
generally favor or generally oppose each one as I read the list:
Restricting the number of children a couple can have.

Favor	25%
Oppose	72
Don't know/Refused	4

N   1,002

April 1992
Gallup Organization

62. Taking all things into consideration, do you think the United States
should develop a Strategic Defense Initiative—Star Wars—or not?

Yes	33%
No	56
Not sure	10
Refused	1

N   1,776

February 1992
Los Angeles Times

63. Do you think homosexuals should be allowed to serve in the United States Armed Forces, or don't you think so?

Should be allowed	47%
Should not be allowed	42
Depends (volunteered)	3
Don't know/No answer	8
N	1,347

May 1992
CBS News

64. Do you think homosexual relations between consenting adults should or should not be legal?

Should be legal	36%
Should not	54
Don't know/Refused	10
N	1,216

September 1991
Gallup Organization

65. I am going to read you a series of statements that will help us understand how you feel about a number of things. For each statement, please tell me whether you completely agree with it, mostly agree with it, mostly disagree with it, or completely disagree with it. School boards ought to have the right to fire teachers who are known homosexuals.

Completely agree	23%
Mostly agree	16
Mostly disagree	28
Completely disagree	28
Don't know	5
N	2,020

November 1991
Princeton Survey Research Associates

D

A Signaling Model of Outside Lobbying

I FORMALIZE the situation between a lobbyist and a policymaker in a signaling model, following the standard framework of Spence (1973) and relying to a considerable degree on Banks (1991) for notation and concepts. Here an interest group (the sender) has private information about its capacity to influence the policymaker's reelection efforts. Its capacity, which is at least partially a function of the state of public opinion at the time, is its type in game theory terminology. The group can send a signal about its type to a policymaker (the receiver), and then the policymaker must make a decision regarding the group's policy goals. The sequence of events conforms to that of other signaling models. The interest group's type is determined by a random process, the interest group decides on a signal (including whether to send a signal), and the policymaker, upon observing the signal if sent (or no signal if not sent), decides whether to support the group's policies or not. The interaction is most interesting when the policymaker's decision hinges on an assessment of the interest group's type.

Consider that an interest group IG can be one of two types, θ^t, where $t \in \{L,H\}$. Low types (θ^L) have low capacity to influence a policymaker's reelection effort, and high types (θ^H) have high capacity to influence a policymaker's reelection effort. IG can take an action OL (for outside lobbying), where the cost is OL/θ^t. Thus, the higher the type, the lower the costs to undertake a given level of outside lobbying. A policymaker D (for decision maker), following the decision by IG, takes an action $a = \{n,y\}$, but is predisposed to choose n. Choosing y supports IG's goals. For convenience, I shall refer to IG as a male and D as a female.

The utilities to IG and D are as follows:

$$
\bullet \; U_{IG} = \begin{cases} V - \dfrac{OL}{\theta^t} & \text{if } a = y \\[2mm] -\dfrac{OL}{\theta^t} & \text{if } a = n \end{cases}
$$

$$
\bullet \; U_D = \begin{cases} \theta^t - k & \text{if } a = y \\[2mm] 0 & \text{if } a = n \end{cases}
$$

V is the value to IG of the policymaker's choosing y. The other term in his utility function is the cost of sending a message. For D, her utility is directly linked to IG's type, and she pays a cost k for changing her mind from n to y. Given the assumptions in the model, k is necessary to analyze the interesting situation where the policymaker has a relevant decision. Otherwise, choosing y for D is a strictly dominant strategy. I shall assume that $0 < \theta^L < \theta^H$, and $\theta^L < k < \theta^H$. This latter condition ensures that D wants to choose y if IG is a high type and n if IG is a low type. Let p be the prior probability of θ^L, and $\mu(OL)$ be the posterior probability of θ^L, where p and $\mu(OL)$ are common knowledge. The relevant concept is sequential equilibrium.

There are three kinds of equilibriums: separating, pooling, and semipooling. In separating equilibriums, the high types use outside lobbying and influence the policymaker to change her behavior, and the low types do not use outside lobbying and the policymaker does not change her behavior. In pooling equilibria, both types do not use any outside lobbying, and the policymaker relies strictly on her priors, p. Finally, in semipooling equilibriums, low types play a mixed strategy (sometimes using outside lobbying), high types always use outside lobbying, and the policymaker plays a mixed strategy (sometimes supporting the group) after observing outside lobbying.

The following result establishes the conditions of the separating equilibriums.

Claim 1: There exists a set of equilibriums such that $OL = 0$ and $a = n$ if θ^L is the group's type, and $OL = OL^*$ and $a = y$ if θ^H is the group's type.

To see that these are equilibriums, note that θ^L prefers $OL = 0$ to $OL = OL^*$ when $0 > V - OL^*/\theta^L$, or $OL^* > \theta^L V$. Likewise, $OL^* < \theta^H V$. Therefore, $V\theta^L < OL^* < V\theta^H$. Intuitively, in this set of equilibriums low types are not willing to pay the costs of outside lobbying to appear like high types, and high types get enough benefit from $a = y$ to pay their relatively low costs for outside lobbying. In other words, it is worth it to high types to pay to distinguish themselves from low types. A range of outside lobbying effort emerges, where below a certain point low types may be willing to pay the cost to appear like high types, and above a certain point high types are not willing to pay the cost to distinguish themselves. Any amount of outside lobbying by the high type within the gap between these two points will form the anchor of the separating equilibriums. D in this scenario chooses y upon observing outside lobbying, and chooses n upon observing no outside lobbying.

The separating scenario depicts a range of outcomes. The equilibriums here are knife-edge, which means the equilibrium equations are not differentiable, and comparative statics cannot be examined. What this means informally is that these equilibriums do not lead to predicted relationships between variables beyond the simple behavioral split between low and high types.

There is also a set of pooling equilibriums, as the following result establishes.

Claim 2: There exists a set of equilibriums where both types, θ^L and θ^H, do $\tilde{O}L = 0$, $p = \mu$, and any OL such that $0 < OL \neq \tilde{O}L$ means $\mu(OL) = 1 - \epsilon$ where $0 \leq \epsilon < OL / (\theta^H V)$. Also, D undertakes the following actions:

- If $\mu < \dfrac{\theta^H - k}{\theta^H - \theta^L}$, then $a = y$

- If $\mu > \dfrac{\theta^H - k}{\theta^H - \theta^L}$, then $a = n$

- If $\mu = \dfrac{\theta^H - k}{\theta^H - \theta^L}$, then D is indifferent between y and n

Here is a simple proof of this second claim. The relationship between μ and the other parameters can be established by setting equal the expected value to D of her two actions. The expected value of choosing y for D is

$$EU_D(y) = \mu[\theta^L - k] + (1 - \mu)[\theta^H - k]$$

The expected value of choosing n for D is

$$EU_D(n) = 0$$

Setting these equal:

$$\mu = \frac{\theta^H - k}{\theta^H - \theta^L}$$

Also, to show that the restrictions on out-of-equilibrium beliefs are sufficient to support the pooling equilibriums, note that for θ^H to choose $\tilde{O}L = 0$, he has to prefer doing nothing to $\epsilon(V - OL / \theta^H) + (1 - \epsilon)(- OL / \theta^H)$, which occurs when $\epsilon < OL / (\theta^H V)$. It can be easily shown that this restriction for the high type is more binding than the restriction for the low type, and so this ensures that neither type wants to undertake any positive level of outside lobbying under the restriction.

Pooling occurs when neither high nor low types use any outside lobbying. Unlike with separation, the policymaker does not know the group's type with certainty after the group's choice of outside lobbying strategy, and the policymaker relies solely on her prior beliefs about the group's true type. Crucial to the result is that D puts a heavy probability on the group being a low type if she observes anything other than the minimum possible level of outside lobbying. Thus high types do not want to use levels of outside lobbying distinctive from low types because the policymaker is going to decide against the group if outside lobbying occurs. Both high and low types might as well save the costs associated with outside lobbying because any outside lobbying they do will either (in the case of the policymaker choosing n based on prior beliefs) cost them resources with no return, or (in the case of the policymaker who would have chosen y based on prior beliefs but then does not after observing the outside lobbying) influence the policymaker in the wrong or unintended direction.

The third result states the conditions for semi-pooling equilibria.

Claim 3: There exists a set of equilibriums where θ^L chooses $\hat{O}L$ with probability α and $OL = 0$ with probability $1 - \alpha$, and θ^H chooses $\hat{O}L$ with probability 1, and $0 \leq \hat{O}L \leq V\theta^L$. Upon observing $\hat{O}L$, D chooses y with probability γ and n with probability $1 - \gamma$, and upon observing $OL = 0$, D chooses n with probability 1. These equilibriums can occur only if $\theta^H - k / \theta^H - \theta^L \leq p \leq 1$ and that any $OL \neq V\theta^L$ means that $\mu(OL) = 1 - \epsilon$ where $0 \leq \epsilon < OL / (\theta^H V)$.

Semipooling equilibriums, in the range specified, exist by the following logic. Note that $\mu(\hat{O}L) = p\alpha / (p\alpha + (1 - p))$. Setting this value equal to μ is necessary to make D indifferent between y and n,

$$\frac{p\alpha}{p\alpha + (1 - p)} = \frac{\theta^H - k}{\theta^H - \theta^L}$$

Then

$$\alpha = \frac{p(k - \theta^H) + \theta^H - k}{pk - \theta^L}$$

If α is greater than this value, D chooses n. If α is less than this value, D chooses y. It easy to show that α is well defined (between 0 and 1) only if $\theta^H - k/\theta^H - \theta L \leq p \leq 1$.

For IG to be indifferent, since

$$U_{IG}(0|\theta^L) = 0$$

then

$$U_{IG}(\hat{O}L/\theta^L) = \gamma \left(V - \frac{\hat{O}L}{\theta^L} \right) + (1 - \gamma)\left(\frac{\hat{O}L}{\theta^L} \right) = 0$$

Or rearranging,

$$\gamma = \frac{\hat{O}L}{V\theta^L}$$

It can be easily shown that γ is well defined only if $0 \le \hat{O}L \le V\theta^L$. Finally, the restrictions on out-of-equilibrium beliefs—any $OL > V\theta^L$ means that $\mu(OL) = 1 - \epsilon$, where $0 \le \epsilon < OL / (\theta^H V)$—correspond to the same logic as that of Claim 2.

In the semipooling equilibriums, high types always use outside lobbying at some level $\hat{O}L$, and low types sometimes use outside lobbying at that level and sometimes do not use outside lobbying at all.

Semipooling equilibriums are appealing because the formulas for α and γ are differentiable, and one can derive comparative statics results. So the results below follow from straightforward differentiation.

1. $\dfrac{\partial \alpha}{\partial p} = \dfrac{\theta^H - k}{(\theta^L - k)p^2} < 0$

2. $\dfrac{\partial \alpha}{\partial k} = \dfrac{(\theta^H - \theta^L)(p - 1)}{(k - \theta^L)^2 p} < 0$

3. $\dfrac{\partial \alpha}{\partial \theta^H} = \dfrac{1 - p}{pk - \theta^L p} > 0$

4. $\dfrac{\partial \alpha}{\partial \theta^L} = \dfrac{p[\theta^H - k + p(k - \theta^H)]}{(pk - p\theta^L)^2} > 0$

5. $\dfrac{\partial \gamma}{\partial \hat{O}L} = \dfrac{1}{V\theta^L} > 0$

6. $\dfrac{\partial \gamma}{\partial V} = -\dfrac{\hat{O}L}{\theta^L V^2} < 0$

7. $\dfrac{\partial \gamma}{\partial \theta^L} = -\dfrac{\hat{O}L}{(\theta^L)^2 V} < 0$

These results yield rich predictions, though testing them is beyond the purpose of this book. The first comparative statics result states that as the probability of a low type increases, outside lobbying among low types decreases. Essentially, the more skeptical the policymaker is about the interest group, the less incentive the interest group has to try to appear like a high type group. It takes too much effort by the interest group to overcome the policymaker's skepticism under many circumstances. The intuition for this result seems fairly clear, although the opposite conclusion—that low types want to use more outside lobbying the more skeptical the policymaker is about the group—may be similarly intuitive. According to the model here, that skepticism has a real deterrent effect. Reputations among some interest groups for not being able to deliver votes on election day or campaign money during the electoral season can help deter these groups from purchasing astroturf support.

The second result is similar in spirit. The higher the cost to the policymaker of supporting the group's policy, the lower the probability that low types will use outside lobbying. Once again, the low type interest group is inclined to use outside lobbying when the reluctance of the policymaker to support the group is not too serious.

The third and fourth results are especially interesting. As both high types and low types increase relative to other parameters, low type groups will use outside lobbying with greater frequency. As the types increase relative to the range of possible types , the policymaker's stake in the decision, it turns out, increases at the same time that the interest group's costs for outside lobbying decrease. So, where a given issue becomes more salient to all sides of a policy debate, outside lobbying should increase among low type groups and policymakers' decisions should be especially sensitive to information gleaned from outside lobbying. Of all the comparative statics results, these two present the clearest testable propositions.

The fifth through seventh results refer to the policymaker's decision to support the group. With the fifth result, the policymaker is more likely to support the group the higher the level of outside lobbying she observes. This occurs because higher levels of outside lobbying become increasingly costly for both high and low types, but they are more costly in absolute levels for low types. The policymaker reasons that as the price of admission for low types gets higher, the less likely low types will try to admit themselves to the class of higher types. The policymaker understands the constraints on low types and makes inferences based on those constraints.

Note that for the sixth result, the value of $a = y$ to the interest group is common knowledge between the players. The result states that as the value of the policy to the interest group increases, the probability of the policymaker supporting the group's policy decreases. Low types are more willing to pay costs to use outside lobbying as high types do. Upon observing outside lobbying, the policymaker places higher weight on the probability that the group is low type than if the value of the policy to the interest group is small. In other words, if a policymaker knows a particular policy is dearly wanted by an interest group, she reasons that the interest group, even if it is a low type, might be willing to pay big costs to appear like a high type. As a consequence, she may be less inclined to support the group even if the group looks like a high type than she would be if she knew the interest group did not value the policy very much.

Finally, the seventh result states that as the low type increases relative to other parameters, the probability of the policymaker supporting the group's policy decreases. This essentially says that when there is not much utility difference for the policymaker between the true type being low or high, then the policymaker is less inclined to pay the cost of supporting the group. Costs for supporting the group stay constant, so these costs loom larger as the utility difference between types decreases.

The third, fourth, and sixth results together introduce the possibility that as the types increase, low types increase their outside lobbying, and policymakers choose to support the group's policies less often. In other words, under increasing stakes for the policymaker, interest groups try harder to convince policymakers that they have a high capacity at the same time that policymakers become harder to convince. Groups shout louder, the volume of total outside lobbying increases on an issue, but policymakers become less inclined to listen and change their behavior. This would explain the vigorous outside lobbying surrounding some issues when these lobbying campaigns in the end change few votes in Congress.

Bibliography

Ainsworth, Scott. 1993. "Regulating Lobbyists and Interest Group Influence." *Journal of Politics* 55:41–56.

Ainsworth, Scott, and Itai Sened. 1993. "The Role of Lobbyists: Entrepreneurs with Two Audiences." *American Journal of Political Science* 37:834–66.

Arnold, R. Douglas. 1990. *The Logic of Congressional Action.* New Haven, Conn.: Yale University Press.

Arrow, Kenneth. 1963. *Social Choice and Individual Values.* New York: Wiley and Sons.

Austen-Smith, David. 1987. "Interest Groups, Campaign Contributions, and Probabilistic Voting." *Public Choice* 54:123–39.

———. 1990. "Information Transmission in Debate." *American Journal of Political Science* 34:124–52.

———. 1993. "Information and Influence: Lobbying for Agendas and Votes." *American Journal of Political Science* 37:799–833.

———. 1995. "Campaign Contributions and Access." *American Political Science Review* 89:566–81.

Austen-Smith, David, and John Wright. 1992. "Competitive Lobbying for a Legislator's Vote." *Social Choice and Welfare* 9:229–57.

———. 1994. "Counteractive Lobbying." *American Journal of Political Science* 38:25–44.

Axelrod, Robert. 1984. *The Evolution of Cooperation.* New York: Basic Books.

Ball, Alan, and Frances Midland. 1986. *Pressure Politics in Industrial Societies.* Atlantic Highlands, N.J.: Humanities Press International.

Banks, Jeffrey. 1991. *Signaling Games in Political Science.* New York: Harwood Academic.

Banks, Jeffrey, and Barry Weingast. 1992. "The Political Control of Bureaucracies under Asymmetric Information." *American Journal of Political Science* 36:509–24.

Baron, David. 1989. "Service-Induced Campaign Contributions and the Electoral Equilibrium." *Quarterly Journal of Economics* 104:45–72.

Bauer, Raymond, Ithiel de Sola Pool, and Lewis Anthony Dexter. 1963. *American Business and Public Policy: The Politics of Foreign Trade.* New York: Atherton Press.

Baumgartner, Frank, and Bryan Jones. 1993. *Agendas and Instability in American Politics.* Chicago: University of Chicago Press.

Becker, Gary. 1983. "A Theory of Competition among Pressure Groups for Political Influence." *Quarterly Journal of Economics* 96:371–400.

Bennett, Linda, and Stephen Bennett. 1990. *Living with Leviathan.* Lawrence: University Press of Kansas.

Bentley, Arthur. 1908. *The Process of Government.* Chicago: University of Chicago Press.

Berry, Jeffrey. 1977. *Lobbying for the People*. Princeton: Princeton University Press.
———. 1989. *The Interest Group Society*. 2d ed. New York: HarperCollins Publishers.
Bianco, William. 1994. *Trust: Representatives and Constituents*. Ann Arbor: University of Michigan Press.
Birnbaum, Jeffrey H. 1992. *The Lobbyists*. New York: Times Books.
Birnbaum, Jeffrey, and Alan Murray. 1987. *Showdown at Gucci Gulch*. New York: Random House.
Blaisdell, Donald C. 1941. *Investigation of Concentration of Economic Power*. Washington, D.C.: U.S. Government, Temporary National Economic Committee.
Bodua, David J. 1983. "Adversary Polling and the Construction of Social Meaning." *Law and Policy Quarterly* 5:345–66.
Bosso, Christopher. 1987. *Pesticides and Politics: The Life Cycle of a Public Issue*. Pittsburgh: University of Pittsburgh Press.
Browne, William P. 1988. *Private Interests, Public Policy, and American Agriculture*. Lawrence: University Press of Kansas.
———. 1995. *Cultivating Congress: Constituents, Issues, and Agricultural Policymaking*. Lawrence: University Press of Kansas.
Bryce, James. [1888] 1912. *The American Commonwealth*. New York: Macmillan and Co.
Cantril, Albert. 1980a. "Introduction." In *Polling on the Issues*. Cabin John, Md.: Seven Locks Press.
———. ed. 1980b. *Polling on the Issues*. Cabin John, Md.: Seven Locks Press.
Carmines, Edward G., and James Stimson. 1989. *Issue Evolution: Race and the Transformation of American Politics*. Princeton: Princeton University Press.
Chong, Dennis. 1991. *Collective Action and the Civil Rights Movement*. Chicago: University of Chicago Press.
Chubb, John. 1983. *Interest Groups and Bureaucracy*. Palo Alto, Calif.: Stanford University Press.
Cigler, Allan, and Burdett Loomis, eds. 1991. *Interest Group Politics*. 3d ed. Washington, D.C.: Congressional Quarterly Press.
Cobb, Roger, and Charles Elder. 1983. *Participation in America: The Dynamics of Agenda-Building*. Baltimore: Johns Hopkins University Press.
Cox, Gary, and Mathew McCubbins. 1993. *Legislative Leviathan*. Berkeley: University of California Press.
Crawford, V., and J. Sobel. 1982. "Strategic Information Transmission." *Econometrica* 50:579–94.
Dahl, Robert. 1956. *A Preface to Democratic Theory*. Chicago: University of Chicago Press.
———. 1961. *Who Governs? Democracy and Power in an American City*. New Haven, Conn.: Yale University Press.
Danielson, Lucig, and Benjamin I. Page. 1994. "The Heavenly Chorus: Interest Group Voices on TV News." *American Journal of Political Science* 38:1056–78.
Deakin, James. 1966. *The Lobbyists*. Washington, D.C.: Public Affairs Press.
Denzau, Arthur T., and Michael C. Munger. 1986. "Legislators and Interest Groups:

How Unorganized Interests Get Represented." *American Political Science Review* 80:89–106.

Dexter, Lewis Anthony. 1969. *How Organizations Are Represented in Washington.* Indianapolis, Ind.: Bobbs-Merrill.

Downs, Anthony. 1957. *An Economic Theory of Democracy.* New York: Harper and Row.

———. 1972. "Up and Down with Ecology: The Issue Attention Cycle." *Public Interest* 28:38–50.

Edelman, Murray. 1964. *The Symbolic Uses of Politics.* Urbana: University of Illinois Press.

Edelman, S. 1992. "Two Politicians, a PAC and How They Interact: Two Extensive Form Games." *Economics and Politics* 4:289–306.

Edsall, Thomas Byrne. 1984. *The New Politics of Inequality.* New York: W. W. Norton.

Elder, Charles, and Roger Cobb. 1983. *The Political Uses of Symbols.* New York: Longman.

Enelow, James, and Melvin Hinich. 1984. *The Spatial Theory of Voting.* New York: Cambridge University Press.

Engler, Robert. 1961. *The Politics of Oil.* Chicago: University of Chicago Press.

Erikson, Robert S., Gerald C. Wright, Jr., and John P. McIver. 1989. "Political Parties, Public Opinion, and State Policy in the United States." *American Political Science Review* 83:729–50.

Ethridge, Marcus. 1991. "Minority Power and Madisonianism." *American Journal of Political Science* 35:335–56.

Farrell, Joseph. 1987. "Cheap Talk, Coordination, and Entry." *Rand Journal of Economics* 19:34–39.

The Federalist Papers. [1788] 1961. New York: New American Library.

Fenno, Richard. 1973. *Congressmen in Committees.* Boston: Little, Brown.

———. 1978. *Home Style: House Members in Their Districts.* Boston: Little, Brown.

Ferguson, Thomas. 1995. *Golden Rule.* Chicago: University of Chicago Press.

Ferguson, Thomas, and Joel Rogers. 1986. *Right Turn.* New York: Hill and Wang.

Fiorina, Morris. 1977. *Congress: Keystone of the Washington Establishment.* New Haven, Conn.: Yale University Press.

Frantzich, Stephen. 1986. *Write Your Congressman: Citizen Communications and Representation.* New York: Praeger.

Gaventa, John. 1980. *Power and Powerlessness: Quiescence and Rebellion in an Appalachian Valley.* Urbana: University of Illinois Press.

Gais, Thomas, and Jack Walker, Jr. 1991. "Pathways to Influence in American Politics." In Jack Walker, Jr. *Mobilizing Interest Groups in America.* Ann Arbor: University of Michigan Press.

Gibbard, Allan. 1973. "Manipulation of Voting Schemes: A General Result." *Econometrica* 41:587–602.

Gilligan, Thomas, and Keith Krehbiel. 1989. "Asymmetric Information and Legislative Rules with a Heterogeneous Committee." *American Journal of Political Science* 33:459–90.

———. 1990. "Organization of Informative Committees by a Rational Legislature." *American Journal of Political Science* 34:531–64.

Ginsburg, Benjamin. 1986. *The Captive Public*. New York: Basic.

Godwin, R. Kenneth. 1992. "Money, Technology, and Political Interests." In Mark Petracca, ed., *The Politics of Interests: Interest Groups Transformed*. Boulder, Colo.: Westview Press.

———. 1992. "The Direct Marketing of Politics." In Mark Petracca, ed., *The Politics of Interests: Interest Groups Transformed*. Boulder, Colo.: Westview Press.

Gold, Howard. 1992. *Hollow Mandates: American Public Opinion and the Conservative Shift*. Boulder, Colo.: Westview Press.

Gorey, Hays. 1975. *Nader and the Power of Everyman*. New York: Grosset and Dunlap.

Grier, Kevin, and Michael Munger. 1991. "Committee Assignments, Constituent Preferences, and Campaign Contributions." *Economic Inquiry* 29:24–43.

Grier, Kevin, Michael Munger, and Brian Roberts. 1991. "The Industrial Organization of Corporate Political Participation." *Southern Economic Journal* 57:727–38.

Hall, Richard, and Bernard Grofman. 1990. "The Committee Assignment Process and the Conditional Nature of Committee Bias." *American Political Science Review* 84:1149–66.

Hall, Richard L., and Frank Wayman. 1990. "Buying Time: Moneyed Interests and the Mobilization of Bias in Congressional Committees." *American Political Science Review* 84:797–820.

Hansen, John Mark. 1991. *Gaining Access: Congress and the Farm Lobby, 1919–1981*. Chicago: University of Chicago Press.

Hanushek, Eric A., and John E. Jackson. 1977. *Statistical Methods for Social Scientists*. San Diego, Calif.: Academic Press.

Hardin, Russell. 1982. *Collective Action*. Baltimore: Johns Hopkins University Press.

Hayes, Michael. 1981. *Lobbyists and Legislators: A Theory of Political Markets*. New Brunswick, N.J.: Rutgers University Press.

Heclo, Hugh. 1977. *A Government of Strangers: Executive Politics in Washington*. Washington, D.C.: Brookings Institution.

———. 1978. "Issue Networks in the Executive Establishment." In Anthony King, ed., *The New American Political System*. Washington, D.C.: American Enterprise Institute.

Heinz, John P., Edward Laumann, Robert Nelson, and Robert Salisbury. 1993. *The Hollow Core*. Cambridge: Harvard University Press.

Herbst, Susan. 1993. *Numbered Voices: Quantification and the Changing Nature of Public Opinion in America*. Chicago: University of Chicago Press.

Hill, Stuart, and Donald Rothschild. 1992. "The Impact of Regime on the Diffusion of Political Conflict." In M. Midlarsky, ed., *The Internationalization of Communal Strife*. New York: Routledge.

Hotelling, Harold. 1929. "Stability in Competition." *Economic Journal* 39:41–57.

Jacob, Herbert. 1988. *Silent Revolution*. Chicago: University of Chicago Press.

Jacobs, Lawrence. 1992. "Institutions and Culture: Health Policy and Public Opinion in the U.S. and Britain." *World Politics* 44:179–209.

Jacobson, Gary. 1980. *Money in Congressional Elections*. New Haven: Yale University Press.

———. 1992. *The Politics of Congressional Elections*. New York: HarperCollins.

Jamieson, Kathleen. 1992. *The Interplay of Influence.* Belmont, Calif.: Wadsworth.

Johnson, Haynes, and David Broder. 1996. *The System.* Boston: Little, Brown.

Jones, Bryan. 1994. *Reconceiving Decision Making in Democratic Politics: Attention, Choice, and Public Policy.* Chicago: University of Chicago Press.

Kernell, Samuel. 1986. *Going Public: Strategies of Presidential Leadership.* Washington, D.C.: Congressional Quarterly Press.

Key, V. O. 1961. *Public Opinion and American Democracy.* New York: Alfred Knopf.

Kinder, Donald, and Jon Krosnick. 1990. "Altering the Foundations of Support for the President through Priming." *American Political Science Review* 84:497–512.

King, Gary. 1989. *Unifying Political Methodology.* Cambridge: Cambridge University Press.

Kingdon, John. 1984. *Agendas, Alternatives, and Public Policies.* Boston: Little, Brown.

———. 1989. *Congressmen's Voting Decisions.* 3d ed. Ann Arbor: University of Michigan Press.

Kmenta, Jan. 1986. *Elelments of Econometrics.* 2d ed. New York: Macmillan.

Knoke, David. 1990. *Organizing for Collective Action.* New York: Aldine de Gruyter.

Knoke, David, and James Wood. 1981. *Organized for Action.* New Brunswick, N.J.: Rutgers University Press.

Kovach, Bill. 1990. "The Impact of Public Opinion Polls." *Neiman Reports* 44:19–21.

Krehbiel, Keith. 1990. "Are Congressional Committees Composed of Preference Outliers?" *American Political Science Review* 84:149–63.

———. 1991. *Information and Legislative Organization.* Ann Arbor: University of Michigan Press.

Kreps, David. 1990. *Game Theory and Economic Modeling.* New York: Oxford University Press.

Lane, Robert E. 1954. *The Regulation of Businessmen.* New Haven, Conn.: Yale University Press.

Latham, Earl. 1949. "Giantism and Basing-Points: A Political Analysis." *Yale Law Journal* 58:383.

Lohmann, Susanne. 1993. "A Signaling Model of Informative and Manipulative Political Action." *American Political Science Review* 87:319–33.

Lowi, Theodore L. 1979. *The End of Liberalism.* New York: W. W. Norton.

Lupia, Arthur. 1994. "Shortcuts versus Encyclopedias: Information and Voting Behavior on California Insurance Reform Elections." *American Political Science Review* 88:63–76.

Mack, Charles. 1989. *Lobbying and Government Relations: A Guide for Executives.* New York: Quorum Books.

Magee, Stephen, William Brock, and Leslie Young. 1989. *Black Hole Tariffs and Endogenous Policy Theory.* New York: Cambridge University Press.

Mahood, H. R. 1990. *Interest Group Politics in America.* Englewood Cliffs, N.J.: Prentice-Hall.

Majone, Giandomenico. 1989. *Evidence, Argument, and Persuasion in the Policy Process.* New Haven, Conn.: Yale University Press.

Makinson, Larry. 1990. *Open Secrets*. Washington, D.C.: Center for Responsive Politics, and Congressional Quarterly.

Mansbridge, Jane J. 1986. *Why We Lost the ERA*. Chicago: University of Chicago Press.

———. 1992. "A Deliberative Theory of Interest Representation." In Mark P. Petracca, ed., *The Politics of Interests: Interest Groups Transformed*. Boulder, Colo.: Westview Press.

Margolis, Michael, and Gary Mauser, eds. 1989. *Manipulating Public Opinion*. Pacific Grove, Calif.: Brooks/Cole Publishing.

Martin, Cathie J. 1991. *Shifting the Burden: The Struggle over Growth and Corporate Taxation*. Chicago: University of Chicago Press.

Matthews, Steven. 1989. "Veto Threats: Rhetoric in a Bargaining Game." *Quarterly Journal of Economics* 104:347–69.

Mayhew, David. 1974. *Congress: The Electoral Connection*. New Haven, Conn.: Yale University Press.

McAdam, Doug. 1982. *Political Process and the Development of Black Insurgency, 1930–1970*. Chicago: University of Chicago Press.

McCarthy, John, and Mayer Zald. 1977. "Resource Mobilization and Social Movements: A Partial Theory." *American Journal of Sociology* 82:1212–41.

McConnell, Grant. 1967. *Private Power and American Democracy*. New York: Alfred Knopf.

McCool, Daniel. 1990. "Subgovernments as Determinants of Political Viability." *Political Science Quarterly* 105:269–93.

McCubbins, Mathew, and Terry Sullivan, eds. 1987. *Congress: Structure and Policy*. New York: Cambridge University Press.

McFarland, Andrew. 1984. *Common Cause*. Chatham, N.J.: Chatham House.

McKelvey, R., and W. Zavoina. 1975. "A Statistical Model for the Analysis of Ordinal Level Dependent Variables." *Journal of Mathematical Sociology* 4:103–20.

McKissick, Gary. 1995. "Policy Entrepreneurs and Recurring Issues in Congress." University of Michigan. Mimeo.

Meier, Kenneth. 1985. *Regulation: Politics, Bureaucracy, and Economics*. New York: St. Martin's.

Meyer, David S. 1993. "Protest Cycles and Political Process." *Political Research Quarterly* 46:451–80.

Milbrath, Lester. 1963. *The Washington Lobbyists*. Chicago: Rand McNally.

Miller, Arthur, Christopher Wlezien, and Anne Hildreth. 1991. "A Reference Group Theory of Partisan Coalitions." *Journal of Politics* 53:1134–49.

Miller, Stephen. 1983. *Special Interest Groups in American Politics*. New Brunswick, N.J.: Transaction Books.

Miller, Warren E., and Donald Stokes. 1964. "Constituency Influence in Congress." *American Political Science Review* 57:45–56.

Mitchell, William, and Michael Munger. 1991. "Economic Models of Interest Groups: An Introductory Survey." *American Journal of Political Science* 53:512–546.

Mizruchi, Mark. 1992. *The Structure of Corporate Political Action*. Cambridge: Harvard University Press.

Moe, Terry. 1980. *The Organization of Interests*. Chicago: University of Chicago Press.

Moodie, Graeme C., and Gerald Studdert-Kennedy. 1970. *Opinions, Publics, and Pressure Groups*. London: Allen and Unwin.

Morris, Aldon. 1981. "The Black Southern Student Sit-in Movement: An Analysis of Internal Organization." *American Sociological Review* 46:744–67.

Morton, Rebecca, and Charles Cameron. 1992. "Elections and the Theory of Campaign Contributions." *Economics and Politics* 4:79–108.

Mutz, Diane, Paul Sniderman, and Richard Brody, eds. 1996. *Political Persuasion and Attitude Change*. Ann Arbor: University of Michigan Press.

Myerson, Roger B. 1991. *Game Theory*. Cambridge: Harvard University Press.

Nader, Ralph. 1965. *Unsafe at Any Speed*. New York: Grossman.

Navarro, Peter. 1984. *The Policy Game: How Special Interests and Ideologues are Stealing America*. New York: John Wiley and Sons.

Nelson, Barbara. 1984. *Making An Issue of Child Abuse*. Chicago: University of Chicago Press.

Olson, Mancur. 1965. *The Logic of Collective Action*. Cambridge: Harvard University Press.

Page, Benjamin. 1983. *Who Gets What from Government*. Berkeley: University of California Press.

Page, Benjamin, and Robert Shapiro. 1983. "Effects of Public Opinion on Policy." *American Political Science Review* 77:175–190.

———. 1992. *The Rational Public*. Chicago: University of Chicago Press.

Page, Benjamin, Robert Shapiro, and Glenn Dempsey. 1987. "What Moves Public Opinion?" *American Political Science Review* 81:23–43.

Penny, Timothy. 1996. *Common Cents*. New York: Avon.

Pertschuk, Michael. 1986. *Giant Killers*. New York: W. W. Norton and Company.

Petracca, Mark P. 1992a. "The Rediscovery of Interest Groups." In *The Politics of Interests: Interest Groups Transformed*. Boulder, Colo.: Westview Press.

———. ed. 1992b. *The Politics of Interests: Interest Groups Transformed*. Boulder, Colo.: Westview Press.

Pincus, Jonathan. 1977. *Pressure Groups and Politics in Antebellum Tariffs*. New York: Columbia University Press.

Piven, Frances, and Richard A. Cloward. 1977. *Poor People's Movements*. New York: Vintage Books.

Poltrack, Terence. 1985. "Influencing the Influentials." *Marketing and Media Decisions* 20:56–116.

Potters, Jan, and F. Van Winden. 1992. "Lobbying and Asymmetric Information." *Public Choice* 74:269–92.

Pym, Bridget. 1974. *Pressure Groups and the Permissive Society*. Newton Abbot, Eng.: David and Charles.

Riker, William. 1983. *Liberalism against Populism*. New York: Freeman.

Ripley, Randall, and Grace Franklin. 1987. *Congress, the Bureaucracy, and Public Policy*. Chicago: Dorsey.

Robyn, Dorothy. 1987. *Braking the Special Interests: Trucking Deregulation and the Politics of Policy Reform*. Chicago: University of Chicago Press.

Rochefort, David, and Paul Pezza. 1991. "Public Opinion and Health Policy." In Theodore Litman and Leonard Robins, eds., *Health Politics and Policy*. 2d ed. Albany, N.Y.: Delmar Publishers.

Rodgers, Daniel. 1987. *Contested Truths: Keywords in American Politics since Independence*. New York: Basic Books.

Rosenstone, Steven, and John Mark Hansen. 1993. *Mobilization, Participation, and Democracy in America*. New York: Macmillan.

Rothenberg, Lawrence S. 1992. *Linking Citizens to Government*. Cambridge: Cambridge University Press.

Sabatier, Paul, and Hank Jenkins-Smith, eds. 1993. *Policy Change and Learning: An Advocacy Coalition Approach*. Boulder, Colo.: Westview Press.

Salisbury, Robert. 1969. "An Exchange Theory of Interest Groups." *Midwest Journal of Political Science* 13:64–78.

Satterthwaite, Mark. 1975. "Strategy-Proofness and Arrow's Conditions." *Journal of Economic Theory* 10:187–217.

Schattschneider, E. E. 1935. *Politics, Pressures and the Tariff*. New York: Prentice-Hall.

———. 1960. *The Semi-Sovereign People*. Hinsdale, Illinois: Dryden Press.

Schelling, Thomas. 1978. *Micromotives and Macrobehavior*. New York: Norton.

Scheppele, Kim, and Jack Walker. 1991. "The Litigation Strategies of Interest Groups." In Jack Walker, *Mobilizing Interest Groups in America*. Ann Arbor: University of Michigan Press.

Schlozman, Kay Lechmann, and John Tierney. 1986. *Organized Interests and American Democracy*. New York: HarperCollins.

Scholten, Ilja, ed. 1987. *Political Stability and Neo-Corporatism: Corporatist Integration and Societal Cleavages in Western Europe*. London: Sage Publications.

Shepsle, Kenneth, and Barry Weingast. 1987. "The Institutional Foundations of Committee Power." *American Political Science Review* 81:85–104.

Smith, Hedrick. 1989. *The Power Game*. New York: Ballantine Books.

Smith, Richard. 1984. "Advocacy, Interpretation, and Influence in the U.S. Congress." *American Political Science Review* 78:44–63.

Smith, Steven. 1989. *Call To Order*. Washington, D.C.: Brookings institution.

Smith, Steven, and Christopher Deering. 1984. *Committees in Congress*. Washington, D.C.: Congressional Quarterly Press.

Smith, Tom. 1985. "America's Most Important Problems." *Public Opinion Quarterly* 49:264–74.

Snyder, James. 1991. "On Buying Legislatures." *Economics and Politics* 3:93–109.

———. 1992. "Artificial Extremism in Interest Group Ratings." *Legislative Studies Quarterly* 17:319–45.

Sorauf, Frank. 1990. "Public Opinion on Campaign Finance." In Margaret Latus and John R. Johannes, eds., *Money, Elections, and Democracy*. Boulder, Colo.: Westview Press.

———. 1992. *Inside Campaign Finance*. New Haven, Colo.: Yale University Press.

Spence, M. 1973. "Job Market Signaling." *Quarterly Journal of Economics* 87:355–74.

Stigler, George. 1971. "The Theory of Economic Regulation." *Bell Journal of Economics and Management Science* 2:3–21.

Stimson, James. 1991. *Public Opinion in America: Moods, Cycles, and Swings.* Boulder, Colo.: Westview Press.

Sundquist, James L. 1968. *Politics and Policy.* Washington, D.C.: Brookings Institution.

Tocqueville, Alexis de. [1835] 1966. *Democracy in America.* New York: Harper and Row.

Truman, David B. 1951. *The Governmental Process: Political Interests and Public Opinion.* New York: Alfred A. Knopf.

Vogel, David. 1987. *Fluctuating Fortunes.* New York: Basic Books.

Walker, Jack, Jr. 1983. "The Origins and Maintenance of Interest Groups in America." *American Political Science Review* 77:390– 406.

———. 1991. *Mobilizing Interest Groups in America.* Ann Arbor: University of Michigan Press.

Waltzer, Herbert. 1988. "Corporate Advocacy and Political Influence." *Public Relations Review* 14:41–55.

White, Halbert. 1980. "A Heteroskedasticity-Consistent Covariance Matrix Estimator and a Direct Test for Heteroskedasticity." *Econometrica* 48:817–38.

Whiteman, David. 1995. *Communication in Congress.* Lawrence: University Press of Kansas.

Wilson, Graham. 1981. *Interest Groups in the United States.* Oxford: Clarendon Press.

———. 1990. *Interest Groups.* Cambridge, Mass.: Basil Blackwell.

Wilson, James Q. 1973. *Political Organizations.* New York: Basic Books.

Wooten, Graham. 1985. *Interest Groups: Politics and Policy.* Englewood Cliffs, N.J.: Prentice-Hall.

Wright, John. 1985. "PACs, Contributions, and Roll Calls: An Organizational Perspective." *American Political Science Review* 79:400–414.

Index

About the Author

Ken Kollman is Assistant Professor of Political Science at the
University of Michigan.